# ISLAM, NATIONALISM AND COMMUNISM IN A TRADITIONAL SOCIETY

*By the same author*

The Sudan Under Wingate

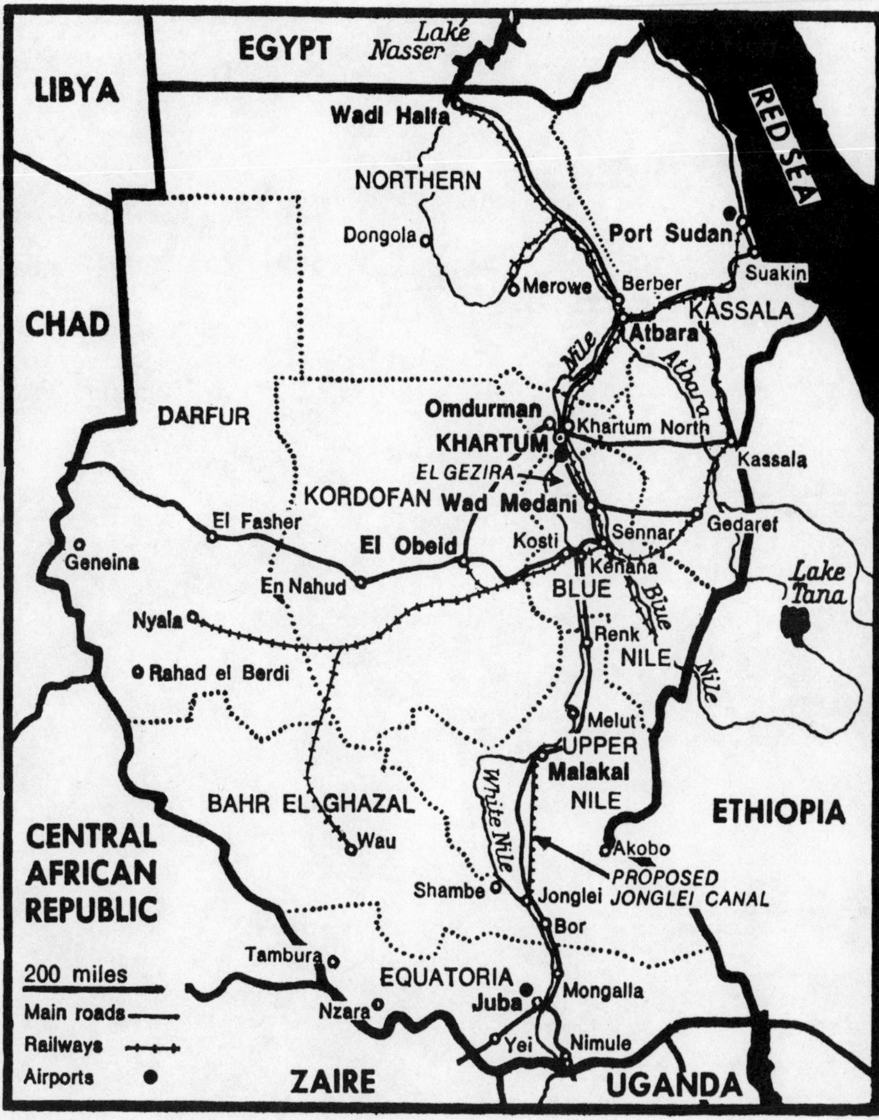

EGYPT
Lake Nasser
LIBYA
Wadi Halfa
RED SEA
NORTHERN
Port Sudan
Dongola
Suakin
Merowe
Berber
KASSALA
CHAD
Atbara
Nile
Atbara
DARFUR
Omdurman
Khartum North
KHARTUM
Kassala
EL GEZIRA
KORDOFAN
Wad Medani
El Fasher
Gedaref
El Obeid
Kosti
Sennar
Geneina
Kenana
Lake Tana
En Nahud
BLUE
Blue
Nyala
Renk
NILE
Nile
Rahad el Berdi
Melut
UPPER
Malakal
White Nile
BAHR EL GHAZAL
NILE
ETHIOPIA
CENTRAL AFRICAN REPUBLIC
Wau
Akobo
PROPOSED JONGLEI CANAL
Shambe
Jonglei
Bor
Tambura
200 miles
EQUATORIA
Mongalla
Juba
Main roads
Nzara
Railways
Yei
Nimule
Airports
ZAIRE
UGANDA


The Sudan

# ISLAM, NATIONALISM AND COMMUNISM IN A TRADITIONAL SOCIETY

## The Case of Sudan

GABRIEL WARBURG

FRANK CASS

*First published in 1978 in Great Britain by*
FRANK CASS AND COMPANY LIMITED
Gainsborough House, Gainsborough Road,
London, E11 1RS, England

*and in the United States of America by*
FRANK CASS AND COMPANY LIMITED
c/o Biblio Distribution Centre
81 Adams Drive, P.O. Box 327, Totowa, N.J. 07511



British Library Cataloguing in Publication Data
Warburg, Gabriel
Islam, nationalism and communism in a traditional society
1. Sudanese Communist Party – History
2. Islam and politics – Sudan
3. Communism and Islam
329.9'624 JQ3981.S873S/
ISBN 0–7146–3080–2



Typeset by Computacomp (UK) Limited,
Fort William, Scotland,
and Printed in Great Britain by
Billing & Sons Ltd, Guildford, London and Worcester

# Contents

# Preface

The studies contained in this volume have one thing in common: they describe the overwhelming impact of Islam on Sudanese society and politics from the formative years of the Sudanese political community until the abortive communist coup in July 1971.

The first study describes the creation of the Umma party and deals with the most important force within the religio-political structure of the Sudan.* It gives an account of the emergence of sectarian politics, in the Anglo-Egyptian setting, and analyses its roots and the reasons for its success.

The second chapter of Part I is primarily an attempt to assess the reasons for sectarianism within the first generation of Sudanese politicians, the so-called 'graduates', largely through a critical examination of the memoirs of Ismā'īl al-Azharī. Al-Azharī exemplifies the failure of the 'graduates' to break loose and to become an independent political force. The four years described in this study are the years when non-sectarian political thinking and action were of paramount importance. Yet it is quite clear that while al-Azharī and his comrades were able to achieve a certain measure of independence, the two 'sayyids', the grand old

* Part I (chapters 1 and 2) are revised texts of the following papers: 'From Anṣār to Umma: Sectarian Politics in the Sudan, 1914–1945', *Asian and African Studies*, vol. 9, No. 3 (1973); 'Sudan Struggles for its Independence', *Hamizrah Hehadash* vol. 25, No. 1–2 (1975) [in Hebrew]. They are included in this volume with the kind permission of their respective publishers and editors. Part II, dealing with Sudanese Communism, was researched and written under the auspices of the Research Institute on Communist Affairs and the Middle East Institute, both at Columbia University, which kindly offered me a research fellowship. It is published in this volume for the first time.

men of the Khatmiyya and the Anṣār, were always behind the scenes when it came to crucial decisions.

Part II of this volume is a study of Sudanese Communism in which I became interested for two main reasons. First, I wanted to find out whether it was possible for a political force which is diametrically opposed to religion to thrive in a traditional and Islamic-dominated society without compromising itself. Secondly, knowing the relatively important role which the Sudanese Communist Party (SCP) played in the 1964 civil revolt which overthrew 'Abbūd's military régime, as well as its direct involvement in the abortive anti-Numeirī coup in July 1971, I was tempted to investigate the real force which is represented by Sudanese Communism.

During the last few years three books have been published dealing with communism in the Sudan, which contain documents of the SCP in their original Arabic.* I was also fortunate in obtaining a number of documents and publications of the SCP from the British Communist Party. All of these sources proved extremely useful for the preparation of this study. However, the gaps which remain in our knowledge of the SCP are still considerable and are likely to remain so in the foreseeable future.

The study on Communism is divided into three main sections. The first (chapter 3) is an historical survey of the SCP, and attempts to analyse the party's role in Sudanese politics, especially in the period following the struggle for independence in 1953–55. In the second section (chapter 4), I have chosen four topics which I regarded as crucial in attempting to understand the ideological framework of the SCP's policies. The first examines the SCP's attitude towards Egypt as well as its views on Arab unity and on the Arab–Israeli conflict. The other three deal with internal Sudanese policies: sectarianism and the SCP's attitude towards Islam; the problem of the South; and the SCP's attitude towards military coups leading to the party's split in 1970.

In section three (chapter 5) I have included five documents published by the SCP, all dealing with the crucial years 1970/71. The first two documents were previously published in Arabic in

* Ḥusayn 'Abd al-Rāziq, *Ḥaqā'iq al-Ṣidām m'a al-Ḥizb al-Shuyū'ī al-Sūdānī* (Beirut 1972); Fu'ād Maṭar, *al-Ḥizb al-Shuyū'ī al-Sūdānī naḥarūhu amm intaḥara* (Beirut 1971); Muḥammad Sulaymān, *al-Yasār al-Sūdānī fī 'Asharah a'wām 1954–1963* (Wād Madanī 1971).

Fu'ād Matar's book mentioned above. The other three are reprinted from the English version, which I obtained from the International Department of the Communist Party of Great Britain.

The reason why the Soviet Union hardly features in my present study is that its relations with Sudan were unaffected by the ups and downs of the SCP. As in other countries in Africa and Asia the communist bloc was unhampered in its dealings with the Sudan by the ideology or policies of the régime. Thus, during the military government of General 'Abbūd, Soviet–Sudanese relations flourished, though the SCP was outlawed and all its known leaders imprisoned. It therefore seemed meaningless to deal with Soviet–Sudanese relations in a study devoted to the internal intricacies of communism in the Sudan.

Finally, I would like to thank Professors Zbigniew Brzezinski and J. C. Hurewitz, both from Columbia University, who advised me during the early stages of my work; as well as Professor Oles Smolansky from Lehigh University and Dr. Wolfgang Berner of the Bundesinstitut für Ostwissenschaftliche Studien, in Köln, for their many useful suggestions made upon reading the first version of my study on Communism.

1978 G.W.

# Sudan in the 18th and 19th centuries*

Prior to the Turco-Egyptian conquest in 1820–21, the Sudan was not a uniform political and governmental unit, and the rule of the Funj Sultanate, from its centre in Sennar, was rule in name alone. The centres of power that arose in various areas of the country were based on the tribal and religious structure prevailing in the country at that time. The exact number of Sudanese tribes during that period is not clear, but can be assumed to have been not less than the 572 tribes counted during the first census in 1956. Most of these tribes (representing approximately thirty per cent of the population) were in the South, and are, therefore, outside the framework of this study. In the area extending north of Baḥr al-'Arab, the tribes were mostly composed of Arabic-speaking Muslims. However, even the population of that area was not homogeneous. Near the Egyptian border lived the Barābra-Nubian tribes, who spoke Nubian dialects in addition to Arabic. To the south of them, on both sides of the Nile, were a number of tribes related to the Ja'aliyyīn group. Although these tribes were largely Arabised and claimed a common forefather – Ja'al, a descendent of 'Abbās, uncle of the Prophet Muḥammad – there is no doubt that their origin is Nubian. The most northern tribe of the Ja'aliyyīn is the Danāqla, which inhabits the district of Dongola. The area south of them, near the bend of the Nile up to Abū Ḥamad, is inhabited by the Rubaṭāb and the Manāṣīr. One of the Ja'aliyyīn tribes, which occupies the area close to the junction of the 'Aṭbarā and the Nile, bears the name of the whole group. Within the Ja'aliyyīn, though not belonging to them, dwells the confederation of the Shāyqiyya in the area between the fourth cataract of the Nile and al-Dabba to the north. All these tribes are

* The following is based on my paper in M. Milson (ed), **Society and Political Structure in the Arab World**, Van Leer Jerusalem Foundation Series, Humanities Press N.Y. 1973, with the kind permission of the publishers.

mainly sedentary and are consequently known by the general name of *awlād al-balad*. Most of the other tribes claiming to be of Arab origin were nomads or semi-nomads. The most important among them were: the Kabābīsh, camel-breeding nomads who roam between the Nubian desert and northern Kordofan; the Baqqāra (colloquial, Baggara), cattle-breeding nomads who inhabit south Kordofan and south Dārfūr; along the Upper Blue Nile are the Rufā'a – one of whose leaders established the dynasty of the 'Abdallāb, which during the Funj sultanate became a centre of power among the Arab tribes. Another tribe of this group which began its rise to greatness during the Funj period is the Shukriyya – whose leader Aḥmad Abū Sinn attained the rank of Bey and the position of governor of Khartoum during the Turco-Egyptian period.[1]

In order to complete this short survey of the northern tribes, three non-Arab tribal groups ought to be mentioned. Firstly, the Fūr, founders of the sultanate of Dārfūr, in western Sudan, who, despite being Muslims, retain their own language up to the present day. The second group inhabits the hill region of south Kordofan, known as the Nuba mountains. The origins of the Nuba are not clear, but it is certain that they, in common with the Fūr, found shelter in the hill region following the penetration of Arab tribes into the Sudan. These tribes speak various dialects and have for the most part retained their pagan beliefs into the twentieth century. The third group, also living in a hill region, are the Beja of the Red Sea Mountains whose origin is Hamitic. As with the Barābra in the North, the Beja have accepted Islam, and to some extent the Arabic language as well. The most Arabised of the Beja tribes are the 'Abābda, who control the Nubian desert pass between Egypt and the Sudan. The most famous and militant amongst the Beja are the Hadendowa, nomads inhabiting the southern area of the Red Sea Mountains up to the 'Aṭbarā River and the delta of the Gash. These tribal groups retained a great deal of independence, recognised even by the Funj sultans. The power of the tribes grew during the hundred years preceding the Turco-Egyptian conquest, as the central authority of the sultanate broke up. The supreme position attained by certain families, such as the 'Abdallāb and the Abū Sinn in the Blue Nile region, has already been mentioned. Similarly, the confederation of the Shāyqiyya was practically independent, while the Ja'aliyyīn created for themselves a political-religious centre in al-Dāmir, at the junction of the Nile and the ʻAṭbarā. Funj rule in western Sudan, particularly amongst the nomad Baqqāra and Kabābīsh, was even more nominal, while the sultanate of Dārfūr had maintained an independent political status since 1596.

While the tribal structure of the Northern Sudan had a lasting impact on future developments, there was another phenomenon of great importance, namely the place of popular Islam in Sudanese society and politics.

This phenomenon is undoubtedly related to the character and methods of Islamic penetration into the Sudan. Islamisation commenced in the seventh century, following the conquest of Egypt by the Arabs and continued slowly until the fourteenth century. At that time, the Christian kingdom of al-Maqurra fell under the control of the Banū Kanz and broke up into a number of Muslim sultanates. Islam continued to penetrate southwards and in the sixteenth century the tribes under the protection of ʻAlwa – the southern Christian kingdom – had also been Islamised. Islamisation progressed gradually during the era of the Funj sultanate, its frontiers stabilizing along the twelfth parallel north. During this period – which lasted some three hundred years up to the Turco-Egyptian conquest – 'holy families', both immigrant and indigenous, started to play a central role in forming the special character of Islam in the Sudan.[2] The 'holiness' of these families was recognised in that their members – apart from being teachers of law and religion, and active in deepening and broadening the scope of Islamic influence – were also regarded as possessors of *baraka*, a power whose source lay in holiness and which brought its holders spiritual and physical happiness. According to belief, *baraka* was inheritable and its beneficiaries tended to claim that they were *ashrāf* (people tracing their descent to the Prophet Muḥammad). It can thus easily be understood that the functions of these leaders far exceeded the teaching of Islam, and they acquired political and social importance in their broadest meaning. By settling amongst the tribes of the northern Sudan, these 'holy families' became part of the ruling hierarchy. One of the best known amongst them was the 'Sons of Jābir', who, during the second half of the sixteenth century, settled among the Shāyqiyya and established a school for teaching Islamic law according to the Mālikī school. One of the

Jābir brothers attained a position of power and wealth which enabled him to maintain forty slaves as bodyguards. Another member of the same family married one of the queens of the Shāyqiyya, while Muḥammad Ṣughayyirūn, also a descendent of Awlād Jābir, settled on the banks of the Nile, south of its junction with the ʻAṭbarā, and opened yet another school for the Jaʻaliyyīn. But, while the ʻSons of Jābir' were teachers of law, who by virtue of their status achieved wealth and power, other saintly families were teachers of religion and heads of Ṣūfī *ṭarīqas* (orders) at one and the same time. One of the most notable examples of this phenomenon were the Majādhīb. Their progenitor was Ḥamad b. al-Majdhūb, a teacher of Muslim Law, who, during his pilgrimage to Mecca, had joined two Ṣūfī *ṭarīqas*. Upon his return to the Sudan, he founded a centre for the teaching of Muslim Law in al-Dāmir, south of the junction of the Nile and the ʻAṭbarā. Aside from his teaching, he also founded a Ṣūfī order, the Majdhūbiyya, a sub-order of the Qādiriyya. At the beginning of the nineteenth century, al-Dāmir was described as a spiritual centre, attracting students from all corners of the Sudan seeking to acquire knowledge and to be accepted, at the same time, into the ranks of the Majdhūbiyya. It is clear that a religious centre with such power acquired a significant socio-political status, not only among the Jaʻaliyyīn where it was located, but also in the Red Sea Mountains, among the Beja who roamed between the ʻAṭbarā and the port of Suakin. It must be added that the disintegration of the Funj sultanate reached its peak exactly in this period, with the rise of the Hamaj dynasty in 1762. The instability of the governing dynasties, as opposed to the stability of the ʻholy families', and of the tribes in whose shadow they dwelt, brought about the rise in tribal-religious power centres as an alternative to political vacuum.

The eighteenth century witnessed the revival of Ṣūfism throughout the Muslim world, and primarily in the Arab provinces. New Ṣūfī orders were founded in the Ḥejaz and spread quickly into other regions, which in many cases led to conflict with local orders. One of these new orders was the Sammāniyya, which was founded in the Sudan in the last quarter of the eighteenth century. Its founder, Aḥmad al-Ṭayyib b. al-Bashīr, established the order's centre near Sennar at the invitation of one of the Hamaj regents. The founder's closeness to the authorities helped the growth of the order's influence, but also aroused the jealousy of the older established 'holy families' of Sennar, primarily the Ya'qūbāb, who had settled in the area as early as the sixteenth century. Hence the Sammāniyya was forced to move its centre further north. Another order established shortly before the Turco-Egyptian conquest was the Khatmiyya, whose founder, Muḥammad 'Uthmān al-Mīrghanī, was a student of Aḥmad b. Idrīs al-Fāsī in the Ḥejaz. After the death of al-Fāsī, he founded his own Ṣūfī order, called the Mīrghaniyya, or the Khatmiyya, with the object of combining Wahhābī principles of puritan reform with Ṣūfī mysticism. The Khatmiyya found its supporters in the northern and eastern Sudan thus immediately coming into conflict with the more established orders, particularly with the Majdhūbiyya.

At the time of Muḥammad 'Ali's conquest in 1820–21, there was no real central government in the Sudan, and the Funj sultanate collapsed without resistance. However, the two alternative power centres, the tribes and popular Islam, had become stronger with the disintegration of the Funj kingdom. The sixty years of Turco-Egyptian rule were characterized by the government's attempts to undermine the power of the local leadership and integrate it into the new Egyptian administration.

It is not surprising, therefore, that while the Funj sultanate vanished from the stage of history without any attempt at resistance, a number of tribes showed violent opposition to the new rulers. The first to oppose the Turco-Egyptians were the Shāyqiyya, who were defeated in battle in November 1820. The results of this battle were important, not because of the defeat itself – hardly surprising in view of the relative strength and the technological superiority of the Egyptians – but rather because the patterns of the relationship between the Turco-Egyptians and the Shāyqiyya were established in an atmosphere of defeat. The courage and fighting ability of the tribe induced the new authorities to decide to exploit them for their own needs. Members of the Shāyqiyya were exempted from tax and conscripted as irregular cavalry (*bāshī būzuq*) into the army of the conquerors. Their main function henceforward was the collection of taxes imposed upon the other tribes – a function which they performed with great cruelty. The hostility of the riverain tribes, such as the Ja'aliyyīn and the Danāqla, to the

Shāyqiyya became an important factor in the Turco-Egyptian régime. Even more important was the rebellion which broke out among the Ja'aliyyīn in October 1822 and rapidly spread to other tribes. The causes were rooted in the Egyptian attempt to impose an administration and a tax system alien to the Sudanese – which undermined the existing political-economic framework and the authority of tribal leadership. While the Funj sultans had been satisfied with a nominal tribute sufficient to maintain their modest capital in Sennar, Muḥammad 'Alī sought to use the Sudan in furthering his plans for the economic and military aggrandisement of Egypt. However, his hopes of finding gold in the Sudan were not to be realised, while large-scale slave hunting would have necessitated conquering the South, which was beyond his power. Thus, the only remaining way to satisfy the administration's needs was through heavy taxation, which would force the tribes, who lacked money, to pay the authorities with slaves or cattle. The suppression of the rebellion took until 1824 and undermined the tribal frameworks, especially that of the Ja'aliyyīn, as well as causing part of the riverain tribes to flee the Sudan. Turco-Egyptian policy did not seek the destruction of the tribes since there was no substitute for them in the realities of the Sudan. However, the new régime was not prepared to recognise centres of power not subject to its authority. The tribes had, therefore, of necessity, to be regarded as administrative units, subject to their shaykhs, not because of the leadership qualities possessed by the latter, but because they represented central government. One of the Jazīra shaykhs was first appointed adviser on tribal affairs to the governor and later became *shaykh mashāyikh al-Sūdān*, but without being given any executive power.[3] While the authorities' control could not be extended to the nomads, the tribal heads of the settled, or semi-settled, tribes became dependent on the central government. The task of collecting taxes was given to the Copts, who acted as assessors, tax collectors (with the help of irregular soldiers), and bookkeepers. Junior Coptic officials lived with the tribes themselves – thus undermining the shaykhs' position even further. Shaykhs who showed an excessive degree of independence were deposed or taken as hostages to Khartoum, and their successors learned their lesson. In some cases, two shaykhs of rival families were appointed to different factions of the same tribe, with the clear purpose of politically weakening the tribe.[4]

The position of the tribes worsened towards the end of Turco-Egyptian rule, especially during the period of the Khedive Ismā'īl. On the one hand, the burden of taxation was increased due to the desperate situation of the Egyptian treasury as a result of wars in Abyssinia and pressure from European creditors. On the other, many tribes were disadvantaged by restrictions imposed on their slave hunting and trading activities. This policy reached its peak with the signing of the Anglo-Egyptian Convention for the Suppression of the Slave Trade in 1877, which was enforced in the Sudan by Gordon Pasha, then governor general, with the help of European officials. The war on slavery hit three main groups, the first two of which had been almost beyond the authorities' scope of control until then. The first were the slave traders themselves with their private armies, mainly composed of the *awlād al-balad* of the dispersion, such as the Danāqla, the Ja'aliyyīn and the Shāyqiyya – some of whom had been forced away from the Nile by population pressure or other economic factors, and had gained control of the slave trade mainly in the Baḥr al-Ghazāl. The second group included certain nomad tribes, such as the Baqqāra and the Kabābīsh, who had helped in transporting the slave convoys northwards and received payment for allowing convoys to pass through their territories. The third group included almost all the settled population living off agriculture, since attempts to restrict the slave trade caused a sharp rise in the price of domestic and agricultural slaves. Therefore, at the time of Ismā'īl's removal in 1879, and just before the 'Urābi rebellion in Egypt, a large section of the Sudanese tribal population was in a state of ferment and opposition to Turco-Egyptian rule was rife.[5]

It is difficult to ascertain the extent to which Turco-Egyptian rule succeeded in undermining the foundations of tribal loyalty in the Sudan. It seems that the settled tribes were more affected because of their proximity to the central government and because of their dependence on the Nile. Until the last decade of the Turco-Egyptian régime, the nomads hardly felt the heavy hand of the administration. The authorities had made no attempt to organise administration among the nomads, neither had they interfered with the powers of their shaykhs. It is known, however, that the authorities did support certain tribal leaders who lacked control over the entire tribe in order to acquire more influence for the central government by dividing the tribes into factions: examples can be found both amongst the Baqqāra of Kordofan and in the confederation of the Kabābīsh, which, during the second half of the nineteenth century, was divided into two groups, one in Kordofan and the other in Dongola. The undefined position of the shaykhs of the two groups is illustrated by the fact that the central authorities organised punitive action against a subtribe of the Kabābīsh without even consulting the tribe's supreme shaykh.[6] Central government interference reached its peak during the rule of Gordon Pasha as governor general, when other tribes, such as the Fūr and the Beja, were affected by pressure from the central administration, particularly in taxation and the war against slave trading. In any event, the power of the tribes decreased – as compared with the beginning of Turco-Egyptian rule – and the tribal map was greatly disrupted by the dispersal of powerful tribes, such as the Ja'aliyyīn, and by the blows dealt to the dispersed *awlād al-balad* at a later date. Conversely, a number of tribes improved their positions as a result of their close cooperation with the authorities. In addition to the Shāyqiyya, the 'Abādba along the Egyptian-Sudanese border also increased in strength by participating in governmental punitive campaigns against other tribes. Their shaykh, Ḥusayn Bey Khalīfa al-'Abbādī, was even appointed governor of Berber. Another tribe which benefited economically and politically as a result of Turco-Egyptian rule was the Shukriyya along the Blue Nile, whose leader, Aḥmad 'Awaḍ al-Karīm Abū Sinn, was appointed governor of the district of Khartoum.

Thus, the authorities tried to integrate the tribes into the administration, but for lack of an alternative were forced to accept their existence. With popular Islam, however, the conquerors had an alternative, which was already activated during the conquest. Three Egyptian *'ulamā'* were attached to the expeditionary force, with the function of explaining to the Sudanese Muslims that their conquest by the Turco-Egyptians was a legitimate act by the lawful ruler of the Muslims, the Ottoman sultan and caliph. It is difficult to suppose that this propaganda was successful among the leaders of popular Islam in the Sudan, especially as from the beginning the so-called 'orthodox' Muslim Egyptian *'ulamā'* were openly contemptuous of the local *fakīs*[7] and of the heads of the Ṣūfī *ṭarīqas*. Matters developed very quickly into open conflict following the Ja'aliyyīn uprising. It will be remembered that the Majdhūbiyya centre was founded in al-Dāmir under the protection of the Ja'aliyyīn. The uprising that broke out in 1822 thus also engulfed the *ṭarīqa*, and, after its suppression and the destruction of the Majdhūbī centre in al-Dāmir, the head of the order, Muḥammad al-Majdhūb al-Ṣughayyir, fled to Suakin and from there to Mecca. He was only permitted to return to the Sudan in 1830, when he discovered that his place amongst the Ja'aliyyīn had meanwhile been taken by the rival order of the Khatmiyya, and he was thus compelled, to be satisfied with the Red Sea Mountains as his area of activities. The hostile attitude of the Majdhūbiyya to the authorities sprang, therefore, from the latter's preferential treatment of another *ṭarīqa*.[8]

Similarly, the heads of most other *ṭarīqas* soon understood that their influence and sources of livelihood were being reduced under the new régime. The new authorities established *Sharī'a* courts, previously unknown in the Sudan, since the heads of the *ṭarīqas* and the 'holy families' had carried out all religious-judicial functions. The new courts, subordinate to government and headed by Egyptian *qaḍīs*, not only undermined the status of the Sudanese *fakīs* but also damaged them economically. Under the Funj sultanate, the heads of the *ṭarīqas* had enjoyed certain economic benefits, such as exemption from taxes, granting of lands (*ṣadaqa*), and even the maintenance of slaves as bodyguards at the expense of the ruler or the head of the tribe in whose area they dwelt. All these were now cancelled, and the *fakīs* became ordinary citizens paying taxes and no longer enjoying any privileges. In the field of education, although the hold of the *fakīs* continued until the rise of the Khedive Ismā'īl, the schools which they headed were now subordinate to the central administration, and Ismā'īl's attempts to create state schools in the Sudan threatened the status of the *fakīs* in this field as well. However, the authorities' policy of creating in the Sudan a local stratum of orthodox *'ulamā'* posed an even more serious threat. To this end, youngsters from the Sudan were sent to al-Azhar, where a special centre had been set up for them, *al-Riwāq al Sinnāriyya*. Upon returning to their homeland after a few years of study, these Azhar graduates were integrated into the structure of the *Sharī'a* courts and into teaching positions in the Koran schools. The growth of a generation of Sudanese *'ulamā'* with roots in Orthodox Islam – Egyptian-style and not in the popular Islam of the Sudan – produced a convenient forum for confrontation between the representatives of the two trends. In certain cases even a rift was brought about within the 'holy families', the outstanding example of which is the Ismā'īliyya order of al-'Ubayyiḍ, which was founded as a sub-order of the Khatmiyya in Kordofan by Muḥammad Ismā'īl b. 'Abdallāh al-Walī in 1842. One of his sons, Aḥmad Ismā'īl, was sent to study in al-Azhar on the initiative of the Egyptian authorities and, on completion of his studies, remained on at this institution as a teacher of Mālikī law. On his return to the Sudan, Aḥmad Ismā'īl al-Azharī was appointed *qāḍī* of al-'Ubayyiḍ and quickly came into conflict with his brother, al-Makkī Ismā'īl, who had become head of the Ismā'īliyya order after the death of his father in 1864. The Mahdist uprising, therefore, found the two brothers in rival camps. Aḥmad al-Azharī rose against the Mahdī, Muḥammad Aḥmad b. 'Abdallāh, to whom he referred as *'al-mutamahdī'* (one assuming the title *mahdī*, 'the heavenly guided'), and found his death in battle against the supporters of the Mahdī in Kordofan. His brother, al-Makkī Ismā'īl, was amongst the first adherents of the Mahdī – even before 'The Revelation' – and brought all the members of his order to the ranks of the Anṣār.[9]

The Khatmiyya, alone among the Ṣūfī orders, enjoyed the clear favour of the authorities. The coming of Muḥammad 'Uthmān al-Mīrghanī to the Sudan almost coincided with the Turco-Egyptian invasion. In the eyes of the inhabitants of the Sudan, the two happenings therefore appeared to be interconnected. In addition, the Turco-Egyptian authorities found no common language with the old established orders of the Sudan, nor with the leaders of the 'holy families', whom they considered superstitious fanatics and ignorant of Islamic law; not so the educated Mīrghanī family, descended from the *ashrāf*, who had come to the Sudan from Mecca, and whose customs and education soon brought about a closer relationship between them and the rulers. The banishment of the Majdhūbiyya leaders from the Sudan at this time created a vacuum which the founders of the Khatmiyya well knew how to exploit. Their influence grew among the riverain tribes, and particularly the Shāyqiyya, who, as protégés of the Turco-

Egyptians, were quick to come to an understanding with the Khatmiyya order. Thus the Khatmiyya's centre, which had been established near Kassala, became a source of spiritual support for the Turco-Egyptian authorities who, in turn, expressed their gratitude by subsidising the order's activities. But far from limiting itself to the vicinity of Kassala, the Khatmiyya succeeded within a relatively short period in gaining adherents in many parts of the northern Sudan.

The process of undermining the status of popular Islam reached its peak during the reign of Khedive Ismā'īl, when the central government tried, by means of economic and educational policies, to drive the Ṣūfī leadership from their traditional positions and impose Azharite Islam, imported from Egypt. However, the Mahdī's uprising put an end to this process before it ripened.[10] *'Ulamā'* al-Azhar – or, in the language of the Mahdī, *'ulamā' al-sū'* (evil *'ulamā'*) – vanished as though they had never been. Some of them fled with their Egyptian masters or fell in battle, others adopted the teachings of the Mahdī and became his disciples. The process of undermining popular Islam was stopped by the Mahdī in its early stages while it still retained its influence. The evidence of Lieutenant Colonel Stewart, who was sent in 1883 by the British Government to report on the situation in the Sudan at the beginning of the Mahdī's uprising, is revealing. Stewart states that the ignorance of the inhabitants hindered all the efforts of Orthodox Islam to penetrate the Sudan, and hence, in his words, 'the enormous influence of the Fakis, or spiritual leaders, who are credited with a supernatural power, and are almost more venerated than the Prophet ...'[11]

The appearance of the Mahdiyya in the Sudan, its success and crystallisation into a political entity, were largely based on the tribal structure of the Sudan and the strength of popular Islam. Faith in a *mahdī* is fairly prevalent in *Sunnī* Islam, but, unlike in the *Shī'a*, it has never become an integral part of *Sunnī* faith. The appearance of a *Sunnī mahdī* was therefore usually restricted to areas far from centres of government and from the influence of Orthodox Islam. It is thus not surprising that the Sudan, soaked in popular mystical beliefs, was ready and prepared for the appearance of the Mahdiyya. During the nineteenth century, several claimants to the throne of the *mahdī* appeared in the Nile Valley and their number increased at the beginning of the twentieth century after the conquest of the Sudan by the Anglo-Egyptian army. The Mahdī himself, Muḥammad Aḥmad be 'Abdallāh, possessed a clearly Ṣūfī background and even before his 'revelation' belonged to, and was appointed shaykh of, the Sammāniyya order. His call to *jihād* against the infidel was primarily aimed at the 'Turks', representatives of foreign rule and so-called Orthodox Islam in the Sudan.[12]

As a Ṣūfī shaykh and member of the Danāqla tribe, the Mahdī understood that his success depended on the support of two central elements in Sudanese society – the heads of the tribes and the leaders of popular mystic Islam. Thus, at the beginning of his call, the Mahdī's letters to the heads of the Ṣūfī *ṭarīqas* are full of symbols taken from Ṣūfism. During the first visit to Kordofan in 1880, even before he had declared his mission, the Mahdī acquired the support of Muḥammad Ismā'īl al-Makkī, head of the Ismā'īli order, and was active among the dispersed *awlād al-balad* who formed the most important social stratum in Kordofan.[13] The three major elements that supported the Mahdī at the beginning of his mission were, therefore, members of his own family, the so-called *ashrāf*, some heads of Ṣūfī *ṭarīqas*, and sections of the *awlād al-balad* in Kordofan and Dārfūr.

The migration (*hijra*) of the Mahdī and his supporters from the island of Abā to Qadīr, in the Nuba Mountains, on 31 October 1881 brought an additional element into his camp – the Baqqāra of Kordofan and Dārfūr. In his letters to the tribal shaykhs and heads of the Ṣūfi *ṭarīqas* during this period, the Mahdī recognises them as his disciples and as the leaders of their respective *ṭarīqas* and tribes amongst their loyal followers. Thus, at this stage, the Mahdī was not yet attempting to impose his mission as the single focus of authority and leadership, but was prepared to accept the existence of additional centres of power, on condition that they declared their loyalty to his movement. This tolerance was already somewhat diminished in 1883 after the Mahdist conquest of al-Ubayyiḍ and the defeat of the Egyptian army under Colonel Hicks in Shaykān. The Mahdī, now controlling all of Kordofan and Dārfūr, and assured of his power, called upon the leaders of the tribes that were still vacillating to join him and carry out the *jihād* in their areas. The undertone of threat in his letters was clear, since he who did not join the Mahdī would henceforward be considered an infidel belonging to the enemy camp. The rebellions in the Jazīra, south of Khartoum, and in Berber, to the north, were the results of the Mahdī's success in the West and the activities of his agents among the tribes. An outstanding example of this was the mission of 'Uthmān Diqna to the Red Sea Mountains in 1883. The success of the Mahdiyya in this area was dependent on recruiting the Beja tribes into the ranks of the Anṣār. Two Ṣūfī *ṭarīqas* were active in the Red Sea Mountains – the Majdhūbiyya and the Khatmiyya. 'Uthmān Diqna was therefore supplied with letters from the Mahdī to the two leaders of the *ṭarīqas*, in which they were called upon to join the ranks of his movement together with their supporters. The response of the Majdhūbiyya was immediate, since their hostility to the authorities who had destroyed their centre at al-Dāmir, and their jealousy of the Khatmiyya, who enjoyed Turco-Egyptian patronage, caused them to regard the Mahdī as an ally against the common enemy.[14] This brought to the Mahdī's camp an element which was important from both the religious and political-military aspects, since the recruitment of the Majdhūbiyya brought many warriors of the Beja, and primarily the Hadendowa, to the ranks of the Anṣār. The leaders of the Khatmiyya refused to join the Mahdī, and their head, Muḥammad Sirr al-Khatim al-Mīrghanī, was later compelled to leave his centre near Kassala and go into exile in Egypt. There is a basis for the supposition that the Mahdi"s approach to the Khatmiyya did not spring from naiveté, as it was difficult to assume that the order's head – so closely connected with the authorities and the orthodox *'ulamā'* – would support an uprising. However, the Mahdī's letters could at this stage, by relying on his great military victories, bring about a split amongst the members of the *ṭarīqa* and undermine their faith in their leadership.

The military administrative organization of the Mahdist state was also on a tribal basis. While the appointment of the Mahdī's *khalīfas* was made in order to emphasize the parallel between the Mahdī and the Prophet Muḥammad, the division of the Mahdī's armies in practice represented the major tribal and cultural divisions of the Sudan: *awlād al-balad* under the red flag of the *khalīfa*, Muḥammad Sharīf, and the Baqqāra under the command of the *khalīfa*, 'Abdallāh al-Ta'īshī, of the black flag. The military-political power of these two camps and the friction between them played a decisive role in the development of the Mahdist state up to its destruction. It has been noted that the powerful groups which first joined the Anṣār were those of *awlād al-balad* who had been badly affected by the suppression of the slave trade in Baḥr al-Ghazāl, Dārfūr, and Kordofan, and brought to the Mahdī's camp their private armies, consisting of slaves. This tribal element, therefore, fulfilled an important role in the first stage of the Mahdiyya, and the majority of the military commanders of the Anṣār were drawn from its ranks. But the recruitment of the Baqqāra tribes after the *hijra* to Qadīr in the Nuba Mountains upset the tribal balance, and the strength of the black flag grew. The attempts of the *ashrāf* and of *awlād al-balad* – based on their tribal-familial closeness to the Mahdī – to achieve supremacy in the state led the Mahdī to condemn his relatives and the men of his tribe in public and declare his full trust in 'Abdallāh al-Ta'īshī as *khalīfat al-mahdī.*[15] Nevertheless, it was clear, even before the death of the Mahdī, that the tribal coalition which had united for the purpose of war against a foreign ruler was destined to bring about open conflict between the two camps, since the religious mission of the Mahdiyya was not sufficient to bridge tribal differences.

The *khalīfa* 'Abdallāh's rise to power constitutes a turning point in the Mahdist state and in its relationship to the two main components of Sudanese society – the tribes and the *ṭarīqas*. While the Mahdī enjoyed an aura of holiness – thanks to his mission and his victories in battle – the *khalīfa* was considered by the *ashrāf* and *awlād al-balad* as a member of a western tribe, ignorant of religious matters, and so primitive that he was not sufficiently proficient in Arabic and did not even know how to read and write. From the beginning, therefore, the *khalīfa*'s foundation of power involved a struggle with his opponents and attempts to neutralise or even destroy them. In the first stage, the *khalīfa* split up the army of the *awlād al-balad*, deposed most of its leaders, and put it under the command of loyal members of the Ta'āisha. In the second stage, he confronted the members of the *ashrāf*, and particularly their *khalīfa*, Muḥammad Sharīf, restricted their power, and turned them into a group deprived of governing functions. At the end of 1886, a year after the Mahdī's death, only two of the *awlād al-balad* commanders were left in their positions, and even they did not threaten 'Abdallāh's rule because of their remoteness from Omdurman.[16]

The next stage of 'Abdallāh's tribal policy was to organise a mass migration of the Baqqāra – headed by his own tribe, the Ta'āīsha – from the West to the central areas of Omdurman and the Jazīra. Two main reasons apparently motivated this step: firstly, the safeguarding of his direct control over the Baqqāra, who being independent nomads were not inclined to accept the orders of central government. The Abū Jummayza uprising in 1887–89 showed clearly that the loyalty of the western tribes to the Mahdist state could be easily upset, should a new religious leader appear who could promise them their freedom. The migration of the Baqqāra to the capital was likely to undermine the powers of their tribal leaders and make them dependent on central government. Secondly, as a son of the west, the *khalīfa* probably preferred the proximity of members of his own tribe to that of the *awlād al-balad*, who were his declared enemies. The migration of the Baqqāra to the east was achieved by means of threats and pressure on their leaders, and in 1888–89 they came to the Jazīra driving some of the local tribes from their lands.[17]

After the battle of Ṭūshkī in 1889 (in which the last military commander of the *awlād al-balad*, 'Abd al-Raḥmān al-Nujūmī, was killed) all the Mahdist armies were put under the command of the Baqqāra, excepting the Beja tribes in the East, whose commander, 'Uthmān Diqna, stayed in his position up to the Anglo-Egyptian conquest. Parallel with the deposition of the military commanders, 'Abdallāh also got rid of the tribal heads who were showing too much independence. Madibbū 'Alī, head of the Rizayqāt – one of the strongest Baqqāra tribes in Dārfūr (who had been among the first to join the Mahdi in that area, thereby helping directly in the downfall of the Turco-Egyptian régime) – was executed in 1886. When it became clear to the *khalīfa* that Madibbū was showing too much independence, and trying to seize power in south Dārfūr, he ordered him brought to Omdurman. On the way to the capital, he was executed by the commander of the Mahdist army in Kordofan. Shortly thereafter, a section of the Kabābīsh in northern Kordofan rebelled, and their leader, Ṣāliḥ Faḍl Allāh Sālim, refused to obey the orders of the *khalīfa*'s messengers. Ṣālih was killed in battle in May 1887, and tribal opposition was broken following a punitive expedition which lasted a year and was assisted by tribes hostile to the Kabābīsh.[18] An additional attempt at resistance to 'Abdallāh's rule and to the Ta'āisha also took place against a tribal-religious background. In November of 1891 the *ashrāf* rebelled, supported by the *awlād al-balad* who were led by the Danāqla, the Mahdī's tribe. The *khalīfa* Muḥammad Sharīf, and the Mahdī's family, had become aware that under 'Abdallāh's régime not only were their rights and status as leaders affected, but they were also dependent on the charity of the Ta'āisha for their livelihood. Tribal support for this group was guaranteed by the fact that the *awlād al-balad* had not only lost their military superiority, but had also been directly hurt by the tax policies and by the loss of lands taken by the Baqqāra. The *khalīfa* 'Abdallāh was informed of the intended rebellion and on the night of 23 November 1891 the rebels, who had found shelter by the Mahdī's tomb, were surrounded and compelled to agree to a compromise – the practical interpretation of which was an end of their hopes of return to power. Father Ohrwalder, one of the Catholic missionaries imprisoned by the Mahdī, who had fled Omdurman during the rebellion, noted justly that the rule of the *khalīfa* 'Abdallāh was now total and that anyone plotting rebellion was doomed to failure.[19]

The situation of the heads of the *ṭarīqas* and of the 'holy families' was not much better. The decline of status of the *ashrāf* after the rise of the *khalīfa* has already been noted, and the fate of other religious leaders was no different. *Fakīs* who showed too much independence, or who for any reason whatsoever aroused suspicion of the *khalīfa*, were wiped out or brought as hostages to Omdurman. Thus al-Manna Ismā'īl, a Sammāniyya shaykh active among the Baqqāra, was executed. At the beginning of the Mahdiyya, he had fought by the Mahdī's side and gained great influence. But, in 1883, when it appeared to the *khalīfa* that al-Manna's influence was undermining his own status, he had him executed. Al-Ṭāhir al-Ṭayyib al-Majdhūb – whose support for the Mahdī had been vital in bringing the Beja tribes to the Mahdist fold – was also compelled to accept the *khalīfa*'s rulings and to desist from any show of independence. The *ṭarīqas*' centres and the graves of their saints were destroyed wherever a suspicion arose that they could become centres of power endangering the supremacy of central government.

If we remember that the supreme judicial power was also in the hands of the *khalīfa* and that the *qaḍīs*, including the *qaḍī al-*

*Islām*, were subservient to his authority, then it becomes clear that the Mahdiyya succeeded exactly where the Turco-Egyptian régime had failed. Over the ten years after their rise to power, the Mahdī and his heir, the *khalīfa*, were able to undermine the two traditional power centres of Sudanese society and impose their rule upon them. By this means the Sudan was united around a new centre of power. The new rulers were assisted in the beginning by the 'holy families' and the traditional tribal framework, but, when the régime had become established, they seemed superfluous, and their removal justified. Thus, a new tribal-religious autocracy was created, which succeeded, by means of inducements, threats, and acts of violence, to unite around itself all the previous frameworks. In 1895, Slatin Pasha was able to sum up his ten years of close connection with the *khalīfa* 'Abdallāh in Omdurman by saying that the power of central government and the fear of the inhabitants of the Sudan was so great that even the most downtrodden amongst them would not rebel unless the *khalīfa*'s final defeat could be guaranteed in advance.[20] Thus, when the Mahdist state came to its end in 1898, it was not the result of internal disintegration, but rather because of the superior military and technological power of the Anglo-Egyptian Army.

# I

# Sectarian Politics in the Sudan

CHAPTER 1

# From Anṣār to Umma, 1914–1945

The establishment of the Anglo-Egyptian condominium once again brought the Sudan under foreign domination and returned the exiled leader of the Khatmiyya, Sayyid ʻAlī al-Mīrghanī, to the country as a protégé of the new rulers. On the other hand, the leading Anṣār – and especially the surviving members of the Mahdī's and the khalīfa's families – were suspect, and remained under constant surveillance by the British-directed intelligence department until the First World War. Thus the twentieth century opened with a clear advantage for the Khatmiyya. Its leader, Sayyid ʻAlī, was the first Sudanese to be honoured with a C.M.G. by Queen Victoria. Moreover, the Khatmiyya, despite the government's tendency to regard Ṣūfism and the local *fakīs* as superstitious fanatics, received special treatment from the authorities, including financial aid.

British officers, from the Governor-General down, filled all the important posts in the administration of the Sudan, and did not intend to rely on their Egyptian partners as co-rulers. They regarded Egyptian maladministration during the nineteenth century as the primary cause of the Mahdist revolt, and were therefore determined to rule the Sudan with as little interference from Cairo as possible. To achieve this aim they needed the support of the Sudanese and tried to foster an indigenous leadership, both tribal and religious, which would gradually assume responsibility in the lower echelons of the administration and thus make the Egyptian presence superfluous. Until the First World War progress along these lines was rather slow. Lack of funds forced the government to concentrate its efforts on the more essential spheres of administration, such as pacifying the country, resettling tribes, and building the basic minimum of an adequate communications system. Moreover, many of the older leaders had collaborated with the khalīfa and hence were viewed with suspicion: the evolution of a new class of leaders required both time and education. Although the authorities attempted to enhance local leadership they did so in a very ambivalent fashion. A 'Board of Ulema' was established in 1900 to advise the government in its religious policy and to mediate between the authorities and the community of believers. In reality, however, the Board was no more than a rubber-stamp for government policy; its members played the 'Vicars of Bray' and had little influence either on the government or on the people.[1]

The government's tribal policy also aimed at re-establishing local leaders but this task was even more difficult. Tribal society and leadership had been greatly disrupted during the Mahdiyya. Moreover, by trying to integrate the tribal leaders into the administration, the government undermined their authority within their tribes, and they tended to assume the role of the British inspectors' messenger-boys rather than becoming leaders in their own right. To use the words of one British administrator '... The equivalent of the Arab type Omda scurrilously known as Kelb el Hakuma [*sic*] was by no means uncommon ...'[2]

Sayyid 'Alī al-Mīrghanī thus enjoyed a clear advantage during that period. He was a highly respected religious leader heading a centralized *ṭarīqa* whose influence had survived the Mahdiyya and was gaining new adherents throughout northern and eastern Sudan. Moreover, during his sojourn in Egypt, Sayyid 'Alī had established close relations with Sir Reginald Wingate, who was to become Governor-General of the Sudan from 1899 to 1916, as well as with other high-ranking British officers. The authorities therefore recognized him as the supreme Mīrghanīst leader, favouring him over his elder brother Aḥmad and other Mīrghanī notables who had remained in the Sudan during the Mahdiyya.[3] In the years before the First World War Sayyid 'Ali emerged as the strongest supporter of the anti-Egyptian policy adopted by the British administration in the Sudan. In this he was even more extreme and more outspoken than the new rulers, whom he accused on more than one occasion of softness and ambivalence in their treatment of the Egyptians. Sayyid 'Alī advocated a complete rupture with Egypt and the establishment of a purely Anglo-Sudanese administration.[4]

This attitude was probably representative of that of a wide cross-section of Sudanese who had either experienced Turco-Egyptian rule in the nineteenth century, or were still feeling the impact of the anti-Turkish (Egyptian) propaganda of the Mahdist state. Egyptian counter-propaganda made little headway with this generation of Sudanese. However, a younger generation was emerging which had been educated in government schools and taught in the main by Egyptian teachers, or had lived side by side with Egyptian officers in the Sudanese battalions of the Egyptian army. These young Sudanese felt more akin to their fellow Muslims and Arabic-speaking Egyptians than to the more aloof and alien English speaking Christian administrators. To the dismay and fear of both the British authorities and the traditional leaders and older generation of Sudanese, Egyptian nationalist propaganda appealed with increasing force to these younger elements.

## THE EMERGENCE OF SAYYID ʻABD AL-RAḤMĀN, 1914–24

Sayyid ʻAbd al-Raḥmān, the Mahdī's son, was born in Omdurman on 15 June 1885, and was thus only thirteen years old when the battle of Karari brought the Mahdist state to an end in September 1898. A few months later he was wounded by British soldiers in a seemingly unprovoked attack in which two of his brothers were killed. All the male survivors of the Mahdī's family were arrested and exiled to Rashīd (Rosetta), but ʻAbd al-Raḥmān, due to his youth, was allowed to remain with the womenfolk of his family on the Island of al-Fīl.[5] In 1906 he made his first visit to Abā Island, where the Mahdist movement had started in June 1881. It was there that he decided to renew his connections with the Anṣār, his father's one-time supporters, and to make Abā the spiritual, social and economic centre of the movement.[6] However, ʻAbd al-Raḥmān and his family were still suspect and were not allowed to leave al-Fīl Island until 1908, when they were granted permission to move to the ʻAbbāsiyya quarter of Omdurman, where they remained under the constant surveillance of the intelligence department. It was in 1908 that ʻAbd al-Raḥmān was allowed to start cultivating the family estates on Abā Island. There the Anṣār were reborn as a religious-political movement.

The outbreak of the First World War changed the fortunes of Sayyid 'Abd al-Raḥmān and his followers. With Turkey joining the Central powers and the declaration of a Muslim holy war (*jihād*) against the Entente's infidels, Great Britain was concerned about the loyalty of its Muslim colonies. In broader terms this brought about a new orientation in Britain's policy towards Islam and the Arabs, culminating in the McMahon-Ḥusayn correspondence and the Sykes-Picot agreement. The Sudan was a focal point in these deliberations, not because of its own importance but as a result of the considerable influence wielded over British policy-makers by Wingate and by certain members of his staff.[7] As far as the Sudan was concerned, a change in policy was clearly warranted. Firstly, in their effort to recruit support against pan-Islamic propaganda originating in Turkey, the British authorities tried to win the loyalty of Sudanese Muslims; and secondly, with Egypt becoming a British protectorate and likely to become independent in the not too distant future, it became imperative to eradicate or at least greatly reduce Egyptian influence in the Sudan. British propaganda was aimed primarily at Sudanese leaders, but was also directed at every sector of the Sudanese people. It was, however, abundantly clear that leaders of popular Islamic organisations of the *ṭarīqa* type enjoyed greater influence than tribal shaykhs or orthodox *'ulamā'*. Among the former Sayyid 'Alī al-Mīrghanī reigned supreme, but it was realized that ex-Madhists, who were known to be both numerous and vehemently anti-Turkish and anti-Egyptian, could provide most welcome support for the new policy. Consequently Sayyid 'Abd al-Raḥmān was allowed to emerge from near-obscurity and to tour the strongholds of the Anṣār, preaching to his followers that the Young Turks were heretics, and that the future of the Sudan would be best secured through loyalty to Great Britain. The Sayyid was, however, shrewd enough to realise that religious and political strength required financial power. He therefore expanded his agricultural enterprises during the war, when both needs and prices ran high, and brought hundreds of Anṣār, especially from the west, to cultivate his fields on Abā Island and on the banks of the Blue and White Niles.[8] He thus emerged from the war a leader in his own right, and by Sudanese standards, a rich man.

Following the end of the war and the dismemberment of the

Ottoman Empire Anglo-Sudanese attention was focused on the renewed menace of Egyptian nationalism and its repercussions in the Sudan. By December 1918 Sir Lee Stack, the Governor-General of the Sudan, had already warned the British authorities of the widespread effects of Egyptian nationalism in the Sudan.[9] The Egyptian national revolt in March 1919 brought matters to a head. Unrest spread through various towns in the Sudan and rumours were spread that, following Egyptian independence, Egypt would assume full control of the Sudan.[10]

Egyptian claims and propaganda centred on several different issues. First, the demand for the 'Unity of the Nile Valley' and the sovereignty of Egypt over the Sudan were reiterated. Second, the British were accused of assuming full control of the Sudan, contrary to the 1899 Condominium Agreement, and of turning the Sudan into a Lancashire-dominated cotton farm (the Jazīra development project was the focus of these attacks). Finally, Egypt accused the British administrators of encouraging '... an artificial Sudanese separatist movement ...' and of '... violently suppressing the manifestations of loyal attachment to Egypt ...'[11] In a manifesto, published by the Wafd in the *Egyptian Gazette* on 6 June 1924, Great Britain was warned that its suppression of pro-Egyptian nationalist feelings in the Sudan would result in trouble. It further promised the Sudanese '... that the day of their emancipation is not far distant ...'

The British authorities in the Sudan reacted vehemently to what they regarded as unlawful interference in the Sudan's internal affairs. They not only accused the Egyptians of spreading propaganda but claimed that Egypt supplied both the brains and the money for anti-British movements in the Sudan. Although no conclusive proof was ever produced for these accusations, and there were repeated denials from Cairo, British policy-makers in the Sudan had no doubt in their own minds that Cairo was the hot-bed of anti-British movements such as the White Flag League, and that the necessary funds for the operations of these movements were smuggled in from Egyptian sources.[12]

How were the British authorities to fight against this annoying interference? The most obvious solution was to get rid, as quickly as possible, of the Egyptian officers serving in the Sudan. The setting up of an independent Sudan Defence Force and the evacuation of the Egyptian army units from the Sudan were suggested by Keown-Boyd as early as March 1920.[13] By August 1924, details for the execution of this plan had been submitted by the Sudanese authorities to Lord Allenby in Cairo.[14] As for the replacement of Egyptian officials by Sudanese, the British proposed to do this at an accelerated pace '... even at a cost of administrative efficiency ...'[15] Thus, the die was cast for the evacuation of the Egyptians from the Sudan long before Sir Lee Stack's assassination, which only provided Lord Allenby with the pretext for putting the policy into effect.[16]

There was, however, another way to combat Egyptian propaganda which could be executed immediately, namely, to recruit all Sudanese leaders who were regarded as loyal to British aims, in order to prove that Egyptian propaganda affected only a small and insignificant part of the Sudanese population. Letters of loyalty from religious and tribal notables poured in from all the provinces, and in April 1919 the Governor-General decided to send a delegation of Sudanese leaders to London to express their loyalty to the British King and government, and to dissociate themselves from Egyptian nationalist claims.[17] The delegation, headed by Sayyid 'Ali al-Mīrghanī, consisted of religious and tribal leaders, but was first and foremost a delegation of the leaders of popular Islamic movements. In addition to Sayyid 'Alī, these included Sayyid 'Abd al-Raḥmān al-Mahdī and al-Sharīf Yūsuf al-Hindī, head of the Hindiyya *ṭarīqa* and one of the most outspoken critics of Egypt in the Sudan.[18]

Sayyid 'Abd al-Raḥmān derived the greatest political advantage from this delegation. Describing the reasons for his anti-Egyptian stand and for his cooperation with the British authorities, the Sayyid wrote that he regarded the White Flag League and other pro-Egyptian elements as off-shoots of Egyptian nationalism which had nothing to do with the true national aspiration of the vast majority of Sudanese, which was independence. Cooperation with the British was dictated by political realities. An armed uprising, as advocated by some fanatics, could only have led to total destruction. By so-called collaboration with the authorities, the Sayyid and his followers hoped to advance gradually towards full independence.[19] Sayyid 'Abd al-Raḥmān and his followers reaped many advantages through cooperating in the anti-Egyptian drive. Firstly, while in London, Sayyid 'Abd al-Raḥmān presented the Mahdī's sword to King George V, thereby assuming the position of the true leader of the Sudanese, and implying the existence of a newly-forged bond between the Anṣār and the British government. Secondly, the Anṣār, which had hitherto been considered an illegal movement, prone to fanaticism, was now regarded by the authorities as an important ally. Thus instead of relying on secret circulars, which he had sent to the Anṣār, beseeching them to keep their allegiance (*bay'a*) with the Imām al-Mahdī, 'Abd al-Raḥmān could now preach openly to gatherings of the Anṣār, and use the Mahdī's prayer-book (*rātib*) without fear of repercussions.[20] But even more important politically was the beginning of a new alliance between Sayyid 'Abd al-Raḥmān and certain sections of the young Sudanese intelligentsia. To counteract 'Alī 'Abd al-Laṭīf and his followers in the White Flag League, the Sayyid helped to found the first graduates' club in the Sudan in 1919, and was instrumental in establishing its first political newspaper *Ḥaḍārat al-Sūdān*, in 1920. The paper, edited by the Sayyid's nephew, Muḥammad al-Khalīfa Sharīf, became the most outspoken organ of 'the Sudan for the Sudanese' movement and succeeded in drawing several of the ablest spokesmen of the younger generation to Sayyid 'Abd al-Raḥmān's side. Among them was Yuzbashī 'Abdallāh Khalīl, who was then an officer in the Egyptian army and was later to become general secretary of the Umma party and Prime Minister of the Sudan after independence. Others included Yuzbashī Ḥammad Ṣāliḥ and Aḥmad 'Uthmān al-Qaḍī, who became editor of *al-Ḥaḍāra* following Sharīf's death and succeeded in establishing close relations with the Wafd, despite his outspoken opposition to the 'Unity of the Nile Valley'.[21]

By the end of 1924, following the removal of the Egyptian army and officials from the Sudan and the virtual annihilation of pro-Egyptian elements among the Sudanese officers and educated classes, Sayyid 'Abd al-Raḥmān had a clear advantage over his main rival Sayyid 'Alī. He had a well organized body of followers in the Anṣār, enjoyed the respect and adherence of leading members of the young intelligentsia, and had the financial means to further his political ambitions. When in September 1924 Sayyid 'Ali al-Mīrghanī declared that he would prefer to see the Sudan under the Egyptian Crown rather than be subject to a Sudanese monarchy headed by Sayyid 'Abd al-Raḥmān,[22] the die was cast for sectarian politics in the Sudan. Thus, by the mid-1920s, while many of the numerous other *ṭarīqas* continued to flourish at the local village level, the Khatmiyya and the Anṣār had emerged as the sole popular Islamic movements contending for political power.

### THE YEARS OF AMBIVALENCE: 1925–1938

Following the expulsion of the Egyptian army and of Egyptian personnel from the Sudan in 1924, the political importance of the two Sayyids to the authorities declined. Moreover, through 'native administration', British officialdom tried to establish direct links with the tribal population, using tribal shaykhs rather than religious leaders as their intermediaries.[23] The adverse effects of this policy were felt by both Sayyids but, while Sayyid 'Alī could easily cope with the new situation, it created a major obstacle for Sayyid 'Abd al-Raḥmān and his Anṣār. Sayyid 'Alī's advantage lay both in his personality and in the organization and distribution of his supporters. The British regarded the Sayyid as the most trustworthy leader in the Sudan, due to the anti-Mahdist and anti-Egyptian inclinations he had shown in the past, as well as to the loyal support he gave the British authorities after the reconquest. Moreover, the authorities knew that Sayyid 'Alī was a man with no political ambitions, and that he would be glad to resume his role as a purely religious leader. As for the Khatmiyya, its support was derived primarily from the more sophisticated population of the 'Three Towns' (Khartoum, Khartoum North and Omdurman) and of the Northern province, and therefore the effect of native administration on its leadership and members was minimal. An official biographical note on Sayyid 'Alī illustrates the views of the British rulers: '... Sayed Ali ... is by tradition and upbringing a conservative. A man of great personal charm and, through his followers, of great influence, he has loyally and consistently supported the Sudan government for the last forty years, though as an onlooker rather than a man of action ...'[24] Hence the Sayyid and the Khatmiyya were never regarded as a political threat and, to the British authorities, even Sayyid 'Alī's interest in Egypt '... did not seem to have political implications ...'[25]

Sayyid 'Abd al-Raḥmān and his Anṣār were in an altogether different category. True, the Sayyid had performed important political services for the British both during the war and during the years of Egyptian agitation which followed it. But now that his services were no longer required he was expected to assume the role of a purely religious leader and to forego his political ambitions. Even as a religious leader Sayyid 'Abd al-Raḥmān's position was far from secure. While the British regarded the neo-Mahdists, as they called the Anṣār, as a legitimate religious sect, fear of fanatic Mahdism was still acute, and they therefore viewed the Sayyid and his followers with suspicion. As early as 1923, the authorities were concerned about the great number of Mahdist pilgrims who had come to celebrate Ramaḍān on Abā Island. Of the 5,000–15,000 pilgrims gathered on the Island, some identified Sayyid 'Abd al-Raḥmān with *Nabī* 'Īsā (the prophet Jesus) who they believed would, with the aid of his Anṣār, drive the Christian-Colonialist power, identified as *dajjāl* (anti-Christ), out of the Sudan. Following a mass demonstration of the Anṣār on Abā Island in 1924, the authorities decided '... to stop these displays which were beginning to disturb the public ...' The Sayyid was ordered to discontinue the pilgrimage and to command his adherents to disperse.[26] A year later, when plans for the establishment of the Sudan Defence Force (SDF) were discussed, the possibility of a Mahdist uprising was taken into consideration.[27] Therefore the authorities did their utmost to keep the Anṣār out of the SDF. The *Secret Sudan Intelligence Reports (S.S.I.R.)*, which had been compiled on a monthly basis since the beginning of 1926, showed the relative strength of the Anṣār in the different units of the SDF, and a special recruiting policy was adopted in order to keep their numbers down.[28]

Government fears of fanatical Mahdism were bound to have repercussions on Sayyid 'Abd al-Raḥmān's position. Although the authorities did not regard the Sayyid as a fanatic, they feared his ambitions and were suspicious of his growing wealth and influence. The forced resignation of Sir Geoffrey Archer, Governor-General of the Sudan in 1925–6, is probably the best illustration of the setback to the Sayyid's fortunes. When at the beginning of 1926 Sayyid 'Abd al-Raḥmān was awarded the K.B.E., senior British officials in the Sudan regarded this as an ample reward for his services. They remarked of the Sayyid that '... from an insignificant Sheikh at £E15 a month he had been elevated by Government to a K.B.E. at £E20,000 a year ...'[29]

They regarded any further encouragement of the Sayyid's ambitions as detrimental to the political-religious balance of the Sudan and its security. Archer visited the Sayyid on Abā Island in March 1926. Instead of playing the visit down, as he had been advised to do by his senior officials, he arrived on Abā in full uniform, accompanied by troops and a host of officials. What had been intended as a courteous visit became an official meeting between two leaders. To make matters worse, Archer made a speech extolling Sayyid 'Abd al-Raḥmān's loyalty and the ever-growing bond between the Sayyid and the British administration. This speech had two important results: Archer was forced to resign and was replaced by Sir John Maffey; and the political ambitions of Sayyid 'Abd al-Raḥmān, which had been the bone of contention between Archer and his advisers, were even more drastically curtailed.[30] The Sayyid was ordered to instruct his supporters on Abā Island and elsewhere to disband their organisations and to refrain from all religious and political activities. Still worse was the restriction of the Sayyid's movements; he was ordered not to leave Khartoum or Omdurman without government permission.[31] The new policy was in fact intended to return the position of the Sayyid and the Anṣār to what it had been prior to World War I. This, however, could no longer be achieved. Although Sayyid 'Abd al-Raḥmān complained constantly of maltreatment by the government, he was shrewd enough to overcome most of these restrictions in subsequent years, aided in no small measure by his growing wealth and by the strength of the Anṣār. Describing Sayyid 'Abd al-Raḥman's character and his ability to flourish despite adverse conditions, Sir Stewart Symes, the Governor-General of the Sudan, wrote in April 1935:

'He has the defects of a Sudanese of his type, the liking of intrigue, vanity, irrelevance and opportunism. On the other hand, he has quick perceptions, panache, and subtle tenacity of purpose ... He has used (or misused) the opportunities ... of laying the foundations of his Mahdist organisation in the provinces ... One moment's relaxation of Government's vigilance and he presents it with some *fait accompli* either in the shape of a new acquisition of land in a forbidden area, or of a large size advertisement of his pretensions to be a national figurehead. His favourite role is that of the loyal supporter of Government who is maliciously misunderstood ...'[32] His ultimate ambition, according to Symes, was to rule the Sudan as his father had done. But as the future of the Sudan had not yet been decided Symes felt that '... it is impossible to decide whether Sayed Abdel Rahman's ultimate ambitions are reconcilable or irreconcilable with the scheme. The Government, therefore, can only allow him to pursue limited ambitions ...'[33] Two years later, with World War II already looming, the government's policy towards the Anṣār was still ambivalent. Symes now defined the Anṣār as '... an administrative embarrassment rather than an imminent danger ...' or as a 'cancerous growth'. He still insisted that the Khatmiyya and its leader, Sayyid 'Alī, were '... politically more desirable ... ,' but declared that the government would not show its preference openly, since only by observing '... a kind of neutrality ...' would it be possible not to antagonise the Anṣār and to justify the government's treatment '... of Mahdist ebullitions in different parts of the country and especially wherever recalcitrant tendencies have been shewn in recent years ...'[34] Consequently Symes ordered that the ban on Mahdist agents operating within the tribes of Darfur, Kordofan and the Funj region be maintained, and declared that Abā Island would not become '... a sanctuary for outlaws and malcontents ...' Although the government was aware that in '... the struggle for ascendancy between Sayed Ali el Mirghani and Sayed Abdel Rahman the political scales may conceivably be weighted increasingly to the latter's advantage ...', it insisted on refuting any '... pretentions of temporal leadership ...' on Sayyid 'Abd al-Raḥmān's part.[35]

The Sayyid and the Anṣār were thus confronted with a concerted effort to limit their activities, not only by forbidding their expansion in the vast territories of the west, but also by trying to mould them into a purely religious, *ṭarīqa*-like movement, contrary to the basic concept of Mahdism, which saw in politics a major aspect of its religious mission. How was Sayyid 'Abd al-Raḥmān to overcome this predicament without antagonising the authorities whose goodwill was essential to his success? The key to the puzzle lay in the economic field and especially in the expansion of the Sayyid's agricultural ventures. For the government, increased cultivation was imperative. Land was the most easily accessible source of income for the impoverished Sudan and Sudanese entrepreneurs were scarce. Moreover, the authorities regarded cultivation as an antidote to involvement in politics and especially to the danger of a fanatic uprising. A cultivator would be more interested in his crops and his profits than in fermenting religious or political trouble. Accordingly, in February 1928, nearly two years after the 'Archer incident' and the resulting setback to Sayyid 'Abd al-Raḥmān's fortunes, Sir John Maffey, the new Governor-General, introduced the following policy: '... I consider that as the Sayed is behaving reasonably in the religious and political field we ought, as a measure of political expediency to bind him to us by economic fetters ...'[36]

The result of this policy was spectacular. In 1928 Sayyid 'Abd al-Raḥmān started a pump-irrigation scheme extending over 200 acres on Abā Island. By 1930 he had expanded this scheme to 2,900 acres and a year later an additional 1,800 acres were added. When Symes wrote his report on Mahdism in 1935 the Sayyid had cultivated '... a gross area of some 15,000 acres (i.e. between 4,000 and 5,000 available for cotton each year) ...' from which he could derive an annual profit of between £E20,000 and £E30,000. Moreover, government laxity enabled the Sayyid to expand into the restricted areas of the Blue and White Niles. He had a pump-irrigation scheme at Gondal, between Wād-Madanī and Sinnār, which had been financed by the government at a cost of £E28,000. On the White Nile, between Abā Island and Geteina, Sayyid 'Abd al-Raḥmān had acquired four large plots for cotton cultivation, using '... the inevitable relative ...' in order to overcome government restrictions and acquire the leases. Even in the Jazīra, where the government had done its utmost to keep the Sayyid out, he had managed by 1931 to lay his hands on some 9,600 acres of cultivable lands. To these considerable profits from cultivation, one should add the *zakāt*, which since 1919 had been collected annually from all the Anṣār, and the presents brought to the Sayyid by his richer adherents on the occasion of *al-'īd al-kabīr*, or during their pilgrimage. Thus by 1935 Sayyid 'Abd al-Raḥmān was a large landowner, and an affluent man by even the most conservative standards.[37]

While the authorities realised quite early that thousands of pilgrims from the west were cultivating Sayyid 'Abd al-Raḥmān's lands, they probably failed to grasp the full political significance of this activity. The Sayyid's motives for encouraging the pilgrimage were regarded primarily as religious and economic, and therefore as quite legitimate. His 'cultivation colonies', where thousands of *fallāta* toiled for a daily ration of grain and some clothing, were commented upon in many intelligence reports in the 1920s. But the main references were to his exploitation of cheap labour, and occasionally to the religious fanaticism which was regarded as an inevitable by-product of immigration from the west. Although they tried to limit the pilgrims' stay on the Sayyid's lands and gave repeated orders that *fallāta* immigration be ended, the authorities were in fact witnessing the growth and enrichment of the Anṣār as a result of their own policy.[38] In binding the Sayyid to the government '... by economic fetters ...', Maffey and his colleagues had enabled him to strengthen and enrich the Anṣār. Sayyid 'Abd al-Raḥmān himself admitted many years later that without his vast cultivation he could never have provided for the Anṣār. However, he denied most vehemently that either he or his followers regarded their relationship as motivated by financial considerations. The Anṣār, he insisted, left their homes and their families, thousands of miles away, in order to seek spiritual guidance, while the Sayyid imbued them with the Mahdist mission and at the same time provided for all their material needs.[39] When in, 1935, the authorities realised that Sayyid 'Abd al-Raḥmān's agricultural exploits were '... actuated by political rather than by commercial motives ...', they again tried to restrict his movements, especially in the *fallāta*-populated areas of Kosti, Sinnār, Singa and al-Qaḍārif.[40] But it was too late; by then the Anṣār were strong enough both in spirit and in wealth to withstand the half-hearted measures of the alien government.

Muḥammad Aḥmad Maḥjūb, a life-long supporter of Sayyid 'Abd al-Raḥmān and one of the most prominent leaders of the Umma party in the post-independence period, wrote in his introduction to *Jihād fī sabīl al-istiqlāl* that the creation of the Anṣār was the Sayyid's greatest achievement. But when it came to defining the Anṣār, even Māḥjūb found himself in difficulties. He limited himself to stating that the twentieth-century Anṣār were not similar to their Mahdist forerunners of the previous century, nor were they a *ṭarīqa*, a political party, or a military organisation. Indeed, their uniqueness lay in that they combined the features of all of these, and in addition, were a viable economic enterprise.

The Anṣār were composed of three main groups:

In the first place there were primitive tribal supporters whose adherence to the Sayyid was based on their belief in the Mahdī and in certain instances tended to border on fanaticism. This group was largely composed of westerners who flocked to the Sayyid *en masse*, despite government measures, since for them '... there was little or no distinction ... between Mahdism and their profession of Islam ...'[41] By 1935 the number of buildings on Abā Island housing western immigrants (*muhājirūn*) had increased from 1,000 to 4,500, while the number of pilgrims continued to be as large as ever (approximately 15,000 a year). Through these pilgrims the Sayyid was able to penetrate the 'forbidden provinces' of Dārfūr and Kordofan and to establish branches of the Anṣār, under selected loyal *khalīfas*, throughout these vast provinces. The *muhājirūn* were utilised in yet another way. In addition to supplying him with the necessary labour-force on Abā, they settled on the Sayyid's orders in many villages in the four provinces of Kassala, Funj, the Blue Nile and the White Nile, thereby opening these villages to Anṣār influence. The authorities discovered the infiltration by the Anṣār in the early 1930s, and ordered all the immigrants to be concentrated into one or two villages in each province. Henceforth the Sayyid's agents were only allowed into the purely Anṣār-dominated villages. Mahdism, however, had already taken root in other villages, and the government's restrictions were of little avail.

The second group consisted of the more sophisticated elements within the tribal population, including many shaykhs of the riverain tribes, for whom the Sayyid's wealth and temporal influence were as important as his religious mission. It was in this sector that 'native-administration' hit the Sayyid hardest, as it sought to establish a direct link between government and tribal leaders which would make the Sayyid's political role superfluous. '... He was frankly hostile to tribal authorities, whose opposition to the spread of his influence he attempted to counter by obstructive criticism and interference ...' After 1931, however, the Sayyid changed his tactics. Instead of hampering the work of the shaykhs he came to their aid, and tried to win their confidence by siding with them in their disputes with the authorities over taxation, and by entertaining them lavishly both in Omdurman and on Abā Island. Having realised that tribal leadership was too weak to constitute a threat to his political ambitions, Sayyid ʻAbd al-Raḥmān became a keen supporter of native administration which, in his words, brought the mass of tribal leaders to the 'Sudan for the Sudanese' camp as allies of the Anṣār.[42] The Sayyid adopted a similar posture with regard to Ṣūfī *ṭarīqas*. Realising that sectarian politics would be fought out between the Anṣār and the Khatmiyya, the Sayyid understood that other *ṭarīqas*, while continuing to fulfil their religious and social functions at the local village level, would not become involved in national politics. The Sayyid therefore assumed the role of mediator in internal disputes of other *ṭarīqas*. He solved a leadership dispute in the Sammāniyya and gave presents and financial aid to the head of the Ismāʻīliyya in Kordofan in order to draw its members away from the Khatmiyya. He also sent agents to Dongola to win the support of Idrīsiyya members, and helped the head of the Aḥmadiyya order in the same province to win a land-dispute.[43] By 1939 the Anṣār had established themselves throughout the rural areas of the Sudan, and had gained many adherents even in the traditionally Khatmī northern province.

The third group from which the Sayyid hoped to draw his supporters consisted of the inhabitants of the towns, especially Khartoum, Khartoum North, and Omdurman. Many of these people still kept their traditional links with tribes and *ṭarīqas*, and could be won over by methods similar to those implemented in the rural Sudan. There was, however, a small but increasingly influential body of educated Sudanese, most of them government officials, whose confidence the Sayyid sought to gain; in order to do so he had to devise new methods. The young intelligentsia was Muslim both in its heritage and its education. However, their Islam was of a more sophisticated brand, and they regarded the *fakī* and his *ṭarīqa* as superstitious relics of the past. Therefore, although he attempted to deepen their knowledge of Islam and their bond to its heritage, the Sayyid realised that the only way to gain their confidence and support was at the political level.[44] It was with this in mind that he helped to found the first graduates' club in 1920 and became involved in the graduates' political debates through his co-ownership of *al-Ḥaḍāra* in the 1920s.

Following Allenby's ultimatum in 1924 and the expulsion of the Egyptians the Sayyid could no longer rely on government support in his dealings with the younger generation. In fact, the government tried its utmost to stop political interference with the intelligentsia. In 1925, a special committee appointed to report on the political situation warned the government that '… it would be entirely misleading to suppose that with the removal of the … opportunity for Egyptian instigation, the Sudan will revert to complete political apathy … There is now in the Sudan a class, small but vocal, and, inevitably possessing influence out of all proportion to its numbers, which has ideas and aspirations …'[45] Sayyid 'Alī al-Mīrghanī, in talking to the Director of Intelligence about the young graduate class, most of whom were government officials, stated even more bluntly: '… The Government's best friends are the tax-payers, and its worst enemies those who receive pay from it …'[46] To avoid further expansion of this class the government decided to limit higher education to technical fields, such as agriculture. In explaining this policy, Allenby wrote: '… I can conceive much harm and no utility from higher education among a people so profoundly backward as the Sudanese …'[47] Native administration, which sought to transfer both judicial and administrative functions to tribal leaders, diminished the need for higher education even further, as '… all education, … whether specialised or not, has been deliberately designed to fit students for definite occupations in after life …' The young graduates aspiring to become 'effendis' were being persuaded by British officials to '… cast off their shoddy European clothes and tarbush and revert to national dress …'[48] The pros and cons of this policy are outside the scope of this study, but for a better understanding of the position of the young intelligentsia, it might be illuminating to cite Sir Miles Lampson's reply to a very critical article by Sir James Currie on education in the Sudan:

> … With regard to indirect rule and the fostering of the tribal system, I believe with Sir J. Currie that we are working against the stream of natural forces at play in colonial and eastern lands today … *Unfortunately a Sudanese intelligentsia already exists*, and it regards this system as directed against its own future development which is bound up with the progress of the Sudan on modern state lines. Again we have adopted this policy, and it must be allowed to run its course.

*Its effects on education must of course be retarding – not altogether a bad thing in the circumstances ...*[49] [italics mine].

A year later, during a special meeting at the British Foreign Office on education in the Sudan, Sir Lancelot Oliphant was even more outspoken. He accused the British authorities of repeating in the Sudan Lord Cromer's erroneous educational policy in Egypt, and warned them that they would have to face the following criticism: '... namely that they had neglected the education of the natives and, instead, had concentrated solely on efficient government, a policy which might lead to the criticism that His Majesty's Government were actuated by self-interest and did not intend to relax their hold on the Sudan ...' In replying to these accusations Sir Stewart Symes, then Governor-General of the Sudan, admitted that since 1924, partly due to the world economic crisis '... education had been rather forgotten ...' but he maintained that efforts were being made to remedy this.[50]

It is therefore immaterial whether native administration and the educational policy which followed it were specifically designed to retard the development of a Sudanese intelligentsia or were the result of '... plain facts and circumstances ...', as claimed by Symes.[51] It is sufficient that even high-ranking British officials like Lampson and Oliphant stated explicitly that progress in education was retarded as a result of this policy, and it is small wonder that the policy was bitterly resented by the educated Sudanese themselves. In 1926 '... hostile criticism of the Government by native officials ...' was reported. The attitude of the graduates was described as '... despairing rather than militant. They feel themselves to be poor, weak and unorganised ... The increase of British officials in the Government is one of the chief sources of discontent ...'[52] Even the graduates' club, which had been founded with so many hopes in 1920, and was defined by one of its leaders as '... the focus of modern political ideas in the Sudan ...', was disbanded in June 1926.[53] With Egypt out of the way, the club, which had originally been encouraged by the authorities as a political expression of 'the Sudan for the Sudanese', had become more of an embarrassment than an asset.

By 1927, Sayyid 'Abd al-Raḥmān was ready to step in, supplying, in his words, 'the roots' to the graduates' 'tree'.[54] Aware that the graduates were hit by native administration just as he was, the Sayyid found a common platform with the young intelligentsia. Furthermore, following the suppression of the anti-British riots in 1924 many of the once pro-Egyptian graduates had become disillusioned with Egypt. Consequently they were drawn to the Sayyid's politics '... of a genuinely Sudanese nationalist movement. For such a movement a leader and figurehead was essential and it was in this capacity the Sayed now offered his services ...'.[55] Sayyid 'Abd al-Raḥmān's real opportunity came in 1931. As part of its general retrenchment policy following the economic crisis, the Governor-General's council decided to lower the starting rates of pay for newly-appointed Sudanese officials.[56] Protests and demonstrations by students and young government officials asking that the new measures be reconsidered were of no avail, and on 24 November 1931, a general strike was declared at Gordon College.[57] The government failed to persuade the students to resume their studies '... An intelligentsia Committee set up by the Omdurman Graduates' Club having failed to deal with the situation (and Sayid Ali having shut himself up in his house at Sinka), the field was clear for Sayed Abdel Rahman ...' whose mediation brought the strike to an end. This gave him '... a hold over the "effendiyya" which he has never lost ... Since then the Sayed has associated himself with every movement sponsored by the Intelligentsia ...'[58] A special committee was set up by the Anṣār to deal with all matters concerning the educated class. Moreover, *dā'irat al-Mahdī* purchased a printing house, to assume overall responsibility for all the Anṣār's publications. This of course further enhanced the Sayyid's position *vis-a-vis* the intelligentsia, as they could now publish their literary and political writings through his good offices.[59] In 1935 Sayyid 'Abd al-Raḥmān founded *al-Nīl*, the first daily Arabic newspaper in the Sudan, as an organ of the Anṣār. The educated class became the natural consumer of the Anṣār's political thinking and the Sayyid assumed his desired role of their leader. By the end of 1935 '... he had more adherents amongst the educated and politically-minded young men, than any other prominent native ...[60] His house, in the 'Abbāsiyya quarter of Omdurman became the meeting place of the politically-minded government officials, and of graduates in general. Many, like 'Abdallāh Khalīl, Muḥammad Aḥmad Maḥjūb, or Ibrāhīm Aḥmad, later joined the Umma and remained ardent supporters of the Sayyid throughout their political careers. Others, like Ismā'īl al-Azharī, 'Abdallāh al-Fāḍil and Yaḥyā al-Faḍlī, who later founded their own political party in opposition to Sayyid 'Abd al-Raḥmān, were among the Sayyid's supporters until 1942, and regular participants in his political *salon*.[61]

This was the political situation in the Sudan when the Anglo-Egyptian Treaty was signed in 1936. For the Sudanese the treaty was a slap in the face: first, because their future had been decided upon without their even being consulted; and second, the phrasing of the Sudanese clause in the treaty was regarded as humiliating. In it the signatories avoided the controversial issue of sovereignty and undertook instead to work for 'the welfare of the Sudanese', implying that the latter were too primitive and ignorant even to be consulted. In reporting on the 'Treaty reactions of the Intelligentsia in the Sudan', the Controller of Public Security had to admit that there was a marked intensification of nationalist feelings and a strong demand that the intelligentsia would have a voice in determining the future of the Sudan. '... The Treaty, in short, had one notable result. It has put Sudanese nationalism on the political map ...'[62]

What ideology could hold together such a variety of Anṣār supporters as the fanatic *fallāta*, the primitive Baqqāra, the settled tribes of the Nile Valley and the young intelligentsia? In studying a selection of Sayyid 'Abd al-Raḥmān's religious and political thinking one is struck by its shallowness and by its complete reliance on nineteenth century Sudanese Mahdism. The Mahdī's *rātib* (prayer book) and his collected *manshūrāt* (proclamations) form the basis of the ideology of the twentieth century Anṣār. Where necessary, apologetics were employed in order to reconcile Mahdist principles with social and political circumstances of the modern Sudan.[63]

A good example of this conflict, and of the way in which it was solved by Sayyid 'Abd al-Raḥmān, is afforded by his interpretation of the Mahdī's *bay'a* (oath of allegiance). Apart from the oath of allegiance with God, His Prophet and the Mahdī, and the forbidding of *shirk* (association), the *bay'a* stated explicitly that believers were to renounce worldly goods and to forsake wealth, for the cause of God. It also implied a clear commitment of the Anṣār to take part in the *jihād*.[64] Sayyid 'Abd al-Raḥmān overcame this predicament by stating that '... the *bay'a* is subordinate to the command of religion and to amendments of the *imām*, in accordance with the circumstances of time ...' The *imām* who supervised the *bay'a* was, according to the Sayyid, not allowed to change its wording. However, in certain cases '... satisfaction of God's will (*murād*) compels (the *imām*) to deviate from it ...'[65] Such a case, stated the Sayyid, was the accumulation of wealth. While at the time of the Mahdī a renunciation of wordly goods was dictated by the war with the enemy, '... now, lawful earning is an obligation especially if the acquisition of such earnings is (undertaken) for the cause of God ...'[66] Regarding the *jihād* Sayyid 'Abd al-Raḥmān claimed that a correct understanding of the Mahdī's intentions would clarify that *jihād* did not necessarily imply holy war, but may just as correctly be interpreted as *jihād al-nafs*. Sayyid 'Abd al-Raḥmān emphasised the dual spiritual and temporal role of his mission. In this he followed in his father's footsteps, stressing the continuity between his own mission and those of the Mahdī and the Prophet.[67] Spiritually his task was to purify Islam and to unite the true believers, the Anṣār, in restoring the debased religion to its former glory. But there was also a political mission inherent in the Mahdiyya: its fight for independence. This again could be accomplished by a continuation of the Mahdī's *jihād*, but only by peaceful means.[68] The conciliatory attitude towards the country's foreign rulers, was, according to the Sayyid, dictated by circumstances and had been part of his policy ever since he had handed the Mahdī's sword to King George V. It was this policy that '... enabled me to achieve the Sudan's independence without revolution and bloodshed ...'[69]

But overriding all arguments was the unifying aspect of the Anṣār's mission. Though employing elements of Ṣūfī symbolism, as his father had, Sayyid 'Abd al-Raḥmān emphasised that the Anṣār were neither a religious order (*ṭarīqa*) nor a sect (*ṭa'ifa*), but embraced all those whom God had chosen from among His believers. Anyone, therefore, who assisted the Anṣār's adversaries or disagreed with them in matters of religion or politics '... has been employed by the enemy for the destruction of truth ...'.[70] This of course included the youth, whose upbringing and education were the guarantee of the Sudan's future. Unlike the older Anṣār who had fully shared the Mahdī's vision, the young generation had '... only seen a glimpse of that light ...' and therefore had to be educated by true believers who could convey to the youth the full impact and glory of the Mahdist mission, through wisdom and preaching.[71]

The emphasis on the oneness of the religious and political mission of the Anṣār as well as the Sayyid's *baraka*, as the Mahdī's son, and his leadership qualities were probably the most important elements in the unity of the movement. The Anṣār were the only organization in the Sudan before World War II which enjoyed mass support based on its popular Islamic mission, and at the same time sought to assume a leading political role. They could therefore appeal with equal authority, to the ignorant tribesmen and to the sophisticated intelligentsia, while each of these groups gave its allegiance to the Anṣār for different religio-political reasons. A well-defined ideology which could unite all the Anṣār was clearly impossible, and hence undesirable.

## THE GRADUATES' GENERAL CONGRESS

The reappearance of Egypt on the Sudanese scene was of little practical consequence. An Egyptian battalion which was allowed to return to the Sudan in 1936 and a few Egyptians who were appointed to government posts were symbols of goodwill rather than a threat to British supremacy. But the presence of Egypt as a political alternative created a new situation, which had similarities to the pre-1924 period. It meant in effect that, in the forthcoming struggle over the sovereignty of the Sudan, Egypt could serve as a partner for Sudanese nationalists. It enabled those who opposed the 'Sudan for the Sudanese' school of thought to re-emerge on the political scene after fifteen years of inactivity, and once again to preach their ideology and politics under the slogan of the 'Unity of the Nile Valley.'[72] Towards the end of the War, Arab unity made its appearance on the Sudanese political scene as a possible alternative to union with Egypt. This was no doubt prompted by events in the Arab world leading to the founding of the Arab League, early in 1945. As elsewhere in the Middle East, Arab unity enjoyed full British approval, especially in the Sudan where it provided a possible solution to the Anglo-Egyptian puzzle.[73]

By 1938–9 the Sudan government had already become aware of evidence suggesting a concerted effort by Egypt to gain a foothold in the Sudan and to assume, in the eyes of the Sudanese, the role of their liberator. In a note on 'Post-Treaty Egyptian relations',[74] the Civil-Secretary, Sir Angus Gillan, enumerated the new dangers which were mainly in the spheres of education, culture and religion. He referred specifically to the proposed opening in the Sudan of an Egyptian secondary school, an Egyptian *ma'had* and an Egyptian library, in which King Farūq and Shaykh Muṣṭafā al-Marāghī were deeply involved.[75] Fārūq even tried to persuade Symes to agree to the appointment of an Egyptian Deputy Governor-General.[76]

But even more important was the change in attitude of the Egyptian government towards Sudanese nationalism. Gillan pointed out that the Egyptians propagated '... the theory of the sister countries joined by ties of blood, water and religion, with the inference of virtual independence except in the matter of sovereignty ...' This line was infinitely more appealing to the Sudanese, since by tying their future to that of Egypt, they could now hope for a more rapid advance toward complete independence, with some loosely defined bonds to the Egyptian Crown. Gillan's statement that '... Egyptian Government senior personnel, civil and military, have all been on their best behaviour and would appear at present to be genuinely anxious to co-operate in a treaty spirit ...' tends to confirm the impression that Egypt was trying to win over Sudanese nationalists by adopting a more realistic attitude.[77]

It is interesting to note that Egyptian efforts in the Sudan tended to ignore the intelligentsia, at least until 1943, and concentrated instead on the more traditional sectors of Sudanese society and leadership. Of special significance was the Egyptian attempt to win over the Sayyids, both by making them Pashas and by publicising their high standing and political importance in the Egyptian press.[78] However, both Sayyids, while pleased with the publicity, declined to take a pronounced pro-Egyptian stand and in fact remained very critical of Egyptian motives and intentions. In 1937 Sayyid 'Abd al-Raḥmān went on a visit to England and Egypt in order to present in person the Sudanese criticism of the Anglo-Egyptian treaty. Although Sayyid 'Abd al-Raḥmān commented favourably on his talks with Butler and other high ranking British officials, he viewed his Egyptian hosts as unrealistic and criticised their plans for unity most vehemently.[79] The Sayyid constantly urged the encouragement of '... Sudanese nationalism as a bulwark against this danger ...' of Egyptian ambitions to rule the Sudan.[80]

Sayyid 'Alī al-Mīrghanī's position was rather more complex. Firstly, because of his role as a religious leader, he tended to retreat from the political scene whenever possible, and had in fact done so since 1924. Secondly he was '... suffering from an illusion that the Government has written him off and is advancing Sayed Abdel Rahman to the foremost position in the country ...'[81] Therefore, although he viewed the ever-increasing impact of Sayyid 'Abd al-Raḥmān with dismay, Sayyid 'Alī refrained consistently from coming into the open. As late as 1944, when asked to comment on the Sudan's future, Sayyid 'Alī '... confined his conversation ... to general observations on the weather in the Sudan, Egypt and England, dealing with the subject pretty thoroughly ...' but refused to be drawn into politics.[82]

It is therefore nearly impossible to define Sayyid 'Alī's political views during this period. His only consistent stand was in opposing Sayyid 'Abd al-Raḥmān and the Anṣār. Sayyid 'Alī opposed the reform of the *ma'had* in Omdurman, stating that under its present leadership it enjoyed a 'golden age', for the simple reason that this reform was supported by Sayyid 'Abd al-Raḥmān. Sayyid 'Alī probably hoped, through his support of the *ma'had's* teachers, '... to capture an institution of considerable social and religious importance ...' and ignored the attacks in the Anṣār's daily *al-Nīl*, which accused him of acting '... against the consensus of enlightened opinion in the country ...'[83] When two years later a close associate of Sayyid 'Abd al-Raḥmān was appointed president of the *ma'had*, Sayyid 'Alī refused to support the institute in any way thereby enabling the Anṣār to accuse him of '... sacrificing public interest to partisan considerations ...'[84]

Even the Italian conquest of the Kassala region in 1940, which included the Khatmiyya centre, became an issue in sectarian politics. Due to the Mīrghanī family connections in Eritrea (the Sharīfa 'Alawiyya, Sayyid 'Alī's cousin, was a well-known supporter of Italian Fascism) Sayyid 'Alī felt that he was suspected by the government. His misgivings were strengthened when Sayyid 'Abd al-Raḥmān was publicised in several BBC broadcasts as 'the religious leader of the Sudan' while his own name was not even mentioned. Next came a bitter attack on Ṣūfism, made by Shaykh Aḥmad 'Utmān al-Qāḍi and published in *al-Nīl*. As the author was both a supporter of Sayyid 'Abd al-Raḥmān and a member of the Central Government Political Department, Sayyid 'Alī felt certain that the attack was inspired by the government.[85] But in January 1941, following the expulsion of the Italians from Kassala, tension was somewhat relieved. A political-intelligence report stated that '... the Sayed's relations with the government have returned to normal and roses from his garden again grace the political breakfast tables of Khartoum ...'[86]

Another of Sayyid 'Alī's activities which clouded his relations with the government was the organisation of a para-military youth section of the Khatmiyya. The so-called 'Mirghanist Shirt Movement', was first organised in February 1940 under the Sayyid's auspices. It was trained by an ex-sergeant of the SDF and paraded '... the streets of Khartoum and Omdurman, in drilled formation, chanting slogans in praise of the Sayed and against all his enemies ... mainly directed against Sayed Abdel Rahman ...'[87] The government was in no mood to tolerate such a movement, especially during the war, even if it belonged to the favoured Khatmiyya. It was assumed that Sayyid 'Alī, having failed to capture the intelligentsia, had decided to concentrate on the less sophisticated youth of the three towns. The authorities, fearing an Ansārī reaction, ordered both Sayyids to refrain from such activities in the future.[88] Yet despite his political setbacks, Sayyid 'Alī maintained his noncommital stand towards both the Sudan government and the Egyptian authorities. During 1944 he strengthened his ties with Egyptian officers and officials in the Sudan as well as with Egyptian leaders and the Egyptian press.[89] But at the same time he stated his support for self-government of the Sudan under British guidance. The definition of Sayyid 'Alī and his supporters, as being '... in a state of indecision and perplexity ...', is therefore probably the most accurate assessment of Khatmiyya politics at the end of World War II.[90]

The establishment of the Graduates' General Congress in February 1938 was facilitated by a number of factors.[91] First, central government authorities had realised that tribal organisation in the Sudan was weakened beyond repair and therefore the '... possibility of evolving a system of genuine local self-government ...' was unrealistic.[92] This did not mean a complete dismissal of tribal leadership, but rather an attempt to look for a possible alternative among the educated class. Second, the threat of war created a situation in the Sudan in which the support of every segment of the population was important to the government, not least the intelligentsia, which was more open to hostile propaganda. Third, the Anglo-Egyptian treaty of 1936 had stirred public opinion in the Sudan to such an extent that the politically-minded intelligentsia could no longer be relied upon to remain passive. Lastly the appointment of Sir Douglas Newbold as Deputy Civil Secretary in 1938 and Civil Secretary in the following year was of great significance. For the first time since the establishment of the Condominium the man who stood at the helm of government was sympathetic to the educated class and tried to understand its aspirations. It would be wrong to define Newbold's predecessors in office as 'reactionaries'. But unlike Newbold, they were creatures of the Wingate era, whose views about the Sudan were largely modulated before World War I. They carried their preference for the honest and primitive tribal population over the 'towny' or 'effendy', into the 1930s.[93] Newbold arrived in the Sudan after the War and thus belonged in a way to a generation with new ideas and perceptions. But he was also by all accounts an extraordinarily humane and able man. Margery Perham, a close observer of British colonialism and of the Sudanese scene over many years wrote of him: '... Newbold showed to me the highest standards I have ever seen in colonial administration ...'[94] Mekki 'Abbās, who as a Sudanese graduate and administrator had many political disagreements with Newbold, wrote of him after his sudden death in March 1945: '... we know that his motive, when he worked himself to death, was not just the discharging of a debt but he had a more sublime motive for working so hard. That was his love for the Sudan ...'[95]

Sayyid 'Abd al-Raḥmān, as noted, had emerged since 1931 as the most powerful political leader in the Sudan, among both the Anṣār and the graduates. The government hoped that, by encouraging the intelligentsia, who constituted the Sudanese official class, to found their own organisation, it would deal a death blow to sectarian politics which the authorities regarded as impairing the progress of the Sudan.[96] Therefore, when the government recognised the Graduates' General Congress in May 1938, it was part of a well-devised plan initiated by the intelligentsia and with the full backing of the authorities. Even the details of the Congress constitution were hammered out '... in friendly collaboration, between the future scourge of the "imperialist oppressors", Ismā'īl al-Azharī, and J. C. Penney, who as Controller of Public Security was immediately responsible for the detection and surveillance of "subversive" political activity ...'[97]

To hope that the weak and politically immature educated class would challenge the authority of the two Sayyids and of their well-organised supporters, without succumbing to sectarianism in the process, was naïve. In 1938 there were about 5,000 'graduates' in the Sudan who, in a total population of six million, accounted for less than one-tenth of one per cent. Moreover, the term 'graduate' included both graduates of Gordon College, which was then the only secondary school in the Sudan, and graduates of intermediary schools. It is therefore no wonder that the government itself, despite its vested interest in the emergence of a non-sectarian intelligentsia, viewed it with certain misgivings. In explaining this new venture in Sudanese politics, the Civil Secretary wrote:

> ... It must not be inferred from the use of this rather grandiloquent title ("Graduates"), that we have already reached a stage in this country at which the intelligentsia are beginning to agitate collectively for political rights and political representation. It is possible that the Graduates' Congress may emerge at some future date as a nationalist organisation with a political programme ... Today ... it neither seeks formal recognition, nor does it claim to represent the views of any but its own members ...[98]

Once again the government's attitude was both ambivalent and unrealistic. It sponsored the intelligentsia as an antidote to sectarianism, but viewed it as too immature to play any significant role in the immediate future. Furthermore, by hoping, as the authorities did, that so-called 'self-imposed terms of reference', would stop the graduates from moving into the political arena, the government ignored both the aspirations of the intelligentsia and the political designs of the Sayyids, and especially of Sayyid 'Abd al-Raḥmān. But even more important was the government's failure to come to grips with the time element. In 1938, just as ten or twenty years earlier, the authorities simply did not foresee a future Sudan which would be administered by its own people without British supervision '... the welfare of the Sudanese people', wrote Symes, 'is likely to be promoted neither by a spectacular process of development nor too rapid innovations. To the Sudan may truly be applied an Arab adage that "haste is of the devil, slow deliberation is of God" ...'[99]

On 12 February 1938 some 1,180 graduates took part in the first meeting of the Graduates' Congress. They constituted themselves into a permanent body with a supervisory committee of sixty and an executive committee of fifteen, to be elected annually. The committees were '... charged with laying down and executing a programme of social reform and bringing to the notice of the Government *the views of the intelligentsia on legitimate matters of public interest* ...'[100] [italics mine]. This very vague definition, which had been insisted upon by the government, before long brought about a split among the graduates and enabled the Sayyids to move in. What is a 'legitimate matter of public interest'? Education, health and welfare were clearly within this definition. Yet from the outset the British regarded the Congress also as an expression '... of an indigenous Sudanese identity, implying rejection of the idea of national absorption by Egypt ...' and consequently a revival of 'The Sudan for the Sudanese' movement.[101] As this was clearly a controversial political issue, it was bound to arouse conflict.

The Egyptian government, sensing in the Congress a threat to its claim for unity, dismissed it as a 'British invention' that '... had been created ... with the object of resisting Egyptian penetration ...'[102] To overcome this suspicion, members of the Congress committee of fifteen tried to convince the Egyptians, both through private talks and articles in the press, that they represented an independent expression of Sudanese nationalism and maintained complete impartiality in the Anglo-Egyptian conflict. Congress leaders saw their chance when 'Alī Māhir, the Egyptian Prime Minister, visited the Sudan at Symes' invitation in February 1940. A tea party was arranged by the Congress for Māhir and his mission, in which some 800 graduates participated. Congress speakers stressed that theirs was the only independent and representative Sudanese organisation, and was not British-inspired. They further emphasised that while Sudanese nationalism did not contradict their brotherly feelings for Egypt, the Sudan and Egypt were two distinct entities.[103] The second and more significant step was undertaken by the Congress when it decided to present a memorandum to ʻAlī Māhir to be submitted to the Egyptian people. The government regarded this as unconstitutional, since it implied ignoring the Governor-General as an intermediary between the Sudan and Egypt. Yet despite a stern warning by the authorities, the committee of sixty decided to present the memorandum to Māhir.[104] The memorandum in itself was unimportant because, as a result of the government's warning, it had been watered down to such an extent '... that the requests embodied in it ... became in themselves innocuous and largely meaningless ...' Even Māhir expressed disappointment at the fact that all the points raised in the memorandum, such as the *maʻhad* in Omdurman or the admission of Muslim 'missionaries' to the southern provinces, had already been settled between him and Symes prior to the submission of the Congress memorandum. The meeting between the Congress and the Egyptian delegation was, however, important as it convinced the Egyptians '... that Congress was the genuine embryo of a nationalist movement and not ... a British anti-Egyptian invention ...'[105] The memorandum itself became significant in a different context. In debating the pros and cons of submitting the memorandum, the committee of sixty had split into two camps. '... The defeat of the more responsible and moderate elements ...' led by Mīrghanī Ḥamza and ʻAbd al-Majīd, both supporters of Sayyid ʻAli al-Mīrghanī, led the authorities to the conclusion that '... both the composition and the functioning of the committee of sixty are extremely unsatisfactory ...' and hence, government intervention was warranted. In a meeting with Congress leaders, Newbold warned them that the government might '... compel the withdrawal of officials from Congress membership, and if need be ... dissolve the Congress itself ...'[106] The Congress, however was threatened from yet another direction as the split within its ranks made it easy prey for the Sayyids.

In January 1940 it had seemed to the authorities that the various groups within the Congress were '... tending to lose all sectarian colour derived from connection with the Holy Men and to assume an independent existence ...' Moreover, the fact that from 1,180 graduates, attending the first annual meeting in February 1938, the number dropped to 400 in 1939 and to only 250 in January 1940, suggested that this was due to the graduates' feeling '... that the Congress has failed, through extreme passivity and moderation, to achieve any results worth while ...'[107] 'Alī Māhir's visit was therefore a turning point as it gave the Congress a new lease of life. The attendance of 800 graduates at the Congress reception for Māhir and the subsequent publicity it received through the submission of its memorandum, enabled the graduates at last to appear on the political scene. This, however, meant the involvement of the Sayyids: first, because the graduates were numerically and financially too weak to make a real impact; second, the Sayyids owned the only non-governmental daily newspapers and the sole Arabic publishing house belonged to Sayyid 'Abd al-Raḥmān; last but not least, many of the graduates, especially the older ones, owed their allegiance to the Sayyids long before the Congress was founded. While their initial attempt to keep sectarian politics out of the Congress was probably quite sincere, it became evident during the first two years of the Congress's existence that this was unrealistic. If the Congress was to become a political factor, despite government opposition, the goodwill and support of either one or both Sayyids was essential. The first opportunity for Congress to become politically involved was offered ironically by Symes himself when on 11 June 1940, he invited Congress leaders, along with the Sayyids and other notables, to acquaint them with Italy's declaration of war, and to win their support for his own proclamation to the people of the Sudan. Congress seized this chance to advertise its role in local politics. Its secretary even suggested to Newbold to permit Congress leaders to broadcast to '... "the people of the Sudan" with the object of giving them such advice and guidance as might be required ...'. This was refused on the grounds that a broadcast '... to "the Sudanese people" was definitely presumptuous and implied an arrogation of status and influence to which Congress was not entitled ...' Instead Congress leaders were advised to publish their proclamation in the Sayyids'-owned *al-Nīl* and *Ṣawt al-Sūdān*.[108]

The split within Congress, between Khatmiyya and Anṣār supporters, occurred during August-September 1940. First came the decision of the committee of sixty to boycott government broadcasts on Sudanese culture. Members of the Congress had been invited to participate individually in preparing these broadcasts but the committee of sixty forbade participation, unless the Congress was also allowed to broadcast in its own name. This caused the resignation of the committee of fifteen which had opposed the boycott and whose members were mostly Khatmiyya supporters. Next came an attempt by the Mahdist-dominated Congress to '... convert it openly into a *political assembly* ...' Using *al-Nīl* for their propaganda they advocated the establishment of a National Front. '... The object ... was to bring the two Sayeds – or Sayed Abd El-Rahman alone – and other elements (such as tribal leaders and urban notables) into open relationship with the Congress ...' and thereby provide it with adequate political backing.[109] Finally an attempt was made both through the press and by circular letters to attract some 3,000 new members into Congress. The tone of the articles and letters implied that the orientation of the pro-Mahdist leadership of the Congress was now primarily political. '... Following these disquieting manifestations the Director of Public Security saw the Congress President and warned him off the political trend ...' Moreover, the government was already so disappointed that it stated bluntly: '... Congress, as it stands now (September 1940), cannot live for long ...' Officially Ismā'īl al-Azharī, the new president of the Congress, agreed to co-operate with the government and to refrain from politics, and even wrote an article to that effect in *al-Mu'tamar*, the new Congress journal.[110] In reality *al-Nīl* and *Ṣawt al-Ṣūdān* provided the platforms from which the rival parties within the Congress could attack each other so that the Anṣār-Khatmiyya feud was once again in full swing.[111]

The elections to the Congress committees held at the annual meeting in January 1941 were contested on a sectarian basis with the Anṣār winning an absolute majority in both. '... They may well show themselves to be an able and irreproachable body', noted the Director of Public Security, 'but the Mahdist label will be tied firmly to all their activities ...'[112] For the first six months after the elections, the Mahdist-dominated Congress seemed to function well. In February 1941 it organised an 'Education Day' in which funds were raised to assist Sudanese non-government schools. The scheme was boycotted by Sayyid 'Alī, due to the Anṣār's domination of the Congress. But its success and popularity among all sectors of Sudanese society proved, as was the intention of the organisers, '... that a Mahdist Congress could do better social work than the mixed assembly of the past years ...' At the same time, public opinion turned against Sayyid 'Alī and blamed him for '... his narrowly partisan and obstructive attitude ...'[113] Another achievement of the new executive of the Congress was its decision to co-operate with the government in broadcasts on cultural affairs, which they previously boycotted. This again became a cause for internal strife as it brought about the resignation of the few remaining Khatmiyya members from the committee of sixty.[114] It therefore seemed that the Anṣār were in full control of Congress. Yet before the end of 1942 the composition of forces within the Congress had been reversed. This development had two major causes. First, many of the so-called supporters of Sayyid 'Abd al-Raḥmān within the Congress were not really Anṣār. They were attracted to the Sayyid as the pillar of an independent Sudan rather than to his religious credo, and thus were quite willing to change sides when the occasion arose. Secondly and in no small measure as a result of the above, Sayyid 'Alī finally decided, in a very hesitant manner, to break away from his many years of political apathy. By doing so he provided the intelligentsia with a political alternative.

The first signs of an internal Mahdist conflict and of its repercussions in Congress came in August 1941. An attempt was made by several leading Anṣār to oust 'Abdallāh al-Fāḍil from his post as Sayyid 'Abd al-Raḥmān's *khalīfa* in Omdurman, and to replace him with al-Ṣiddīq, the Sayyid's son. The conflict was not resolved until 1943, probably because Sayyid 'Abd al-Raḥmān did not want to commit himself openly in a conflict involving his own son. But during the following two years the Anṣār were considerably weakened as a result of this discord, and their supporters in the Congress were divided into two opposing camps. Those backing al-Fāḍil were headed by Ismā'il al-Azharī and Yaḥyā al-Faḍlī, while their rivals included Ibrāhīm Aḥmad, then president of the Congress, who had the backing of Aḥmad Yūsuf Hāshim, editor of *al-Nīl*, and head of the very strong Hāshim clan.[115] Matters came to a head in the Congress elections of December 1942, when the Azharī-Faḍlī party emerged victorious. To the outsider it appeared that the internal rift between the two Mahdist blocs in the Congress and the appearance of two additional groups, *al-Mu'tamirīn al-aḥrār* and *Abu rūf*, '... completely superseded the old sectarian division ...'

Moreover, the attendance of some 1,250 members at the Congress' annual meeting, many of whom were artisans, merchants and even illiterates seemed to imply '... a great deterioration and a fundamental change in the character of Congress ...' The Director of Public Security even suggested that the interplay of private animosities would soon bring about the collapse of the Congress.[116]

It seems therefore that by the end of 1942 the government had written off the Graduates' Congress as a potential political organisation of any significance. The events which brought about the final verdict against the Congress started, as has been noted, in 1940 and came to a head in April-May 1942. At the beginning of April 1942 the committee of sixty, under the presidency of Ibrāhīm Aḥmad, formulated a memorandum containing twelve demands, ostensibly in the name of the Sudanese people, and submitted it to the government. Many of these dealt with clearly political matters such as the right of self-determination, immediate steps toward self-government, and the revision of Southern policy. From a governmental point of view it was therefore unacceptable both in content and in form. On 24 April the memorandum was returned by Newbold to Ibrāhīm Aḥmad with a curt letter stating the government's reasons for refusing to accept or to discuss its contents.[117] Newbold instructed all provincial governors and heads of departments to refuse to discuss the memorandum as the Graduates' Congress had in his words '... deliberately and after due warning forfeited its confidence ...'[118] What had prompted the Congress, under the moderate leadership of Ibrāhīm Aḥmad, to venture into the forbidden sphere of politics? According to Huddleston, then Governor-General, and Newbold, the memorandum was inspired by several factors: the promises made by the Atlantic Charter declaration; the part played by the SDF against Italy in the East African Front; and finally the passage through the Sudan of Sir Stafford Cripps, who on his return trip from India, gave an interview to the vernacular press on 4 April 1942 in which he stated that the Sudan's participation in the War effort '... will gain it a place in the new era which we all hope to see in the world when we have finished with the evil forces ...'[119] But the government was still disturbed by the fact that the 'comparatively moderate' committee of sixty, under an '... enlightened president, should have been stampeded into addressing to the Governor-General a letter containing extravagant and ill considered claims …'[120] The answer to this may be sought in the internal conflict in the Congress, between the Ibrāhīm Aḥmad camp and the followers of Ismā'īl al-Azharī. A hint, suggesting this, can be found in Sayyid 'Abd al-Raḥmān's memoirs in which he stated that the Congress memorandum was prompted by an article inspired by him, and published in *al-Nīl* at the beginning of 1942. By refusing to accept the memorandum or to discuss its very moderate and legitimate demands, the government, according to the Sayyid, was trying to humiliate and discredit the leadership of Congress, and thus played into the hands of the extremists.[121] To follow the line of reasoning suggested by the Sayyid, it is possible to surmise that Ibrāhīm Aḥmad's submission of the memorandum was partly the result of his strife with al-Azharī, in which he enjoyed the Sayyid's full backing. A further, and more reliable proof to that effect can be found in Ibrāhīm Aḥmad's own conduct in the months May-September 1942. Following a private meeting with Newbold, in which an understanding was reached, Ibrāhīm Aḥmad tried to convince the committee of sixty to accept the compromise. He failed, however, due to the opposition of al-Azharī and his supporters, and had to retreat from his previous position.[122] Ibrāhīm Aḥmad's reluctance to force the issue may have been prompted by the preparations for Congress elections which were already in full swing, and by a realisation that a conciliatory line might play into the hands of his rivals. As noted above, both he and his followers were defeated and, to quote the Director of Public Security, '… the notoriously unstable Azhari …' was once again president backed by a committee of sixty which with few exceptions was '… a very poor lot …'[123]

## THE EMERGENCE OF SECTARIAN PARTIES

By the end of 1942, the government entertained no further hopes from the Congress. Plans for establishing advisory councils both in the provinces and in the central government were well under way. They were intended not only as a first step toward self-government, but also as a framework in which the 'more responsible' graduates alongside tribal and religious leaders could be associated with their own government. However, the authorities realised that it would take a year or two before an effective central advisory council could be established. If Congress should attempt during that period to step into the vacuum, the government intended to act firmly under the motto 'trespassers will be prosecuted'.[124]

Under al-Azharī's leadership, the Congress tried in the meantime to assert itself as an independent political force. In July 1943, al-Azharī visited Egypt with two other leading members of Congress. In a series of interviews with leading Egyptians, including Prime Minister Naḥḥās Pasha, he tried to convey the impression that they were the legitimate spokesmen of Sudanese nationalism.[125]

In November 1943, following long deliberations with the defeated group of graduates under Ibrāhīm Aḥmad and Aḥmad Yūsuf Hāshim, Sayyid 'Abd al-Raḥmān finally decided to sever his connections with the al-Azharī-Faḍlī group. He had been reluctant to withdraw his support earlier because of al-Azharī's success. But now the combination of several factors made an immediate decision imperative. First, the resignation of Ibrāhīm Aḥmad and his supporters from the committee of fifteen made the feud between the two camps so intense that it became impossible to support both sides. Second, the government's plan for an advisory council, which had the Sayyid's full support, was boycotted by the al-Azharī-dominated Congress. Third, the Sayyid disapproved of al-Azharī's flirtations with the Egyptian leadership. Lastly, there was the internal struggle within the Anṣār in which, as has been pointed out, the whole conflict had originated. By the end of 1943 it became apparent to Sayyid 'Abd al-Raḥmān that 'Abdallāh al-Fāḍil, his *khalīfa* in Omdurman, was exploiting his connections in Congress in order to secure his position as the Sayyid's successor. Sayyid 'Abd al-Raḥmān was therefore compelled to overcome his previous reluctance; he had to intervene so that he could secure the position of his son, al-Ṣiddīq and so he ordered al-Fāḍil to resign from both committees of the Congress and to devote himself fully to his duties within the Anṣār. This in turn prompted Sayyid 'Alī to '... emerge from a long period of political inactivity ... (and) to promise his support to Azhari ...'[126]

During the following two years, the story of the Congress was one of continuous internal strife, openly directed by the two leaders of popular Islam. Al-Azharī's 1943 election victory was turned into defeat when Muḥammad Khalīfa Sharīf, Sayyid 'Abd al-Raḥmān's nephew, stepped in and 'convinced' several of al-Azharī's supporters to desert him, thus securing the re-election of Ibrāhīm Aḥmad to the presidency. But Aḥmad's position was extremely shaky. His policy was largely dictated by the al-Azharī group, who continued to hold the majority in the committee of sixty.[127] Moreover, Ibrahīm Aḥmad himself was critical of Sayyid 'Abd al-Raḥmān's political line as well as of his open intervention in the Congress. He realised that the Sayyid's '... separatist attitude towards Egypt gave the impression that he hoped to become King of an independent Sudan ...' and thus played into the hands of al-Azharī and his Khatmī supporters.[128]

In the 1944 Congress elections, the newly formed Ashiqqā' party, led by al-Azharī and with the support – both moral and financial – of Sayyid 'Ali al-Mīrghanī, won an overwhelming victory.[129] For Ismā'īl al-Azharī it was also a personal triumph: he beat Ibrāhīm Aḥmad, his rival for the presidency, by nearly 1,500 votes. What were the reasons for the overwhelming Khatmiyya-Ashiqqā' victory? '... The Ashigga won', wrote the Director of Public Security:

> (a) because the Mirghanists are a majority in the Three Towns ...
> (b) because the Ansar did not enter the field in earnest until a short time before the elections ... whereas the Mirghanists had been solidly supporting the Ashigga throughout the year.
> (c) because quite apart from sectarian support, they were a better organised and more united party ... and had behind them the bulk of the younger graduates ...[130]

However, this is not an entirely satisfactory explanation as it tends to ignore Sayyid 'Abd al-Raḥmān's predominance within the intelligentsia in the preceding years. The following reasons for the decline in the Anṣār's popularity among the graduates should be considered. First, many of the intelligentsia feared and opposed the renewed importance of tribal leaders which they felt was implied by the creation of the central advisory council in May 1944. While the council enjoyed the full backing of Sayyid 'Abd al-Raḥmān, Sayyid 'Alī viewed it with suspicion because the Anṣār predominated among its members.[131] Similarly, many of the graduates, who were not necessarily Khatmiyya followers, found themselves on the latter's side in the 1944 elections, in order to express their anti-government and anti-Anṣār feelings. Second, the intelligentsia by and large favoured some connection with Egypt, primarily as an ally against prolonged British domination. In many cases, fear of an Anṣār-dominated monarchy under Sayyid 'Abd al-Raḥmān gave an added impetus to some form of alliance with Egypt and hence to the support of the Ashiqqā'.[132] Finally, the death of Sayyid 'Abd al-Raḥmān's brother, whose funeral coincided with the Congress elections, kept many of the leading Anṣār fully occupied, thus indirectly helping the Ashiqqā'-Khatmiyya coalition.[133] So the collaboration between an important section of the intelligentsia and Sayyid 'Alī al-Mīrghanī can best be described as a marriage of convenience – which applied equally to both partners. Sayyid 'Alī stated quite frankly, in private conversation with the Commissioner of Police, that he had no interest in or political affinity with the Ashiqqā', and that his only motive was '... to prevent Sayed Sir Abdel Rahman from capturing the Congress as he had already captured the Advisory Council ...'[134]

To the internal strife which had already torn the Congress apart, two elements were now added; pressure from the British authorities to confine Congress membership to the educated classes only; and a demand by Egyptian politicians that the Congress declare itself openly in favour of union with Egypt. Early in 1945, the Governor of Khartoum alerted al-Azharī to the fact that the Congress elections of the preceding November had been unconstitutional as '... many of the new "members" ... did not possess the prescribed or any educational qualifications ...'[135] This was followed by an even more explicit statement to the effect that the government had decided to withdraw its recognition of the Congress as it was no longer a true representative of the educated classes.[136] Although an attempt was made by al-Azharī to come to terms with the government, from then on the latter tended to ignore the Congress. Apart from occasional rebukes, it paid little attention to the Congress's political ventures.[137]

The problem of the Sudan's sovereignty and its relations with Egypt assumed increasing importance as the Allies' victory in the war became apparent. The Sudanese realised that as soon as the war would be over, a new Anglo-Egyptian treaty was likely to be negotiated. They wanted to assure their own participation in the forthcoming negotiations and, if possible, to present both Egypt and Britain with a united Sudanese front. To achieve this, al-Azharī had to compromise, as neither of the Sayyids was likely to support his previous policy of complete unity. In December 1944, despite mounting pressure from Egypt, al-Azharī made a public statement to the effect '... that the aim of the Ashigga is not fusion with Egypt but Dominion status under the Egyptian Crown and flag ...' He put forward two arguments in support of this aim: '... a) that alignment with Egypt is a necessary safeguard against incorporation in an African system; b) that Egypt is the Sudan's only link with the Arab World ...'[138] Early in April 1945 a resolution was passed by the Congress committee of sixty stating that '... Sudan shall be ruled by a Sudanese democratic government within a union with Egypt under the Egyptian Crown ...' While most of the Egyptian press greeted this resolution favourably, reactions in the Sudan varied between '... indignation and a certain amount of ridicule ...'[139] Indeed, the indignation within certain sections of the graduates, especially those aligned with the Anṣār, was so great that al-Azharī feared that both he and the Ashiqqā' would be defeated in the forthcoming elections if he didn't compromise.[140] He therefore decided to set up a 'United Parties Committee', composed of three representatives from each of the six factions represented in the Congress, to try to work out a formula which would be acceptable to all concerned. On 25 August, a compromise was devised which called for '... the establishment of a free, democratic, Sudanese Government in union with Egypt and in alliance with Great Britain ...'[141]

Although they called the resolution ambiguous and vague, the British authorities regarded it as moderate enough to be accepted by the Sudan government. However, they expressed doubts on Egyptian reactions to 'a free democratic Sudan' which, in fact, denoted independence and ignored the Egyptian Crown.[142] Yet, on the very same day that the 'United Parties' Agreement' was adopted by the Congress, a secret session of the committee of fifteen passed a resolution calling for '... the formation of a democratic Sudanese Government in a union with Egypt, under the Egyptian Crown ...' Al-Azharī communicated this resolution to the Prime Ministers of both Great Britain and Egypt, ignoring the compromise reached by the United Parties Committee.[143] This gave the authorities the opportunity to discredit the Congress completely. First, by leaking al-Azharī's letter to the opposition within the Congress, they helped to create an uproar against the Ashiqqā' in the Anṣār-Umma dominated press. Second, in replying to al-Azharī, the government was able to ignore the resolution and to state quite bluntly that it was unconstitutional and did '… not appear to enjoy the confidence of more than a section of the Graduates' Congress itself …'[144] Al-Azharī's belated reply was apologetic rather than convincing. He claimed that 'union with Egypt under the Egyptian Crown' was just a more accurate definition of the word 'union' used by the 'United Parties Committee'.[145]

The government, however, was in no mood to pursue the argument. Congress elections were due in November, and, with strife within Congress at its peak, it was quite uncertain whether the organisation would survive until the end of 1945. The pro-Anṣār elements within the Congress knew that they would be defeated in the elections. They therefore tried to come to an agreement with the Ashiqqā' regarding the allocation of seats on Congress committees. Failing to achieve this, they decided to boycott the elections in order '… to make it clear to the world that the Congress of 1946 … was a single party (Ashiqqa) organisation and that it could no longer rightfully call itself the Graduates' Congress …'[146] In fact, the Congress, though still in existence, ceased to play any role in Sudanese society or politics from 1946 onward. The Umma and the Ashiqqā' became the dominant organisations in the political arena, with the two Sayyids continuing to pull the strings.

The founding of the advisory council and the decline in the stature of the Congress intensified the political activity of the two Sayyids. While the vocal intelligentsia continued to dominate the growing political press, the centre of the religio-political activities tended to shift to the rural areas. This came about partly by the founding of the advisory council in which tribal and other rural leaders were predominant. The 'unreliability' and 'inconsistency' of the intelligentsia, as far as the leaders of sectarian politics were concerned, were probably contributing factors.

Both Sayyids congratulated the Sudan government on its decision to set up an advisory council. But whereas Sayyid 'Abd al-Raḥmān did so wholeheartedly, Sayyid 'Alī expressed certain reservations. He was aware of the Anṣār's strength in the countryside, and therefore emphasised that the council's success would depend '... on the quality of those chosen to be members ...'[147] Moreover, having initially agreed to accept the government's invitation to become an honorary member of the advisory council alongside Sayyid 'Abd al-Raḥmān, Sayyid 'Alī later withdrew, due to the preponderance of Anṣār on the council. It was only after much prompting that he finally attended the opening session of the advisory council '... though it was evident that he viewed the whole affair with extreme distaste ...'[148] The weakness of the Khatmiyya in the countryside, and hence on the advisory council, persuaded Sayyid 'Ali to throw his weight behind the Ashiqqā' party and at the same time to try to strengthen his standing in rural Sudan. An uprising on Tuti Island in April 1944 was exploited by Sayyid 'Ali for Khatmiyya propaganda. He tried to give this local incident '... a national colour and lift it from the administrative to the political plane ...'[149] In June Sayyid 'Ali undertook a propaganda campaign in the Northern Province to prove his political supremacy among the members of the Idrīsiyya order. The campaign was intended to counter a visit by Sayyid 'Abd al-Raḥmān to 'Aṭbarā, al-Dāmir and Berber, all of which were regarded by Sayyid 'Ali as his own 'special reserve'.[150] By August Sayyid 'Ali was considering the severance of his connections with the Ashiqqā', and plans for a new Khatmiyya party called *al-Sha'b* were well under way. His aim was to rid himself of the unreliable al-Azharī-clique and of its pro-Egyptian programme. At the same time he hoped to formulate a policy which would enable him to win over certain sections of the rural population and to mend his fences with the government.[151]

Sayyid 'Abd al-Raḥmān, though still disappointed with his political setback in the Congress, had regarded the political scene since 1943 with growing optimism. First, because the advisory council was dominated by Anṣār supporters, and secondly because the opening statement of the Governor-General in the first session of the council coincided with the Sayyid's own views. Huddleston emphasised in his speech '... that the aim of the Government is to create a self-governing Sudanese nation ...' thereby implying clear support for Sudanese independence.[152] However, the split within the Anṣār supporters in Congress made it clear to the Sayyid that an organisational reform of the 'Sudan for the Sudanese' camp was urgently required. The close link between the Anṣār apparatus and the Congress had been resented even by such staunch supporters of the Sayyid as Ibrāhīm Aḥmad. It had been partly responsible for the emergence of the Qaummiyyūn and the Aḥrār, which appeared on the political scene in 1944. Both supported Sudanese independence but resented the close connection with the Anṣār.[153] Therefore a political party had to be founded which would unite all the pro-independence groups without being identified with Sayyid 'Abd al-Raḥmān's religious mission. In August 1944, the Sayyid invited a number of senior Congress members and tribal leaders to discuss the proposal. The gathering came to the conclusion that the first step should be '... the publication of a new independent daily, quite separate from the Sayed and *El-Nil* [the Anṣār's daily] and able to express the views of the responsible graduates and tribal leaders ...' By December most of the provincial members of the advisory council had agreed to join the new venture. They declared their willingness to contribute the necessary funds for the publication of *al-Umma*, the daily organ of the 'Sudan for the Sudanese' camp, which henceforth was to be known as the Umma party.[154]

The choice of the name, *al-Umma*, is significant as it suggested a link with nineteenth century Mahdism and its belief in the establishment of an Islamic Community (*Umma*). It was also significant in the political sense as it implied adherence to the concept of Islamic unity and to anti-sectarianism, while advocating a separate Sudanese national entity.[155] By February 1945 preparations for the foundation of the Umma were completed and 'Abdallāh Khalīl, the party's first secretary, applied in writing for the required government licence for its establishment. The Umma's constitution, which was also submitted to the government, spoke as follows on the party's aims:[156]

> ... *The principle of the Party*: 'The Sudan for the Sudanese'.
> *Object of the Party*: 'To work for the independence of the Sudan within its recognised geographical frontiers, while preserving friendly relations with Britain and Egypt ...'

Membership in the Umma was stated to be open to '... all adult Sudanese who believe in the principle and object of the party ...'

while the party's control and management was to be vested in a committee. Throughout the constitution there was no mention of Sayyid 'Abd al-Raḥmān, the Anṣār, or sectarian divisions in the Sudan. The party's founders, probably intending to emphasise its non-sectarian composition, even asked Sayyid 'Alī al-Mīrghanī to join its ranks. '... The Sayed received them well, expressed, in his usual platitudes, his sympathy with the project and concluded by saying that he would reserve his judgement until their words and intentions had been translated into actions ...'[157] The only indication of the Umma's apparent dependence on Sayyid 'Abd al-Raḥmān was, significantly, in the financial sphere. The party's funds, as stated in its constitution, were to be derived from: '... a) Membership fees amounting to 5 P. T. (piastres) to be paid once in life; b) Subscriptions; c) Donations ...'[158] A party propagating separatism and relying on donations in order to cover its expenses and to finance its daily newspaper, must have been assured by Sayyid 'Abd al-Raḥmān of his support. Already in April 1945 the Sayyid realized that '... the Umma Party is seriously embarrassed by its close connection with the Mahdist Daira ...' He therefore stated that he would support any other movement working for the well-being of the Sudan, and instructed leading Anṣār not to become openly involved in the Umma's politics.[159]

However, the Anṣār-Umma connection could not be hidden from either friend or foe. In the Sudan, the Umma party was regarded by many as a government creation aiming at the establishment of a Sudanese monarchy under Sayyid 'Abd al-Raḥmān. As rumours to that effect circulated freely without being denied either by the Umma or by the Sayyid himself, many moderates were driven into the Ashiqqā' party out of fear of a Mahdist revival. By June 1945, tensions rose to such a pitch that the government decided to intervene and to deny publicly its intentions to support a Mahdist monarchy.[160] At the same time the authorities warned both Sayyids to cease their involvement in party politics in order to avoid a religious-inspired upheaval. The government feared that '... the adherence to two rival political parties of thousands of illiterate and semi-illiterate tribesmen and provincials, to whom politics are meaningless, and by whom the jargon of the party canvasser can only be interpreted as a "call" to support their own particular Holy Man, must lead eventually to a wavering in the state of public security ...'[161]

The ambivalent attitude of the authorities toward the Umma was reminiscent of their attitude towards Sudanese nationalism in the 1920s. The government viewed the emergence of a pro-independence party with favour. They regarded the attempt to unite tribal leaders and graduates in one political party as an encouraging development, but they feared and disliked the sectarian connection which, as they should have known, was the only factor which could hold the party together. In a lengthy letter, tracing the history of Sudanese politics to the 1924 mutiny, Sir James Robertson, the Sudan's Civil Secretary, described the Anṣār-Umma connection as a natural reaction to the Khatmiyya's support for the Ashiqqā'. But he complained that the main political issue ' "separatism" versus some form of union with Egypt – is being hopelessly obscured by the old Mahdist/Mirghanist rivalry ...'. Furthermore, Robertson admitted that the government's support for the Graduates' Congress and the Advisory Council was meant to '... damp down the Sayeds' rivalries and to form some sort of a united front which would devote its immediate energies to the practical realisation of our internal self-government programme ... These hopes were defeated by the intransigence of the Sayeds ...'.[162]

At the end of the World War the Sudan government faced a grave dilemma in its internal policies. Its attempts to form a non-sectarian political leadership had failed. Egypt was clamouring for a new treaty and was openly supporting the Ashiqqā' and other pro-unity groups in the Sudan. The Muslim Brothers were attempting to organise a Sudanese branch of their movement, while labour unrest, especially among railway workers, seemed to signify communist infiltration. The Umma party thus remained the only political force of any consequence which advocated policies similar to those of the government. Hence despite their distrust of Sayyid 'Abd al-Raḥmān and his personal ambitions, the authorities regarded their support of the Umma as inevitable as it was their '... main defence work against the Egyptian invasion ...'[163]

## CONCLUSION

The two main characteristics of the Sudanese political scene during the pre-independence period were the strength and flexibility of popular Islam; and the inability of the authorities to comprehend it and to formulate policies which made sense in the Sudanese context. Looking at the evolving Sudanese scene in perspective it seems only too obvious that the various attempts undertaken by the British authorities to encourage the growth of a non-sectarian Sudanese leadership were an exercise in futility. Native administration could have been a sensible policy if it had been confined to the purely administrative needs of tribal society. However, it made no sense, and could achieve few results by attempting to elevate tribal heads to the level of national political leaders. The disruption of tribal leadership, as opposed to the growing stature of the leaders of popular Islam, made the outcome of any rivalry between these two forces a foregone conclusion. And yet the British authorities never gave up. They realized the weakness of tribal leadership in the 1930s; yet they set up the advisory council only to discover once again that by and large tribal leaders were the political pawns of the Anṣār, and to a lesser degree of the Khatmiyya. As late as 1951, when a tribal-oriented party, The Socialist Republicans, was founded, the British still toyed with the idea that the 'silent majority' would at last come into its own. Its defeat in the 1953 elections at last brought about the realisation that this hope had been illusory.

Similarly, the government's attempt to foster a separatist Sudanese nationalism among the intelligentsia, combined with the decision to keep the Graduates' Congress out of politics, seems a contradiction in terms. And yet experienced British administrators, who had spent many years in the Ṣudan, initiated these policies and continued to support them even after their failure had become apparent.

Two major reasons go some way to explain this phenomenon. First, the complexities of Anglo-Egyptian relations, both in Egypt itself and in the Sudan, hindered the evolution of purely Sudanese policies. By virtue of the Condominium agreement, Britain, and to a lesser extent Egypt, were restricted in their dealings with the Sudan question. Both before and after the 1936 agreement British policy-makers in the Sudan were forced to pay heed to the repercussions of their Sudanese policies in Egypt. This in turn brought about a misinterpretation of Sudanese political trends and aspirations. Slogans such as 'the Sudan for the Sudanese' or 'the Unity of the Nile Valley', were interpreted by Britain and Egypt as supporting or opposing their continued presence in the Sudan or their future ties with that country. Yet in reality both were expressions of Sudanese aspirations towards self-government and independence; the difference between the two schools of thought was in how to achieve this aim, and as to who would rule the Sudan rather than in the aim itself. The ease with which Sudanese leaders, such as al-Azharī, changed sides in the years 1943–1956 would support this view. Instead of interpreting his inconsistency as signifying weakness of character or personal ambition, it could be understood as a choice between two different paths leading ultimately to Sudanese independence.

The second and more important reason was a misconception of the political role of popular Islam in the Sudan. The authorities' persistent attempts to confine Sayyid 'Abd al-Raḥmān al-Mahdī to what they regarded as his 'natural role' of religious leadership can be explained only as a total failure to comprehend the essence of Mahdism. The Anṣār of the twentieth century, as had their forerunners in the Mahdist state, comprised a Muslim movement in which religion and politics could not be separated from one another. And similarly Sayyid 'Abd al-Raḥmān's religious ambitions could only be interpreted in political terms. Moreover, Mahdism had been the only force which had succeeded in bringing independence to the Sudan in the nineteenth century. Therefore, it was only natural that neo-Mahdism would identify itself with its forerunners, both ideologically and politically, and would assume a similar role against those who had crushed the Mahdist State. The fact that Sayyid 'Abd al-Raḥmān discarded his father's militancy and chose the peaceful path toward independence was largely the result of his realistic appraisal of the political and military scene in the Sudan.

British misinterpretation of popular Islam in the Sudan was the result of a number of factors. First, their experience in Egypt since 1882 tended to suggest that it was possible to divorce Islam from politics. Second, during the first decade after the reconquest, British assessment of Sudanese popular Islam was largely based on their dealings with the Khatmiyya order and its leader Sayyid 'Alī al-Mīrghanī. But historically the Khatmiyya, unlike the Anṣār, had always been a supporter of the status quo and hence a collaborator with the established order. Politically the Khatmiyya had seen its role as an intermediary between its members and the rulers rather than as an active combatant for political power. Therefore the British view of popular Islam, based on their understanding of the Khatmiyya and other Ṣūfi orders, led to a misunderstanding of the Anṣār. Last but not least, the British governors sought to establish in the Sudan a social structure and a government of which they could be proud and which, in their view, would be capable of modernising the country. Tribal administration, both in its early stages of indirect rule and especially after the founding of the rural and central advisory councils, was a crucial part of this scheme. It intended to associate the rural population with the type of government most suitable for them. Again, the attempt to associate the intelligentsia with the Sudan's education, culture and welfare was regarded as an essential step in the process of modernisation. But there was no place for popular Islam, in its sectarian manifestations, within this scheme. The Sayyids were regarded as a hindrance to modernisation, both socially and politically, and the separation of 'Church and State' was viewed as essential in the Sudan no less than in England. The British authorities never realised that the centres of popular Islam, though clinging to tradition, were assuming an important modernising role. The achievements of Sayyid 'Abd al-Raḥmān in the fields of agriculture, education and publishing, provide adequate proof that the Anṣār were striving to adjust their movement to the needs of modern society. An outstanding feature of this modernising trend was the prominence of the intelligentsia in both the Anṣār and the Khatmiyya. Side by side with the traditional functions of a popular Islamic movement, which had in essence remained unchanged since the nineteenth century, the Khatmiyya and the Anṣār evolved new forms of organisation and allowed a certain flexibility in their ideologies, which had never really been well-defined, in order to attract the 'new men' to their ranks.

It was therefore impossible to divorce the social and political development of the Sudan from its sectarian divisions. Since the 1920s there had always been individuals and groups who had tried to break out of the 'magic sectarian circle' but they were too weak and too divided to have any impact on the political scene. In Sudanese politics, during the pre-independence period, it mattered little whether one belonged to a tribe or to the Graduates' Congress, or whether one advocated unity with Egypt or opposed it. Ultimately what counted was whether one supported the Anṣār or opposed them. Those who opposed them and wanted to maintain a political impact, had to seek shelter with the Anṣār's only rival – on the broad back of the Khatmiyya.

CHAPTER 2

# Ismā'īl al-Azharī and the Struggle for the Sudan's Independence

## THE EARLY YEARS

One of the groups which tried to break loose from the religious leadership was the young intelligentsia, consisting primarily of high-school and college graduates who reached maturity after the Anglo-Egyptian conquest. Thus they were not burdened by memories of the past rulers, whether Mahdist or Egyptian, and sought the swiftest road to independence. This, they believed, could be achieved through the 'Unity of the Nile Valley' as propagated by Egyptian nationalists, with whom they had a common language, religion and ideology.

However, several attempts of these young graduates to found their own political organisation failed because of their weakness and the supremacy of the Khatmiyya and the Anṣār. Only in 1938, when the number of graduates had increased considerably, did they succeed in establishing the 'Graduates Congress'. The rise and decline of this Congress and its attempt to play a major political role in the crucial post-war period, is closely connected with the career of Ismā'īl al-Azharī. As one of the only Sudanese graduates of the American University in Beirut, al-Azharī assumed the leadership of the Congress and became the main spokesman of the pro-Egyptian camp in the years prior to independence.

Ismā'īl al-Azharī[1] was born on October 29, 1900, in the house of his grandfather, also called Ismā'īl al-Azharī, one of the most prominent '*Ulamā*' and *Muftī* of the Sudan in the years 1924–1932.[2] His childhood was passed in a traditional orthodox atmosphere – he was sent to study at the *Khalweh* of the Ismā'īliyya Order and then to a *Madrasa* in Omdurman, his aim being to follow in the steps of family tradition and complete his studies at al-Azhar. His grandfather, however, interfered with this intention, and the course of Ismā'īl's studies was changed. He was first sent to Gordon College where he took the special study-course for *qāḍīs* and later, in 1921, he completed his studies at the Teacher's Seminary and began to teach in Government primary schools. The second turning-point in his life came in 1927, when he was sent together with the first Sudanese students to study at the American University in Beirut. In addition to his studies and his first contact with Arab students from other lands, the AUB became al-Azharī's first political battle-ground, when al-Azharī tried – unsuccessfully – to stand for the elections to the office of President of the Students' Union.[3] Al-Azharī completed his studies in Beirut in 1930, arriving in Sudan in time to offer his help and advice to the students of Gordon College in their first strike against the British in 1931. This year also saw the beginning of al-Azharī's political activity in the Sudan, on his election as chairman of the 'Graduates Club' in Omdurman, which was then already split between the supporters of the Khatmiyya order and the Anṣār – the great foci of power of popular Islam in the Sudan.

Al-Azharī later said that he had immediately become aware of the dangers inherent in a possible invasion of political life by religious factions and saw as his mission the prevention of the Anṣār and the Khatmiyya from influencing college graduates, thus facilitating their unification for the good of their country.

In the years 1935–1938 al-Azharī taught at Gordon College and continued as Chairman of the 'Graduates Club' in Omdurman, the President being the British Headmaster of the College. In 1938 the Government of the Sudan agreed to have a graduate as the Club's president, and thus al-Azharī became the first Sudanese elected as the Club's President. The Club served al-Azharī as a stepping stone to the 'Graduates' Congress' founded in 1938, the aim of which was to unify the graduates of all schools in the Sudan in one organisational framework, regardless of factions. The declared aims of the Congress were to promote education and culture. However, political targets were evident from the start; this was primarily due to the fact that the Anglo-Egyptian Treaty of 1936, which determined the Sudan's future without consulting its people, still rankled with all political circles in the Sudan, in particular with the intelligentsia which considered itself the flag-bearer of Sudanese nationalism.

Al-Azharī was active in the process of founding the Congress and was one of its first four presidents for in order to prevent factionalism, the graduates decided to rotate the presidency among four members. In 1942 the Congress submitted a memorandum to the Governor-General of the Sudan in which the Congress made political demands, thus claiming to act as a spokesman of the Sudanese nationalist movement. This caused a split among the graduates into two factions: a moderate stream which included most of the Anṣār supporters, and a more extreme stream which in 1943 founded the Ashiqqā' party which despite its proclamations denouncing factionalism had to seek the patronage of the Khatmiyya order and its leader, Sayyid 'Alī al-Mīrghanī. According to al-Azharī, al-Ashiqqā' had been established by members of the Graduates Club in Omdurman even before the founding of the Congress, and, due to their organisational ability, had succeeded in the elections to most of the Congress's institutions. But until 1943, they had hoped to act exclusively through the Congress and to that end, utilised and exploited the more senior and moderate members, who were trusted by the British. However, when they saw that compromise was to no avail, the Ashiqqā' asked the Egyptians for their support in setting up an autonomous Sudanese government under the aegis of the Egyptian Crown. Al-Azharī was chosen by the Party to represent it in the negotiations with the Egyptians, but on arrival in Cairo he conducted the negotiations in the name of the entire Graduates' Congress. Al-Azharī claimed that at the time the Ashiqqā' were very close to Sayyid 'Abd al-Raḥmān al-Mahdī, and that he had consulted the Sayyid before leaving for Egypt, but Sayyid 'Abd al-Raḥmān later came out openly against the aims of the negotiations; again according to al-Azharī this precipitated the split between the Ashiqqā' and the Mahdi and his Anṣār.

## AL-AZHARI'S RISE TO PROMINENCE

In 1945 the supporters of al-Mahdī founded the Umma party and this in fact brought about the gradual decline of the Graduates' Congress. From that date until 1954, al-Azharī and his fellow members of al-Ashiqqā' were the chief proponents of union with

Egypt. Against this background it is easy to understand the split which occurred in the united Sudanese mission which went to Cairo in 1946 to plead the Sudanese case, in preparation for the negotiations between Ismā'īl Ṣidqī, representing Egypt, and the British Foreign Secretary, Ernest Bevin. According to al-Azharī a clearly-stated declaration on the unity of Egypt and the Sudan, was the only way that could have saved the Sudan from 'the claws of the British lion'.

Indeed such a resolution was passed on 3 October 1945 and became known as the 'Covenant of the United Parties'. Signed by the leaders of the six political parties active in the Sudan, including, of course, the Ashiqqā' and the Umma, the Covenant declared as its aim:

> '... The establishment of a free, democratic Sudanese Government in union with Egypt and alliance with Great Britain ...'[4]

This, of course, did not correspond fully with the views of the Ashiqqā' or the Graduates' Congress, who opposed an alliance with Britain and foresaw '... the formation of a Sudanese democratic Government in a union with Egypt, under the Egyptian crown ...' Once the United Parties delegation arrived in Egypt, it became quite clear that there was a difference in the interpretation of the so-called 'union with Egypt.' While al-Azharī and his colleagues gave full support to the Egyptian claim and accepted a United Nile Valley under King Fārūq, the Umma delegates in Cairo were unwilling to commit themselves to any form of unity and hastened back to Khartoum. However, the Umma Party delegation which returned from Cairo to Khartoum to receive new instructions from its leader, failed to have the line supporting unification approved, as a result of British pressure. Consequently, according to al-Azharī, the Umma Party split up the united mission. Al-Azharī himself went to London with Ismā'īl Ṣidqī and his delegation, afterwards giving his full support to the Egyptian version which interpreted the protocol of Anglo-Egyptian agreement signed by Bevin and Ṣidqī as a victory for the cause of the 'unity of the Nile Valley'. However it should be noted that al-Azharī tried in vain to meet the British Foreign Secretary, Ernest Bevin, while in London and that Egyptian demands for sovereignty over the Sudan, were largely responsible for the ultimate failure of the 1946 Anglo-Egyptian agreement.

Al-Azharī's political rivals, headed by 'Abd al-Raḥmān al-Mahdī, played a quite different role during these crucial months. According to al-Mahdī, he and his fellow-supporters had always been against any definition that would seem to empower the Egyptian King with any authority over the Sudan. Such authority could have only one result – the end of Sudanese nationalism, independence and sovereignty. This was the reason behind the objection to al-Azharī's attempt to rally an all-embracing Sudanese support for the unification of the Nile Valley under the Egyptian Crown. The resolutions laid before the United mission which had left for Cairo in 1946 were therefore limited to the Sudanese claim for self-determination and independence. When the split became a reality, al-Mahdī and his followers set up an 'Independence Front' and organised massive demonstrations against the draft agreement in all the major Sudanese towns. The Sayyid himself sent telegrams to Clement Attlee, Prime Minister of Britain, and to Ṣidqī Pasha, Prime Minister of Egypt, requesting them to meet with him as soon as practicable in order to hear his views about the agreement.[5] In November 1946 the Sayyid and his delegation left for London via Cairo. The Government of Egypt completely ignored their presence, but the Governor-General of the Sudan, at the time staying in Cairo, encouraged them to present their claims to Attlee, while warning them that there was no chance whatsoever for any change in the Anglo-Egyptian draft agreement so recently achieved.

According to the Sayyid, his talk with Attlee lasted for about two hours and at its close the British Prime Minister remarked that '... the Egyptians persisted in their claim for sovereign rights over the Sudan for seventy years. He went on to ask: where have you been all that time? ...'[6] The Sayyid replied that the British were to blame for the absence of the Sudanese from the negotiation table since 1899. And now a new climax had been reached; Britain and Egypt had agreed to take away from the Sudan its very right to exist independently, and without even bothering to consult its people. The Sudanese, the Sayyid proclaimed, would not meekly accept the Egyptian crown or any other foreign rule over their country and would fight for independence with all their power. The Sayyid also pointed out the glaring discrepancy between the beginning of the Ṣidqī-Bevin protocol which mentioned 'the unification of Egypt and the

Sudan under the Egyptian Crown' and its end which spoke of the right of the Sudanese to decide their political future. The practical implications of this discrepancy were, according to the Sayyid, that the Sudanese right of self-determination was conditional upon the unification of the Sudan with Egypt and that any attempt to deviate from the latter principle would be regarded as unlawful and unacceptable by the Egyptians. According to the Sayyid he left the meeting with Attlee confident that he had won. Indeed, the controversy over the interpretation of the agreement between the governments of Egypt and Britain, as to the right of the Sudanese to self-determination on the one hand and the unification of Egypt and the Sudan on the other, led to the shelving of the agreement.[7] There is no doubt that Sayyid 'Abd al-Raḥmān's staunch opposition to the Egyptian claim of sovereignty over the Sudan contributed to the failure of the agreement.

The next controversy between the Umma and the Ashiqqā' parties revolved around the setting-up of the Legislative Assembly. Discussions about the matter began at the Sudan Administration Conference in April 1946 and came to an end with the founding of the Assembly in 1948.[8] Al-Azharī and his followers had four objections to the Legislative Assembly. First, they claimed that the Assembly was not representative at all since its members were elected according to criteria set down by the British rulers. Second, the discussions of the Legislative Assembly were circumscribed as its directives prevented the Assembly from discussing foreign affairs, including talks with Britain and Egypt about the Sudan's future. Third, because the British Governor had the right to veto the Assembly's decisions, its authority in the sphere of self-government was virtually non-existent. Finally, in view of the fact that the Legislative Assembly was set up in the face of Egyptian opposition, it could be seen as another attempt to turn the Sudan into a British colony. The Ashiqqā', therefore, boycotted the Assembly and by this act – according to al-Azharī – they dealt it a fatal blow.[9]

A somewhat similar, although more ambivalent, stand was taken by the leader of the Khatmiyya Order, Sayyid 'Alī al-Mīrghanī. The Khatmiyya leaders took part in the discussions on the Legislative Assembly, but the Sayyid himself openly expressed his reservations about its establishment. His main objection was to the proposal that tribal chiefs could stand for election as the representatives of the rural areas in which they resided. Despite this, several Khatmiyya leaders did take part in the Legislative Assembly which began its activities in December 1948.[10] Sayyid 'Abd al-Raḥmān al-Mahdī and the independence parties did support the setting-up of the Assembly and saw it as a meaningful step towards Sudanese independence. It was, according to al-Mahdī, the first administrative framework in which all the political and religious circles of the Sudan conferred together, and thus the British were prevented from instigating quarrels between religious leaders and tribal chiefs or between the traditional leaders and the young intelligentsia. The only reason al-Azharī and his followers opposed the Legislative Assembly, Sayyid 'Abd al-Raḥmān al-Mahdī maintained, was because of their fear that the Assembly would lead the Sudan away from Egypt, thus bringing it closer to independence.[11]

A crucial event in the Legislative Assembly, an event described by the Sayyid as an historical victory of the Umma Party but which al-Azharī viewed as a personal triumph and a failure of the Legislative Assembly took place on 15 December 1950. Two days earlier, an Umma member put before the Assembly a draft resolution requesting that the Governor-General of the Sudan demand from Britain and Egypt to grant the Sudan independence forthwith. Despite all the pressure exerted by the British authorities on the members of the Assembly and despite the authorities' claim that, in the absence of a Khatmiyya representation, the Assembly could not be regarded as a truly representative body of the Sudanese people, the resolution was adopted with a majority of one vote.[12] As mentioned before, Al-Azharī regarded this episode as unequivocal proof that his stand was sound. Firstly, the British admitted, as he had claimed all along, that the Assembly did not represent all the people of the Sudan, and secondly – and most importantly – the British attitude in this affair proved to even the most ardent pro-British elements among the Anṣār that Britain could not be relied upon. Sayyid 'Abd al-Raḥmān, however, viewed the affair as justifying his own course: all the British pressure notwithstanding, the Umma Party did obtain a majority in the Assembly for its demand for immediate Sudanese independence; furthermore, cooperation with the British had a priori been one of the means to achieve maximum self-government, the ultimate aim being independence. Hence, cooperation within the framework of the Assembly had made it possible for the Sudanese to achieve a tangible partnership in governing their country and thus bring nearer the ultimate transition to independence.

Sayyid 'Abd al-Raḥmān did concede that the British henceforth did everything in their power to obstruct him and to break the Umma Party apart. They founded the so-called Socialist-Republican Party and proposed to the tribal chiefs and village notables, who had been Umma members up to that stage, to leave their Party and represent the rural population themselves. The British attempts failed however, according to the Sayyid, because most of those who did join the new Party returned to the Umma shortly afterwards, since their historical ties with the Anṣār and their Mahdist faith were stronger than the British inducements.[13] Moreover, the Sayyid maintained it was the resolution that made the British, albeit reluctantly, set up a committee for drafting a constitution for the Sudan as early as 1951, a constitution endorsed in April 1952, and which later became the basis for Sudanese independence.[14]

There is no doubt that al-Azharī and 'Abd al-Raḥmān al-Mahdī are both guilty of disregarding the external factors which exerted a decisive influence over events in the Nile Valley. The United States, which at the time did everything in its power to save the Fārūq régime in order to hitch Egypt to the wagon of American strategic policy in the Middle East, pressured Britain to make concessions to Egypt with regard to the Sudan's future. This pressure brought about an unsought for result. It accelerated the process of transition to partial autonomy and to a unilateral British proclamation on the right of the Sudanese people to self-determination. Britain knew that the United States would be unable to make an open statement against this policy, although the American Embassy in Cairo continued secretly to support the demands for the unity of the Nile Valley.[15]

## THE YEARS OF AMBIGUITY

On 8 October, 1951, when it finally became clear that the Anglo-Egyptian negotiations on the future of Sudan had reached a dead end, the Egyptian government headed by Naḥḥās, unilaterally abolished the Condominium Agreement of 1899, and the Anglo-Egyptian treaty of 1936. A week later, King Fārūq ratified a resolution of the Egyptian Parliament to the effect that the King of Egypt would henceforth rule as King of Egypt and the Sudan and thus implement the unification of the two countries after fifty years of struggle. The constitution of a united Egypt and Sudan, as ratified by the Egyptian Parliament, without Sudanese consultation, raised a storm of objection in the Sudan, which swept before it not only the militants for Sudanese independence such as the Umma Party, but also the leader of the Khatmiyya Order and the political parties that had previously spoken up in favour of union with Egypt. All that is, except for the Ashiqqā' Party headed by Ismā'īl al-Azharī, which found itself in total isolation.[16]

The British government's reaction was firm, since this course of events played into its hands in its struggle against American pressure. On 9 October the Governor-General of the Sudan proclaimed that the 1899 and 1936 pacts were still valid and that the Government of the Sudan would continue to help the people to achieve full self-government. Two days later the British Government stated that it would continue to support the right of the Sudanese to determine their political future in an atmosphere of full freedom.[17]

But just as the Sudanese parties objected to Egypt's unilateral decision, they were also not prepared to recognize the authority of Britain in the newly-created situation. They claimed that the abolition of the Condominium by the Government of Egypt rendered void the authority of the Sudan's Governor-General. This was the reason behind the Sudanese proposal, sent to the United Nations, to appoint an international committee which would replace the Governor-General and implement the right of the Sudanese people to self-determination not later than December 1953. In April 1952, the Legislative Assembly of the Sudan approved the draft resolution for the transition to self-government and the document was sent to Britain and Egypt for ratification or amendment.[18]

This put Egypt in a predicament, because when it had proclaimed the abolition of the Condominium it had – to all practical purposes – waived its right to approve or reject the proposals as to the Sudan's future. The government of Egypt, headed by Najīb al-Hilālī (who replaced Naḥḥās following the events of 'Black Saturday' in January 1952), therefore invited Umma representatives in the hopes of reaching an agreement on the future of the Sudan. The Egyptian Government thought that an agreement with the main faction supporting the independence of the Sudan, would facilitate a demand for the curtailment of the powers of the British Governor-General during the transition period, especially if such a demand was presented in the name of a united Egyptian-Sudanese front.[19] On 27 May 1952 a high-level Umma delegation, headed by 'Abdallāh al-Fāḍil, left for Cairo to conduct negotiations with the Government of Egypt. At the conclusion of the negotiations, on 28 June, the parties arrived at an agreement on most points, Egypt for the first time recognising the right of the Sudanese to self-determination and supporting a referendum which would decide the future of the Sudan. The remaining differences revolved mainly around the status of King Fārūq during the transition period; the al-Hilālī Government demanding that the Sudanese recognize him as King of the Sudan, at least temporarily and symbolically, until the referendum were to take place, since otherwise Egypt would have no legal status in the Sudan in the interim period. The Umma delegation rejected this proposal forthwith and instead proposed, as an interim arrangement, the appointment of a tripartite committee made up of an Egyptian, a British and a Sudanese representative, to assist the Governor-General of the Sudan and to oversee his actions in the transition period.[20]

Less than a month after the negotiations were concluded, Fārūq was driven into exile. Further negotiations were postponed until October 1952 and were then conducted by General Muḥammad Najīb, the new President of Egypt. The main obstacle to an agreement – King Fārūq – having now been removed, Najīb and his fellow-officers assumed that his deposition, together with the right of self-determination granted to the Sudanese would improve prospects for a favourable Sudanese decision on the unification of the Nile Valley. This assumption was based – among other things – on the familiarity of Najīb and his fellow-officers with the mood in the Sudan and on statements by the spokesmen of the Umma delegation who said time and again that any Egyptian attempt to delay recognition of the rights of the Sudanese to self-determination would incite anti-Egyptian feelings in the Sudan and impair future relations between the two countries.[21]

According to al-Azharī Britain initiated the talks mentioned above between Najīb and the Umma. During a visit of Sayyid 'Abd al-Raḥmān al-Mahdī to London Sir Anthony Eden, the British Foreign Secretary, advised the Sayyid that he stop over in Cairo on his way back to the Sudan in order to discuss the Sudan's future with Najīb. Al-Azharī claimed that Britain's intentions were as usual perfidious, for the British assumed that an agreement between the Umma and Egypt was not feasible and once the talks broke down, the British would remain in power.[22] However, al-Azharī's claims cannot be corroborated from other sources and they appear unreasonable. First, the talks between the Sayyid and Eden took place on 11 November 1952, whereas the talks between the Umma representatives and the Egyptian Government had resulted in an initial agreement on 19 October. Second, ever since the foundation of the Socialist-Republican Party, relations between Sayyid 'Abd al-Raḥmān and the British were very strained and they knew that he would do his utmost to have them ousted from the Sudan.[23] It is true that Eden had expressed a hope, in his discussions with the Sayyid, that the latter would visit Cairo on his way home to the Sudan and reach an agreement with Najīb on the Sudan's future. But Eden assumed that such an agreement was not only possible but would also help the British to stabilise their relations with Egypt before the impending talks about the British evacuation of the Suez bases.[24]

On 19 October the first agreement between the Umma representatives and the other Sudanese parties who favoured independence, on the one hand, and the representatives of the Egyptian Government, on the other, had been signed. On 10 January 1953, the agreement was ratified by the Government of Egypt and by representatives of all the parties of the Sudan. The agreement granted the Sudanese the right of self-determination and stipulated a transition period of not more than three years, during which parliamentary elections were to be held and a Sudanese government formed. All the military forces of Britain and Egypt were to be evacuated and all the British and Egyptian officials serving in the Sudan were to be replaced by Sudanese officials. A special clause stipulated that if no suitable Sudanese officials could be found for certain jobs the vacancies were to be filled by officials from neutral countries. The agreement also stated that at the end of the transition period the people of the Sudan should decide their own future by referendum. But the greatest slight to Britain – according to al-Azharī – was the curtailment of the powers of the Governor-General of the Sudan during the transition period implicit in the agreement. First, it imposed upon the Governor-General two international commissions that were to supervise the Sudanese administration on the one hand, and the general elections on the other. Second, a clause originally inserted to meet a British demand, that the Governor-General be given special rights in the Southern Provinces of the Sudan, was rephrased in such a manner that the South was not mentioned.[25] A month later the main outlines of this agreement were endorsed by the Anglo-Egyptian treaty on the future of the Sudan, thus bringing to an end the 1899 Condominium agreement.

The course of events from the signing of the agreement until the proclamation of Sudanese independence on 31 December 1955 was as follows: The general elections to the Sudanese Parliament were held in November-December 1953. Out of a total number of 97 MPs, 51 members of the National Union Party (NUP) which was formed as a result of a union between the Ashiqqā' and the other parties favouring union with Egypt were elected, whereas the Umma Party, the main opponent to union with Egypt, won only 22 seats. As a result the NUP headed the Sudanese Government in the transition period and it might have been assumed that this would lead the Sudan towards union with Egypt. But instead of striving for union with Egypt, a process of erosion began which undermined the government's previous position. On 1 March 1954, thousands of the Anṣār came out on the streets to demonstrate against a union with Egypt – on the very day that the festive opening ceremony of the Sudanese Parliament was to take place, in the presence of the Egyptian President, Muḥammad Najīb. The demonstrations, which turned into bloody clashes, with many wounded and killed, resulted in the cancelling of the ceremony and brought about a more sober view of the differences of opinion in the Sudan. It became evident that any attempt to unite the Sudan with Egypt could only result in civil war. Even more important was the fact that many of those who had supported a union with Egypt had not regarded it as a political end but merely as a means in the struggle for independence. Moreover, a considerable number of those in favour of a union had wanted the British out of the country but feared that the Anṣār and their leader Sayyid 'Abd al-Raḥmān would then take over. Once it became clear that the British were in fact leaving and that the Sayyid and his followers constituted only a small minority in Parliament, Egyptian 'assistance' was no longer required and the slogans urging union became redundant. The leader of this group, Sayyid 'Alī al-Mīrghanī, head of the Khatmiyya Order, withdrew his support from the NUP in 1954, and arrived at an unexpected agreement regarding independence with his long-time rival, Sayyid 'Abd al-Raḥmān al-Mahdī, in October 1955. Several other, and less important, causes also had an effect. Foremost among them was the ouster of Najīb, popular with the Sudanese because of his half-Sudanese origin and his education at Gordon College; the attitude of many Sudanese politicians was much less warm to the Nasser régime. The suppression of the Muslim Brothers in Egypt in 1954 also evoked an unfavourable reaction. Moreover, Egypt was accused of intervention in the course of the Sudanese elections in favour of the NUP when the Egyptian press and radio conducted a propaganda campaign under the slogan of the 'Unity of the Nile Valley', in contravention of the gentleman's agreement signed between Egypt and the Sudanese parties.

In April 1955 the Sudanese Prime Minister and leader of the NUP, Ismā'īl al-Azharī, proclaimed his support for independence, thus removing all doubts as to the Sudan's future. On 19 December it was decided that no referendum was to be held and that Parliament itself, representing the Sudanese people, would determine the Sudan's future. On 31 December 1955, Parliament unanimously ratified the temporary constitution of the Democratic Sudanese Republic and the flags of the Sudan were hoisted on the flagpoles which had flown the Egyptian and British flags ever since 1898.[26]

## UNION WITH EGYPT DISCARDED

The memoirs of Ismā'īl al-Azharī add a personal note to this affair and shed light on the process of changing postures within the ruling party. Al-Azharī contends that his party had already taken a stand on the question of union with Egypt in the election campaign of 1953. While the NUP had proclaimed its loyalty to the Anglo-Egyptian agreement and in particular to the clause stipulating the right of self-determination, it had done little to propagate its declared stand concerning union with Egypt.[27] Al-Azharī notes the fact but offers no explanations and the reader cannot but reach his own conclusion, namely that the NUP was wary of the slogan of union with Egypt because it realised that its unpopularity would endanger votes in the impending elections. It can also be surmised, as events have subsequently shown, that even the party leadership was not unanimous in its views about the future of the Sudan.

The main problem with which al-Azharī had to deal, both before the elections and after, was to safeguard the unity of the party and in particular to ensure the continued support of 'Alī al-Mīrghanī, without which his rule was jeopardized. Sayyid 'Alī demonstrated his power in the elections of the representatives of the NUP to the Supervising Committee of the Governor-General. The party's candidate, who had been duly elected by its leadership, had to step down in favour of Sayyid Dardirī Muḥammad 'Uthmān, whom Sayyid 'Alī named as more suitable for the job.[28] Sayyid 'Alī's power was even more manifest when al-Azharī formed his first government, and had to take heed of Sayyid 'Alī and one of his close followers, Mīrghanī Ḥamza, in order to safeguard the integrity of the party. Moreover, on the day the government was formed and after its presentation to the Governor-General and to Sayyid 'Abd al-Raḥmān, al-Azharī was summoned to the house of Sayyid 'Ali al-Mīrghanī. There he was told by one of the Khatmiyya leaders that to all intents and purposes Sayyid 'Alī was the true leader of the Sudan and al-Azharī must, therefore, report to him about all his actions and hold himself responsible to him. Al-Azharī stressed that Sayyid 'Alī himself kept silent and made no demands on him.[29] However, there was no doubt about the fact that al-Azharī knew that Sayyid 'Alī and the Khatmiyya were the real source of his power and that without them the Sudanese intelligentsia was powerless.

On the other hand, al-Azharī had also to take into account Sayyid 'Abd al-Raḥmān and the large number of his followers, in particular among the tribal population. Although the NUP did gain a majority during the elections, the bloody clashes on 1 March 1954 between those in favour and those opposed to union with Egypt left no doubt that the Anṣār would not be overly fastidious in choosing the means for obstructing the proposed union.[30] With this in mind, al-Azharī treated his rivals from the Umma Party rather gingerly, and unlike his fellow party members, who demanded the arrest of all the Anṣār leaders, al-Azharī insisted that the affair be conducted as a routine legal case without harming the leaders of the opposition.[31]

How was it, therefore, that the NUP changed its stand from outright support for the unification of the Nile Valley, to a proclamation on the independence of the Sudan? The answer to this question is furnished by the party leaders, the heads of the Khatmiyya and by Sayyid ʻAlī himself, who had never regarded the union with Egypt as a political aim in itself, but rather as a means for obtaining independence from Britain and preventing the Anṣār from taking over. As early as August 1950, *Ṣawt al-Sūdān*, the main Khatmiyya publication, proclaimed that despite the Order's support for the slogan of union with Egypt the Khatmiyya demanded that the nationality and sovereignty of the Sudan be preserved and that it had no intention of leaving the future of the country in the hands of Egypt.[32] Even in the course of the 1953 elections, Mīrghanī Ḥamza, one of the Khatmiyya and NUP leaders, proclaimed his support for close relations with Egypt but not to the point where independence would be lost. The Sudan, he said, must set up independent government and military bodies.[33] Debates within the NUP culminated in the second half of 1954, when the Khatmiyya leaders demanded a clear declaration in support of independence, while others in the party, such as Muḥammad Nūr al-Dīn, insisted on implicit commitment to union with Egypt.

Al-Azharī tried to evade a decision in order to avoid a split. During his visit to London as Sudan's Prime Minister, in October 1954, he stated at press conferences that the Sudan would not give up its entity and would not exchange one imperialist rule for another, but he consistently claimed that his party had not yet decided on its future relations with Egypt.[34] In late 1954 it was evident that the NUP was in danger of a split. This started with a series of articles by Khalafallāh Khālid, one of the Khatmiyya leaders, published in *Ṣawt al-Sūdān*, in which Khalafallāh stated that he and his followers would oppose any solution that did not ensure the Sudan's independence.[35] A short while later, in December 1954, the break culminated with the dismissal of three Khatmiyya leaders, Mīrghanī Ḥamza, Khalafallāh Khālid and Aḥmad Jalī, all ministers in al-Azharī's government, from their ministerial offices and the accusation by the Prime Minister of their support for the policy of the Umma. The three men reacted by publishing a proclamation charging al-Azharī and his supporters with an attempt to enslave the Sudan to Egyptian rule.[36] This step forced al-Azharī to state his position more clearly, since it was quite clear that Sayyid 'Alī and the rank and file of the Khatmiyya were behind the three ousted leaders. In late December 1954 al-Azharī explained the principles governing his policy in an interview to the daily *al-Ayyām*, stressing that the party had not yet taken a decision on these matters.[37] His statement included the following points: First, the Sudan should adopt a republican régime headed by a President, government and an independent Parliament. Second, the special relationship between the Sudan and Egypt would be coordinated through a sort of a Supreme Council which would meet at least once a year in order to discuss matters of common interest, such as defence, foreign relations and the use of the Nile waters. The recommendations of the Council would then be brought before the governments of Egypt and the Sudan which would be empowered to adopt, reject, or propose amendments to, them. The editorial board of *al-Ayyām*, which regarded this statement as a revolutionary turning-point in al-Azharī's views, asked the leaders of the Khatmiyya and the Anṣār to comment on them. The Khatmī leaders treated al-Azharī's statements with suspicion and commented that al-Azharī had been known to deny one day the statements he had made the day before. But the Umma leaders welcomed his statement, saying that their Party was fighting for the independence of the Sudan and would be very pleased if al-Azharī and his supporters would take a similar stand.[38] The danger to the continued rule of al-Azharī was evident, since a reconciliation and rapprochement between the Khatmiyya and the Anṣār could in practice mean the collapse of the parliamentary majority upon which the NUP relied.

The process of rapprochement between the two religious

orders had begun even before the elections, when Sayyid Abd al-Raḥmān announced in August 1953 that he and his party were in favour of a democratic-republican régime in an independent Sudan.[39] The importance of this announcement lay in the fact that it put an end to the rumours and the suspicions among the Khatmiyya and other anti-Anṣār elements, that Sayyid 'Abd al-Raḥmān wanted to become Sultan or king of the Sudan once independence had been achieved.[40] His true aim, according to his announcement, was to see the flag of Islam hoisted on the flagpoles of an independent Sudan and to see all those who had shed their blood for his father the Mahdī, win the freedom for which they had been fighting.[41]

The attempted ouster of the President of Egypt, General Najīb, in February 1954 and the persecution of the Muslim Brothers, were also exploited by the Umma Party for instigating a schism between the Khatmiyya and al-Azharī's supporters within the NUP. In a manifesto signed by Ṣiddīq al-Mahdī, the son of the Anṣār leader and the head of the Umma Party, it was stated that events in Egypt clearly proved that those people of the Sudan who did not want to share a fate similar to that of their persecuted Egyptian brethren, must opt for independence before it was too late.[42] The party spokesmen claimed that the so called revolutionary government of Egypt would follow in the steps of previous Egyptian governments and do everything to achieve a union, which would mean, in practice, the loss of Sudanese independence, sovereignty and national entity.[43]

This was the background against which the first split in the NUP took place, to be followed by al-Azharī's proclamation that he supported independence for the Sudan. The Egyptian reaction was sharp. Ṣalāh Sālim, the 'dancing colonel' then in charge of Sudanese affairs on behalf of the Egyptian Revolutionary Command Council (RCC), announced that Egypt would not agree to any compromise in the matter of unifying the Nile Valley and even boasted that he could 'wipe al-Azharī off the face of the earth'.[44] Sudanese reactions to the Egyptian attacks on al-Azharī were on two levels: in the NUP, a majority was formed supporting his stand as regards the independence of the Sudan; then, various organisations such as the Students' Union, the Federation of Trade Unions and the Jazīra Cotton Growers' Association publicly declared in January 1955 their full support for Sudanese independence.[45] At the end of the same month a meeting of all Sudanese parties in favour of independence was held. The meeting decided to adopt as a platform the three following principles: (1) Full independence; (2) Safeguarding of the common rights of all inhabitants; (3) No military pacts were to be joined and no foreign aid accepted that might affect the sovereignty of the Sudan.[46] In these circumstances, the parliamentary faction of the NUP decided on 8 April 1955, to support the full independence and sovereignty of the Sudan while favouring cooperation with Egypt on the economic and military levels.[47]

These events in fact amounted to a decision as to the Sudan's future, but the Egyptian authorities could not yet reconcile themselves to such unexpected developments. At the Bandung Conference in April 1955, Nasser made no contact with al-Azharī, who represented the Sudan. The Egyptian leadership made every effort to isolate its former ally, Ismā'īl al-Azharī, and help to form a majority within the NUP that would support union with Egypt. Even worse was the propaganda campaign conducted by the Egyptian radio and press concerning the problem of the Southern Sudan. The Egyptians accused the al-Azharī government of neglecting the South and claimed that the problem of the South would find its solution only if the area was made autonomous and connected by federal ties to a united Egypt and Northern Sudan. The Egyptian propaganda was translated into most Southern dialects in order to win over its population. A delegation from the South was invited to Egypt, where it was given a warm welcome and subsequently announced its support for a union of the Sudan and Egypt. The Egyptians thus indirectly helped to inflame tempers in the South, which led, in August 1955, to the rebellion of the Southern battalions and the beginning of the civil war in this area.[48] The Egyptian government went even further, voicing demands, through the semi-official *al-Jumhuriyya*, that al-Azharī resign and new elections be held in view of the fact that al-Azharī and his party had won the previous elections on a platform that supported union with Egypt.[49] Soon after these demands were made, on 28 August 1955, Ṣalāh Sālim, who had been in charge of Sudanese affairs in the RCC, was dismissed and a more moderate stand taken by the Egyptian government, namely that the Sudanese people had the right to determine their own future without pressure. But the harm had already been done and distrust between the two governments continued. This manifested itself, among other things, in another split within the NUP, one of its leaders, Muḥammad Nūr al-Dīn, leaving the party because of its alleged betrayal of its support for the 'Unity of the Nile Valley'. This made it possible for al-Azharī to form and head a unified parliamentary bloc favouring independence, which gave the government a decisive majority in Parliament. On 16 August the Sudanese Parliament decided to approve a proposal by al-Azharī demanding the immediate evacuation of the British and Egyptian forces from the Sudan as a step towards implementation of the Sudanese people's right to self-determination.[50]

Throughout the course of these events Sayyid 'Alī al-Mīrghanī kept completely silent. Other Khatmiyya leaders, such as Mīrghanī Ḥamza, did express their views in favour of independence for the Sudan, but in the pro-Egyptian group there were also leaders who claimed to represent the views of Sayyid 'Alī. As if to add to the general confusion among his followers, Sayyid 'Alī broke his silence in mid-August 1955 and published a manifesto in which he proposed that all parties in the Sudan support a referendum to determine the future of their country. This statement was rather puzzling both in its content and its timing, for it was made at a time when all Sudanese parties, including the NUP, had already declared their support for independence; a referendum was therefore unnecessary and could even give rise to divisiveness. Moreover, while the people of the Sudan expected Sayyid 'Alī to voice his opinions as to the future of their country, he said nothing about the main problem – union with Egypt or independence.[51] Three days later, the revolt in the South started and it became evident that a referendum in that area would be impossible in the forseeable future. Despite this, Mīrghanī Ḥamza, leader of the splinter group which had left the NUP earlier, proposed on 29 August in Parliament to adopt Sayyid 'Alī's proposal concerning a referendum and this was carried by a decisive majority. The motives behind this decision were primarily based on internal party politics. The NUP could not afford to oppose the Sayyid's proposal and thus jeopardise the continued support of the Khatmiyya. The proposal was therefore adopted although many of those who had voted in favour openly criticised it.[52] Sayyid 'Abd al-Raḥmān, who did not want to endanger the consensus reached among all the parties as regards independence, proposed that the referendum should concern itself only with the question of the form of government to be adopted by an independent Sudan and not with independence itself, on which general agreement had already been reached.[53]

On 26 October the two Sayyids signed a document in which they pledged themselves and members of their families to refrain from political and party activities. The initiative to sign such a pledge came from the Mīrghanī family, whose members were never openly involved in active politics and such a pledge could only be of help to them.[54] The Mahdī's family was, however, playing an active role in the political arena and Ṣiddīq al-Mahdī, 'Abd al-Raḥmān's son, was leader of the Umma party. It must therefore be assumed that 'Abd al-Raḥmān's approval of this pledge came because of the transition to independence and his desire to form a united front of the two important religious sects which would ensure a straight majority in any referendum to be held on the future of the Sudan.[55] About a fortnight later, on 12 November, Sayyid 'Alī proclaimed his support for a national coalition and a national policy agreed upon by all political streams. This was presumably a direct result of the arrangement made between him and Sayyid 'Abd al-Raḥmān. The Umma party did everything in its power to force al-Azharī into forming a coalition in which the Umma would participate. It did manage, on 10 November, to overthrow the al-Azharī government by a no-confidence vote. But despite the pressure of Sayyid 'Ali, al-Azharī adamantly refused to include the Umma in his new government although he proclaimed his willingness to adopt a 'national policy', in line with the demands made by Sayyid 'Alī. There is no doubt that al-Mīrghanī could have mobilised a majority from among the Khatmiyya supporters inside the NUP, that could have formed a coalition government composed of the Anṣār and the Khatmiyya, with al-Azharī and his followers finding themselves in the opposition. Such strategems were, however, not in line with the Sayyid's inclinations – he never gave the Khatmiyya politicians clear directives, preferring to leave the decisions in their own hands. Thus, after a reconciliatory meeting between the Sayyid and al-Azharī it was agreed that the latter continue as prime minister with Khatmiyya support, and instead of a national coalition an inter-party committee would be set up to advise the prime minister in the transition period leading to independence.[56]

Even at this late hour al-Mīrghanī still refrained from announcing his outright support for independence and continued to favour a referendum, that was – by almost overall agreement – unnecessary and possibly damaging. The first hint of a shift in the Khatmiyya stand came on 3 December, when the two Sayyids published a manifesto to their followers and to all the Sudanese people asking them to bury their differences and work together for the achievement of full sovereignty. Although Sayyid 'Alī, even in this manifesto, still refrained from using the word 'independence', he also did not implicitly mention his former demand to hold a referendum and thus left the initiative to the Government and Parliament.[57] It was, in fact, the British that drove the Sudanese Parliament into making a decision: first, by announcing that Britain would accept any decision taken by the Sudanese, whether in parliament or by referendum, the British strengthened those opposing the referendum – much to Egypt's dismay; second, on 13 December the British Governor-General handed in his resignation to the British and Egyptian governments, and two days later departed from the Sudan on his way home. In the Sudan his departure was taken as a step heralding independence, and on 15 December al-Azharī announced that the independence of the Sudan would be proclaimed four days later by the Sudanese Parliament.[58] On 19 December 1955 Parliament decided to ask Britain and Egypt for recognition of the independence of the Sudan, and elected an all-Sudanese five-man committee representing all shades of political thinking to head the country until the constitution was ratified and a President elected. The speed with which this decision was passed was due – according to al-Azharī – to fear of missing the propitious moment. According to al-Azharī, he had been notified by the Egyptian representative in the Governor-General's committee that Egypt would not agree to a Sudanese decision on independence as long as a British Governor-General was still at his post in the Sudan. Thus the announcement by Sir Knox Helm that he was resigning gave the Sudanese Parliament the opportunity it had been waiting for, and before Britain or Egypt could decide on a new Governor-General, the five-man committee took over all his powers, thus making the appointment of a new Governor-General both superfluous and unlikely. Both governments of the Condominium could only give their blessing to the fait accompli and on 1 January 1956 the independent Sudanese Republic was born.[59]

The history of the Sudan during the transition to independence clearly shows that despite the emergence of political parties and the holding of parliamentary elections, political power in practice remained in the hands of the religious leadership and its two centres, the Khatmiyya and the Anṣār. The rise of the Sudanese intelligentsia, in the form of the Ashiqqā' Party, led various historians to the logical, though mistaken, view that this was a clear sign of the decline of the political influence of the traditional power groups. The British did everything in their power in order to break up the political influence of Sayyid 'Abd al-Raḥmān al-Mahdī, and the founding of the Republican-Socialist Party in 1951 was part of that plan. But in practice no tangible change in the structure of the forces operating in the Sudan could be felt, since each political group formed in time became part of the traditional power set-up. The fight for independence, except for external factors over which the Sudanese had no control, was therefore a sequel of the struggle between the power centres active in the Sudan since the First World War. Even Britain and Egypt became pawns in the hands of these forces. After the British betrayal of 'Abd al-Raḥmān al-Mahdī in 1951, he turned his back on them and already in 1952 he tried to reach an agreement with Egypt. Sayyid 'Alī al-Mīrghanī, having used the Egyptians to prevent Sayyid 'Abd al-Raḥmān and the Anṣār from taking over the Sudan, forsook them in 1954 when it became clear that this danger had passed. An examination of the moves which led to the proclamation of the Sudan's independence in December 1955 shows that the consensus reached between the Sayyids, concerning a coordinated policy on which both agreed, was far more important than decisions made by government or Parliament. Al-Azharī knew the rules of the game, and he was constrained to ensure Khatmiyya support for every major political decision. His stubborn refusal to form a national coalition despite the demand of Sayyid 'Alī was due to his familiarity with the Sayyid and of his conviction that the latter would not interfere when essential matters were not at stake. It was the compromise reached on 3 December 1955 between the two Sayyids which really paved the way to independence. Al-Azharī and the 'secular' national group which he had tried to form and to represent was thus forced into an increasingly narrow manoeuvring position. This became even clearer after independence, when on 5 July 1956 a coalition of the Umma and the People's Democratic Party (PDP) – the political parties representing the Anṣār and the Khatmiyya respectively – overthrew the al-Azharī government and returned the rule to those who really held the power.

# II

# Sudanese Communism

CHAPTER 3

# The Rise and Decline of the Sudanese Communist Party

## THE FORMATIVE YEARS

The study of so-called parliamentary politics in the Sudan seems to suggest that sectarianism was so powerful that the democratic system imported from the West had little chance of success. At the same time, while al-Azharī and his colleagues were attempting to break loose from their traditional leaders, there appeared in the Sudan another alien political force trying to implant the communist creed in a society which seemed rather unprepared for its message.

Although it is generally accepted that the Sudanese Communist Party (SCP) was founded in 1946, earlier attempts to plant communism in the Sudan go back as far as the post-World War I period. The upsurge of nationalism in Egypt, culminating in the National revolt of 1919, had its repercussions in the Sudan. The Sudan at that time was ostensibly ruled by Great Britain and Egypt which had conquered the country in 1898 and, having destroyed the independent Mahdist State, had established the so-called Anglo-Egyptian Condominium. Yet, in fact, England was the real ruler of the Sudan and every attempt was made by the British administrators to diminish Egyptian participation in the country's administration to vanishing point. This policy seems to have been generally acceptable to the older generation of traditional Sudanese leaders for a number of reasons. Firstly, many of them still remembered the Egyptian rulers of the Sudan in the pre-Mahdist period and hence feared that the 'Unity of the Nile Valley' and other expressions of Egyptian 'brotherhood' with the Sudan were in reality covers for expansionist ambitions. Secondly, it was quite clear that Britain was the senior partner in the Sudan and that through its virtual rule over Egypt, the latter was in no position to provide any meaningful help to the Sudanese. However, many of the younger educated Sudanese did not share this view. Not burdened by historical memories, they felt more akin to the Muslim Arabic-speaking Egyptians and were inspired by the ideas of Egyptian nationalism and its anti-British struggle for independence. The White Flag League, which was the first expression of modern Sudanese nationalism, was thus influenced and inspired by Egypt and to a certain extent also received direct aid from Egyptian nationalist sources. The leaders of the White Flag League had little support outside the small and politically immature intelligentsia and the handful of Sudanese army officers who founded it. England had therefore no difficulty in crushing the movement and, following the expulsion of the Egyptians from the Sudan in 1924, Sudanese nationalism of the intelligentsia brand vanished from the political scene for the next fourteen years.

However, during the five years of the White Flag League's existence, communist elements succeeded in infiltrating the movement.[1] These elements included Egyptian students studying in Europe, communists in Egypt who were cooperating with the extreme wing of the *Wafd* and young Sudanese who had been influenced by communists mainly from central European extraction, who were employed as officials by the Sudanese Railways department in 'Aṭbarā. However, due to British supremacy both in Egypt and the Sudan, and as a result of the narrow base the White Flag League had in the Sudan itself, the impact of communism was negligible. After the crushing of the League and the departure of the Egyptians, communist propaganda and infiltration were conducted from the Soviet diplomatic mission in Jedda, using as its base of operations in the Sudan, pro-communist elements within the Egyptian *Wafd* and European officials in 'Aṭbarā, the headquarters of the Sudan's railways. The Red Sea port of 'Aṣmara served as an alternative route for infiltrating into the Sudan from Jedda.[2]

The major communist propaganda was in the economic sphere, in which it was emphasised that Britain was doing its utmost in order to make the Sudan economically independent of Egypt and conversely to tie the Sudanese economy to the British Empire. The building of Port Sudan in the Red Sea in 1910 and the cultivation of long staple cotton in the British-financed Jazīra project after the war, were cited as examples of this policy. An Intelligence Report, in June 1926, stated that Soviet agents had been planted in the Sudan and that anti-British propaganda in the Sudan had been traced to the Third International and to its agents in Egypt and the Sudan.[3] In reality all these attempts were of little significance and their sole result was that a few additional officials, charged with tracing communist agents, were employed in the British Intelligence Departments in Egypt and the Sudan. By the beginning of 1928, the Third International terminated its activities in the Nile Valley and as far as the Sudan was concerned the re-appearance of communism had to be postponed for another fifteen years.

Communism re-emerged in the Sudan during World War II when several British officers and at least one school master, who were members of the British communist party, started propaganda among Sudanese intellectuals and students. The Wādī Sayyidina Secondary School, north of Khartoum, many of whose graduates pursued their studies at Khartoum University, became a hot-bed for communists and supplied the members of the first communist cell which was founded at the University in 1946. Another group of Sudanese students founded a communist cell at Cairo University, during the same year. These two groups included many of the future leaders of the SCP such as: 'Abd al-Khāliq Maḥjūb, al-Tījanī al-Ṭayyib, Aḥmad Sulaymān and 'Azz al-Dīn 'Alī 'Āmir.[4] Through its Egyptian cell the movement had connexions with the *Mouvement Démocratique de Libération Nationale*, one of the factions of the Egyptian communist party.[5] As they were not allowed to function legally and influenced by their Egyptian comrades, the young Sudanese communists named their organization the 'Sudanese Movement for National Liberation' (SMNL). In March 1946 the SMNL organised the first political demonstration to be held in the Sudan since 1924, under its anti-imperialist banner. But already in 1947 the party suffered its first serious crisis. 'Opportunist elements' had infiltrated the central committee of the SCP which as a result was unable to reach a decision regarding the future of the Sudan. Some of these 'middle class opportunists' went so far as to support the 'Unity of the Nile Valley' under the Egyptian Crown and were therefore known as 'Royalist Communists'. Following the purge of this group the party succeeded in expanding and attracted many of the members and leaders of the newly founded trade unions to its ranks. Moreover, the party now had its own periodical, *al-Kādir*, through which it preached its principal political beliefs to the Sudanese people. These included the fight against imperialism and the struggle for the Sudanese right of self-determination. Hardly two years had passed before the SCP was in the midst of another turmoil which was only resolved at the third congress of the party, in 1956. At the centre of the crisis was a so-called 'revisionist group' led by 'Awwaḍ 'Abd al-Rāziq, the party's secretary general. According to Maḥjūb, the discussion with the 'revisionists' centred around the party's role within the peasants' movement as well as their doctrinaire interpretation of Marxism.

It was during the early years of its existence that the SCP succeeded in breaking out of the small circle of its supporters from the intelligentsia and to establish itself among workers and peasants, a step which lies at the root of the SCP's relative strength in later years.

The beginnings of trade unionism in the Sudan took place in 1946, thus coinciding with the establishment of the first communist cell in Khartoum. In July 1946 the 'Workers' Affairs Association' (WAA) was founded as the spokesman of the Sudan's railway workers. It was no coincidence that the first attempts at trade unionism in the Sudan took place in 'Aṭbarā, a fairly new town which had developed as the centre of the expanding Sudan railways. Out of a population of some 40,000, over ninety per cent consisted of railway employees and their dependants. Moreover, owing to its special character, the town's traditional centres of loyalty – tribe, family and religious leadership – were all weakened by new forms of solidarity.[6]

The fact that the Sudan railways were chosen as the centre of the trade unions was a good omen for the young movement. In a country that stretches over a million square miles, the smooth running of the railways is of crucial importance to the administration and security as well as to the economy and well-being of the population. Moreover, in the Sudan, whose industry was in its initial stages of development, the railways presented the largest concentration of labour which could be organised in the new unions.

Recognising the importance of the railways and the potential strength of a railway union, if properly organised, the British management refused to recognise the WAA despite its moderate demands. It was only after a mass demonstration on 8 August 1947, followed by a general strike and the arrest of the union's leaders that the government at last relented. By that time, however, the leadership of the union was already in communist hands. The SCP's position was further enhanced by the refusal of the railways management to negotiate with the workers regarding wages and working conditions. The railways, it was stated, were a branch of the Sudan civil service and hence any negotiations had to be conducted directly with the government. In this way the workers' struggle for better wages and better conditions of employment became part and parcel of their nationalist struggle against a British-controlled government.[7] One of the leaders of this struggle who later became a trade union leader of world renown was al-Shafi' Aḥmad al-Shaykh, a leading member of the SCP and of its central committee. Al-Shafi' played a predominant role in the development of Sudanese trade unions not only among town workers but also among the cotton growers in the Jazīra and elsewhere. In 1948 he led the struggle against the British-inspired Trade Unions Law and succeeded after a one-day strike of all Sudanese workers to force the government to modify its original draft and thus enable the relatively free development of trade unions.[8]

These were the major factors which turned the Sudanese trade unions into a militant political force. From 1950, the trade unions were linked together in the Sudan Workers' Trade Union Federation (SWTUF) in which the railway workers played a predominant role. In December 1951 the SWTUF decided to take an active part in Sudanese politics. Prompted by the unilateral abrogation by Egypt of the Anglo-Egyptian treaty of 1936, the SWTUF declared that its objective was to defeat imperialism and to achieve for the Sudan the right of self-determination. To achieve this end, 'The United Front for the Liberation of the Sudan' was established and all workers' and peasants' unions were called upon to establish national committees in order to function within this Front which was initiated and run by communists.[9]

The year 1952 saw the first attempts of the SWTUF at organising peasants and agricultural workers. Existing organisations, such as the Jazīra Tenants' Association, were branded as fake organisations imposed by the authorities. In August 1952, the Northern province tenants held their first conference at 'Aṭbarā, under the auspices of the railway workers. This was followed by the Nūba Mountains cotton cultivators, whose congress, in May 1953, was attended and addressed by the president of SWTUF. Finally, the Jazīra cotton growers joined the ranks of the newly founded 'United Front for the Liberation of the Sudan'.[10]

It is hard to determine the extent of communist influence or control of either the trade unions or the tenants' associations. The SCP claimed during the 1953 elections to be spokesman of the 'Anti-Imperialist Front' consisting of workers, peasants and intelligentsia applying in the Sudan 'the successful tactics of the Chinese communist party ...'[11] It is known, however, that communist attempts to exploit the trade unions for political aims, failed in many instances. In April 1952, the SWTUF threatened a general strike for an unlimited period unless its chief officers were released from jail within forty-eight hours. However, the strike had to be called off as some of the most powerful unions were not willing to support what they regarded as a political strike.[12]

The declining prestige of the SWTUF and of the SCP within the Federation became even clearer in 1953. When the Anglo-Egyptian agreement was signed in February 1953 granting the Sudanese the right to self-determination, it was hailed by the major political parties as a victory for Sudanese nationalism. The SCP and following it the SWTUF, condemned it as an Anglo-Egyptian imperialist plot and called for a three-day general strike in protest. The strike had to be called off due to lack of support and the SWTUF executive had to announce that every worker had the right to hold his own political views.[13]

These few examples, as well as the close links between SWTUF and the World Federation of Trade Unions in Prague, tend to imply that while the SCP was well established within the Trade Union Federation and its cadre, it lacked similar influence among the rank and file membership of the trade unions themselves.

The first general elections ever were held in the Sudan in 1953. Outwardly, the issue on which the election was fought seemed to be the future of the Sudan: an independent sovereign state or some form of union with Egypt. In reality, however, it was a fight between the two major religious sects, the Khatmiyya and the Anṣār, as to who would rule the Sudan. Towering over Ismā'īl al-Azharī's NUP which advocated union with Egypt, and 'Abdallāh Khalīl's Umma party which sought complete independence, were the two dominant leaders of Sudanese Islam and politics, Sayyid 'Alī al-Mīrghanī and Sayyid 'Abd al-Raḥmān al-Mahdī. The NUP's victory in these elections was an expression of fear of Anṣārī-Umma domination and of mistrust in its ability, after some thirty years of collaboration with the British, to lead the country to real independence. Once a Sudanese government had been installed, al-Azharī and his NUP cabinet sought to Sudanise the administration as quickly as possible and were in no hurry to further the cause of union with Egypt for which they had previously fought. In May 1955 al-Azharī announced that the Sudan would seek complete independence. The old nationalist slogan 'Unity of the Nile Valley' had been discarded and on January 1, 1956 the Sudan became an independent sovereign state.

The SCP had sided with the anti-unionist camp during the elections, in which it participated under the banner of the Anti-Imperialist Front (AIF). The sole representative of the Front to be elected to parliament was Ḥasan al-Ṭāhir Zarūq, a leading communist and an outspoken critic of Ismā'īl al-Azharī's NUP government. The Front's opposition to al-Azharī's and later to 'Abdallāh Khalīl's governments, was all-embracing, but one of its main foci was the fight for democratic rights and for the freedom of expression and organisation in the Sudan.[14] In this battle the SCP managed to gain the support of many non-communist professionals, especially journalists, who feared that the law of subversive activities formulated by the British might be used by the government in order to stifle the opposition. In October 1954 this law was revoked by al-Azharī who probably sought to isolate the communists through the introduction of an explicitly anti-communist law. However, once again the SCP managed to break out of isolation. On January 24, 1955, the editors of most of the newspapers and periodicals sent a memorandum to al-Azharī warning him that his policy was undermining the freedom of expression and hence the effectiveness of the Sudanese press.[15]

The fact that this move, which was initiated by 'Azz al-Dīn 'Alī 'Amir, a leading communist, received the active support of all opposition groups, including the Umma and the Anṣār, was a remarkable achievement for the AIF. A few days later, the Front achieved an even greater success with the establishment of the so-called Independence Front. This new Front included the Umma, the Republican Socialists, the Republican Party and the AIF itself. The Independence Front was therefore an expression of organised opposition to al-Azharī rather than a united ideological or political Front. The agreement between the participants centred around the following points: complete independence; guaranteed democratic rights; non-participation in military pacts; and opposition to economic aid which could affect the Sudan's sovereignty.[16] In its first public declaration to the people of the Sudan, the new Front demanded the evacuation of all foreign armies from the Sudan. British imperialism and Egyptian military dictatorship were singled out as the most dangerous adversaries of Sudanese independence. Ironically, the word *Jalā'* (evacuation), which had been the Egyptian slogan against British military presence in the Suez Canal zone, was now employed against the Egyptians themselves.

The AIF withdrew from the Independence Front in September 1955, some eight months after its foundation. It accused the Umma party of not adhering to the Front's programme, especially regarding non-participation in military pacts and the guaranteeing of democratic rights.[17] The real reason, however, was probably different. A Front, wherein communists became partners of the Umma and the Republican Socialists, the 'arch-reactionaries' of the Sudan, aroused criticism and created friction within the SCP itself.

During the parliamentary crisis in November 1955 which nearly brought about the downfall of al-Azharī's NUP government, the AIF refused to support the Independence Front in its attempt to replace al-Azharī and abstained during the crucial vote of confidence. In explaining this policy the AIF stated that it was fighting for principles and not for or against personalities. The real issue was a united Sudan which could bring the anti-imperialist battle to its logical conclusion, rather than a mere change of government. Only a national-coalition government could, according to the AIF, realise the true national objectives.

However, since both the government and the opposition disagreed with the principles of the AIF, the latter abstained from voting[18] and thus helped al-Azharī to remain in office until after the declaration of the Sudan's independence.

## THE FIRST PARLIAMENTARY GOVERNMENT 1956–1958

Throughout the period of transition (1954–1956), the AIF had remained consistent in its opposition to Egypt, which it accused of having imperialist designs on the Sudan. It was also more outspoken than any other party in its demand for a just and democratic solution of the Southern problem.[19] The AIF's impact was, however, marginal due to its numerical weakness, and its repeated attempts to become part of a larger progressive-nationalist front ended in frustration. With the decline in the NUP's fortunes, in 1956, and especially after al-Azhāri's replacement by 'Abdallāh Khalīl and his Umma-dominated coalition in July of that year, the AIF renewed its attempts to become part of a National Front. 'Abd al-Khāliq Maḥjūb, the SCP's new secretary general, regarded a front wherein the 'reactionary pro-imperialist' Umma party would be replaced by the NUP and by the newly-founded Khatmiyya-supported People's Democratic Party (PDP), as heralding a new era in Sudanese politics.[20]

However, once again the AIF's hopes of a progressive National Front, wherein it would participate, failed to materialise. Instead, the PDP, on which the AIF had pinned its main hopes, joined the Umma party in an unholy alliance which ruled the Sudan until the military coup which put an end to the first parliamentary experiment in November 1958. The two partners were most ill-suited to form a coalition. Firstly, the old feud between the Anṣār and the Khatmiyya was still ripe and in consequence created immediate frictions between the Umma and the PDP. Secondly, there were considerable differences in the political outlook of the two parties, especially in the field of foreign relations. While the Umma advocated a close link with the West and the acceptance of American aid under the Eisenhower doctrine, the PDP was in favour of strict adherence to the principles of 'positive Neutralism'. Similarly, the PDP advocated a much closer relationship with Egypt which included adherence to Egyptian policies both in the Arab world and the Afro-Asian bloc. The Umma on the other hand was suspicious of Nasser's ambitions and opposed to his policies. The only factor which united the two parties was their desire to rule and their opposition to al-Azharī and the NUP. In June 1957 the Umma-PDP coalition introduced a new electoral law which increased the number of constituencies from 97 to 173 and adjusted them to the figures of the population census taken in 1956. The increased weight of the rural population in the elections enabled the Umma to acquire 63 seats while the PDP gained 26, thus giving them a working majority in parliament.

The AIF had fought against the new electoral law both before it was introduced and after, stating that an Umma victory was imminent unless a realignment of the opposition could be brought about. It maintained that despite its disunity, the opposition was much stronger than the Umma. However, since parliament had been dissolved, the Umma was in a position to run the country without opposition and to prepare the elections in a way which would give its own candidates the best chance. This it hoped to achieve by deepening the rift between the NUP and the PDP, its two main rivals. Therefore the only chance for the opposition lay in unity, and the SCP committed itself to fight towards that end.[21] In October 1957, as the elections drew nearer, the AIF approached the president of the PDP, al-Sayyid 'Alī 'Abd al-Raḥmān as well as the party's spiritual leader, Sayyid 'Alī al-Mīrghanī and called upon them to save the Sudan's independence by creating a united front with the NUP and other opposition groups in the forthcoming elections. The AIF claimed that through its partnership in the coalition government with the Umma, the PDP had given its support to policies to which it was opposed in principle. Thus the government's support of the Eisenhower doctrine would not have been possible without the PDP's backing, while the government's lack of support for Egypt, during the Suez Campaign in 1956, was also not in keeping with the convictions of the majority of Sudanese people, including the PDP itself. The AIF accused the PDP that by enabling the Umma to rule the country without parliamentary control it had helped to prepare the elections in an undemocratic manner. Furthermore, through its decision to run in the elections in a united front with the Umma, the PDP had thrown its weight behind the reactionary forces and against the nationalist front. The AIF concluded by asking the PDP to reconsider its position. However, as mentioned above, these attempts were of no avail as the PDP had already committed itself to a continuation of its alliance with the Umma. In consequence, the AIF was obliged to contest the elections once again under its own banner and failed to get even one of its candidates into the new house of representatives.

Another issue which probably affected the outcome of the general elections in favor of the Umma was the 'Egyptian border incident'. On the eve of the elections, and without any prior warning, the Egyptian government claimed that all areas north of parallel 22 were Egyptian territory. These areas had been administered as part of the Sudan ever since the reconquest in 1898. The issue was brought before the United Nations' Security Council and both countries moved their troops to the disputed areas. Not surprisingly, anti-Egyptian propaganda flourished, tempers were running high in the Sudan, and the matter dominated the election campaign. The AIF alongside other opposition parties appealed to Egypt to drop its claim until after the elections. The Front accused the Umma party of exaggerating the incident out of all proportion in order to serve its imperialist allies and to rouse the Sudanese against their Egyptian brethren. Border incidents did occur between neighbours, stated the AIF, and ought to be solved with patience and understanding. Thus, the Sudan should not give up its territory to any one, not even to its brother Eygpt, but the crisis should be regarded as artificially created and not as a real one. Its sole purpose, so the Front alleged, was to prove to the Sudanese prior to the elections that the Umma was a patriotic party fighting for independence, while everyone in the Sudan well remembered that the Umma had supported Britain all along the line and was in fact opposed to real independence. The present Umma complaint to the United Nations' Security Council was again aiding the imperialists in their anti-Egyptian policy.[22] *Al-Mīdān*, the communist daily newspaper published a declaration of the Egyptian government which stated that it would postpone its territorial claims until after the Sudanese general elections. The declaration maintained that the Egyptian forces would never attack their Sudanese brethren but were ready to aid the Sudan in defending itself against the common imperialist enemy. The Egyptian government, the declaration went on to say, had taken this decision following the appeals of Sayyid ʻAlī al-Mīrghanī, Sayyid Ismāʻīl al-Azharī and other Sudanese personalities, who had asked Egypt to refrain from giving any opportunity to the pro-imperialist forces in the Sudan who were exploiting the present dispute for their selfish political ends.[23]

After the general elections, in which the Umma-PDP alliance emerged victorious, the AIF published a declaration accusing the PDP and the NUP of causing the debacle and calling upon the supporters of these parties to bring pressure to bear on their leaders in order to re-unite the nationalist front.[24] However, the spiritual leaders of the Anṣār and the Khatmiyya expressed their full satisfaction with the election results, stating that these would enable the Sudan to continue its peaceful development under a truly democratic government, which had the support of all classes of Sudanese as well as the blessing of the two Sayyids.[25] The AIF of course disapproved of Sayyid ʻAlī al-Mīrghanī's view and called upon him, as spiritual father of the Sudanese both in the past and the present, to bring about a reunification of all nationalist forces by rejoining the Khatmiyya with their brethren of the NUP.[26]

Parliamentarism in the Sudan had, however, only another nine months of grace during which the political and economic situation deteriorated rapidly. A few days after ʻAbdallāh Khalīl's new government had assumed office, the council of ministers approved an agreement with the United States for economic and technical aid to the Sudan despite protests from the opposition. The pro-Egyptian wing of the PDP was in the meantime pressing for closer relations with the United Arab Republic (the UAR) which had been founded in February 1958 as the result of a union between Syria and Egypt. There were troubles in the internal front too. First, the presidential issue had to be decided and the Umma majority was pressing for the election of Sayyid ʻAbd al-Raḥmān, the Anṣār's leader, as a non-executive president. This of course was totally unacceptable to Sayyid ʻAlī al-Mīrghanī as well as to the NUP and PDP. Secondly, the country's finances were going from bad to worse. Cotton prices were falling on the world market and the Government had decided not to sell the 1957 crop, which had been very poor, until prices would rise again. Consequently the country's foreign currency reserves had decreased from £62 million to £8 million and there was fear of a budget deficit for the first time since 1932. Lastly, the Southern problem which had been shelved since the 1955 uprising rose to the fore in December 1957. The Constitution Committee had rejected the Southerners' demand for regional autonomy and consequently the Southern members boycotted the Committee. In the February 1958 elections, the new southern Federal Party, in a united front with the AIF fought for a federal government and for the recognition of Christianity alongside Islam as a state religion, as well as English as an official language on a par with Arabic. The popularity of these demands in the South became clear when the Federalists won forty out of the forty-six seats which had been allocated to the South in Parliament. However, these demands were rejected out of hand by 'Abdallāh Khalīl's new government, and when it became clear that the Constituent Assembly would endorse the new constitution, the Southern MPs left Parliament on June 16, 1958.

This was the situation with which 'Abdallāh Khalīl had to cope from the beginning of 1958, and to make it worse he did not enjoy the confidence of the PDP members in his own cabinet either. Even within the Umma there was strong opposition to 'Abdallāh Khalīl. Headed by al-Ṣiddīq al-Mahdī, the eldest son of the Anṣār's spiritual leader, the opposition demanded an Umma-NUP coalition as the only alternative to political chaos. But 'Abdallāh Khalīl rejected any accommodation with al-Azharī and instead adjourned parliament and sought a solution with the help of the army.

The AIF and the Federation of Sudanese Trade Unions who had been campaigning against the Eisenhower doctrine and the American aid programme since February 1957, were the first to warn against a military take-over. Towards the end of October *al-Mīdān*, the SCP's organ, warned the Sudanese people that an imperialist plot against the Sudan's independence was imminent. This was followed by a more direct warning, issued a few days later, stating that with the weakening of the Umma, the imperialist agent in the Sudan, the US might be tempted to support a military coup which would secure its position in the Sudan. Citing the recent coups in Burma, Ceylon and Pakistan, the AIF claimed that the Americans had now reached a new stage in their imperialist intervention whereby the US assisted coups not only against nationalist democratic régimes but also against pro-imperialist governments once it became clear that they could no longer serve American interests. Therefore the Sudanese people were called upon to defend their independence, their democracy and their constitution.[27]

The expected military coup took place two weeks later and the testimonies of its leaders tend to support the accusations about Umma complicity in plotting the coup. According to a report prepared under the auspices of the Ministry of Justice, after the deposal of General ʻAbbūd by the popular uprising of October 1964, ʻAbdallāh Khalīl and several other Umma leaders including al-Ṣiddīq al-Mahdī took part in numerous meetings with ʻAbbūd and other senior officers prior to the November 1958 coup. It appears that while al-Ṣiddīq was opposed to non-parliamentary government and was only willing to grant the military the office of Minister of Defence, the others headed by ʻAbdallāh Khalīl supported a military take-over.

Following al-Ṣiddīq's departure from the Sudan, ostensibly for medical treatment, the remaining Umma leaders undertook to convince ʻAbbūd that the army had to assume power in order to save the country from chaos. These charges were vehemently denied by ʻAbdallāh Khalīl and the whole truth will probably never be known.[28] However, on 17 November 1958, Parliament was dissolved and General Ibrāhīm ʻAbbūd, leading a supreme council of army officers, was named head of state.[29]

## THE FIRST MILITARY REGIME 1958–1964

The military régime which was to rule the Sudan for the next six years, had more in common with the politicians of the al-Azharī and ʻAbdallāh Khalīl type than with the 'Free Officers' who overthrew the Egyptian monarchy in 1952 or those who assumed power in the Sudan in 1969. The social background, education and political outlook of ʻAbbūd and his colleagues were similar to those of the politicians who had preceded them. They felt, however, that they would succeed where their predecessors had failed, as they believed themselves to be unhampered by sectarian-political divisions and free of civilian corruption. On the morning following the coup, the new Junta received the unequivocal blessing of the Khatmiyya order, to which most of the officers belonged, as well as a more reluctant blessing from the Anṣār.[30]

It took the main political parties more than two years to organise an opposition to the military régime which consequently had this period in which to formulate its policies and to offer solutions to what it regarded as the country's most urgent problems. These included:

a. The setting up of representative government through a system of local, provincial and central councils. This pyramid-shaped structure, the military believed, would give wider representation to the people, especially of the countryside, and would be more suited to the Sudan than a Westminster type parliament. The programme took, however, too long to mature and by the time the régime was ready with its plans, public resistance to military rule had grown to such an extent that the councils were boycotted by most of the political leadership and thus failed to achieve their primary aim.

b. In the economic field the régime first sought to solve the immediate problems resulting from the poor cotton prices and the deficit in the Sudan's budget. These goals were largely achieved within one year and the trade balance of the Sudan in 1959 was favourable after two adverse years. The régime next initiated new development plans, especially in the fields of agriculture, irrigation and industry, which culminated in 1961 in a very ambitious ten-year development plan, calling for a capital outlay of some £600 million. However, most of the planned projects were unproductive at least in the first few years and thus by the time the military régime was replaced in 1964, criticism of its economic policies was mounting. This criticism received an added impetus from the poor cotton crops in the years 1963–1964 which in turn brought about heavier taxation and the introduction of income tax for the first time in the Sudan.

c. The problem of the South was viewed by the military régime as artificial and apt to be solved within a united Sudan. Not unlike their predecessors, the military regarded a separatist solution or even a federal one as unacceptable and harmful to the future of the Sudan. But unlike the politicians, 'Abbūd and his colleagues were not hampered by political considerations in their dealings with the South. The missionaries were expelled, education was unified and Arabic was introduced as the medium of instruction instead of English. Southerners who resisted were dealt with in a military fashion, namely arrest or expulsion. Those who took to arms were hunted down wherever possible and the villages sheltering them were burnt. The results were the deepening of the Southerners' hatred of the Arabs in the North and armed resistance instead of political strife. The military's failure in the South was in the long run one of the main reasons which brought about the régime's downfall.

d. In the field of foreign relations two main problems had occupied and divided the previous régime: the Sudan's position vis-à-vis the superpowers and its relations with the Arab world and primarily with Egypt. The military declared a policy of positive neutrality and non-alignment. It preserved close relations with the West and at the same time opened the door for the Soviet bloc and even for Communist China which for the first time provided economic and technical aid to the Sudan. With regard to Egypt the régime reached what it regarded as a satisfactory settlement of the border dispute and of the division of the Nile waters which were to be saved through the building of the high dam at Aswan. It also received from Egypt £15 million for the resettlement of the Nubians who were dispossessed through the building of the Aswan dam. On the whole 'Abbūd pursued a much more balanced line of policy as between Africa and the Arab World, emphasising the Sudan's role in Africa wherever possible and maintaining neutrality in inter-Arab feuds. The régime could therefore claim a favourable balance in its external relations. This, however, was overshadowed by mounting criticism of all the régime's policies and by a growing dissatisfaction on the internal front which came to a boiling point in 1964.

The SCP alone among the political parties opposed the military régime immediately after the November 1958 coup. This was probably the result of the communists' preparedness and experience in clandestine activities. Moreover, while the other politicians were biding their time and were hoping, at least until 1960, that the army would return to its barracks once it had completed its job, the SCP had no such illusions. It had opposed the coup on principle even before it had occurred, and therefore had nothing to lose through its continued opposition. Within the first month of military government the authorities arrested all the known communist leaders on whom they could lay their hands, and on 3 December 1958, all trade unions were banned.[31]

During the first two years 'Abbūd and his colleagues were busy overcoming their enemies from within the army while the SCP was too weak to fight the régime single-handed. The party even decided to call upon all trade union members to compete in the elections held in 1960. This limited co-operation advocated by the SCP despite its opposition to the régime's trade union law and the arrest of all leftist trade union leaders, soon paid off. The proven strength of the SCP within the unions forced the régime to modify its anti trade union law.[32]

In November 1960, the Front opposing the military rule was founded and on the 29th of that month it published its first declaration signed by the leaders of nearly all the disbanded political parties headed by al-Ṣiddīq al-Mahdī, leader of the Anṣār since his father's death. The only notable exception were the Khatmiyya leaders headed by Sayyid 'Alī al-Mīrghanī. The signatories of the declaration expressed their regret that the army had, despite its promises, not introduced a constitution nor returned the reins of government to the civilian authorities. It therefore demanded an immediate fulfilment of the above and the return of the army to its prime duty of preserving the country's security.[33] The SCP gave its full support to the Front's declaration. It called upon its members and upon the mass of the Sudanese people to fight for the Front's demands and to collect tens of thousands of signatures on petitions which would be handed to 'Abbūd.[34]

The Front of the Opposition Parties (FOP), as it came to be known, sent a second letter of protest to 'Abbūd in January 1961. This time it accused the military of creating an atmosphere of terror in the country in which innocent people were being arrested and well-known patriots branded as traitors. The letter stated that 'Abbūd and his collaborators would be held responsible for their deeds and that, by ignoring the collective views of the people of the Sudan, as expressed by the FOP, the military were isolating themselves.[35]

A few weeks after the second memorandum was sent, al-Ṣiddīq al-Mahdī started negotiating with the military about the future régime in the Sudan, but the result until al-Ṣiddīq's death on October 8, 1963 was nil.[36]

A few months earlier, the régime had retaliated against the growing ferment among workers, students and peasants by arresting twelve leading politicians of the FOP and exiling them to Juba in the Southern Sudan. The immediate reason for their arrest was their protest against the torture of a witness in a political trial, who happened to be a communist. Among those arrested were the leaders of all political parties, including the SCP, with the notable exception of the PDP-Khatmiyya leaders who were still supporting the regime.[37] But even in exile there was no agreement between the traditional leaders of the Umma-NUP brand on one hand and those of the professional associations and the SCP on the other. The former were still hoping for some sort of accommodation with the régime, while the latter favoured an open declaration of intent to overthrow it.

The formation of a broad opposition had enabled the SCP to break out of its isolation and to initiate a more effective programme of harassment of the régime. The first to act were the trade unions whose leader al-Shafi' Aḥmad al-Shaykh had been arrested on 8 December 1958, and sentenced to five years imprisonment. In June 1961, the railway-workers' union, the strongest and most militant in the Sudan, declared a one-week general strike, demanding a fifty per cent increase of their wages and threatening to strike one week per month until their demands were met.[38] Next to act were the students whose president al-Aḥmadī was a member of the SCP. Following the students' demonstration in the streets of Khartoum, the régime banned their union in October 1961, interfered with meetings, and forbade the publication of wall-newspapers on the campus.[39]

In 1963 trouble spread to the Jazīra where elections to the Tenants Union had been forbidden by the government. Inflation and falling cotton prices had combined to lower the income of the farmers. They demanded a higher share in the profits and when this was refused declared a general strike at the height of the picking season. The immense damage which this strike would have caused to the Sudanese economy could only be avoided by armed interference or capitulation. The government chose the second alternative and also allowed the postponed elections to the Tenants Union to be held. The result was a victory for the communists whose leader, al-Amīn Muḥammad al-Amīn, was elected president of the Tenants Union. This was due primarily to his militancy in the past and to the consistent support the SCP gave to the tenants' demands.[40]

During 1962 the SCP launched an all-out attack against the government's economic policies. It accused the 'Abbūd régime of exposing the country's economy to capitalist exploitation. Thus the loans of £21 million which had been granted to the Sudan by the US in the years 1959–1961 were, according to the SCP, intended not for useful economic development but for paving the way for imperialist penetration. All the development projects in the public sector were controlled by western foreign capital. Thus in building up Sudanese industry, which had hitherto been practically non-existent, the capitalists concentrated on new cotton growing and ginning projects in Manajīl and Khashm al-Ghirba instead of laying the foundations of more essential and basic industries. Moreover, interest on capitalist loans was between 5–10 per cent which meant that, including debt redemption, the Sudan would have to pay £26 million annually, i.e. more than half its yearly budget. Even in those few cases where industrial plants were built, such as the new textile factory, which was the biggest industrial plant in the Sudan, its ownership and management were in American hands and in consequence its profits went to the US and were of little use to the Sudan. The only loans advantageous to the Sudan were, the SCP maintained, those from the communist bloc, headed by the Soviet Union. These loans were granted at an interest rate of two per cent and the ownership and management of the projects they helped to finance were in Sudanese hands. According to the SCP, 'Abbūd had been forced to accept these loans as a result of public pressure.[41] While criticism of this kind was at least in part justified, it failed to recognise that most of the industrial development projects were still in their building or running-in stages and thus could hardly be evaluated on purely economic terms. Moreover, the participation of the communist bloc, including Yugoslavia, was quite substantial and had been brought about by the initiative of 'Abbūd himself. A criticism which could have been voiced against the régime's development projects was that they were too ambitious and at least in part badly planned. This was true especially of the new dam at al-Ruṣayriṣ which, for lack of money to complete the irrigation works, became a 'white elephant' instead of turning into an immediate source of revenue.[42]

'Abbūd's 'new democracy' which sought to establish a pyramid of democratic institutions throughout the Sudan, starting from the village through the provincial councils and ending at the national level, was labelled by the SCP as a farce. The communists claimed that the Sudanese had been fighting for freedom and democracy for nearly twenty years, and 'Abbūd's 'new democracy' was no better than the British so-called democratic Advisory Council in 1943 against which the people of the Sudan had fought and won. Democracy could not be achieved under a dictatorship nor could it thrive while newspapers were banned, trade unions and political parties forbidden, and hundreds of political leaders rotting in prisons.[43] True democracy, according to the SCP, could only be brought about through the combined struggle of the workers, peasants, students, nationalist merchants and the nationalist intelligentsia, under the leadership of the working class, the most revolutionary of all. 'Abbūd, according to the SCP, was trying to use democratic slogans in order to save his régime, but every freedom loving Sudanese knew that these slogans were nothing but pretence and that dictatorship was the true aim of the military despots and their imperialist overlords.[44]

Yet despite its opposition to 'Abbūd's so-called 'new democracy', the SCP did call upon the Sudanese to take part in the elections to the local councils in 1963, and described the boycott of these elections, which had been declared by the major political parties, as an exercise in futility. The communists insisted that while only a general political strike could bring about an end to the military régime, it was useful to exploit any loophole offered by the military, in order to fight against it. A boycott could only lead to the domination of the councils by the régime's agents whereas an election victory of the Democratic Front would turn the councils into a real force fighting the régime from within.[45] In January 1963, the central committee of the SCP decided to leave the FOP and concentrate all its efforts within what it defined as the 'Revolutionary Democratic Movement'. The reasons for this decision were, according to the SCP, connected with the death of al-Ṣiddīq al-Mahdī and with the subsequent decline of the FOP's militancy. Amongst other things the SCP accused the Front of giving in to the military régime's decision to cancel the Independence celebrations in 1962. Moreover, after the release of the party leaders from Jūba, the FOP agreed to 'Abbūd's request not to celebrate their release despite an earlier decision to the contrary. But the SCP's main criticism was directed against the Front's negative attitude towards the declaration of a general political strike which had been proposed by the communists, who regarded a strike as the best and only way to overthrow 'Abbūd, and had decided to devote all their time and energy toward this end.[46]

Communist criticism of the régime emphasised its economic failures and denounced the decline in the standard of living caused by inflation. It attacked the government's so-called subservience to the West and the growing impact of the United States on the Sudanese economy and politics. Finally, it attacked the government for its anti-democratic actions leading to the imprisonment of hundreds of innocent people, annihilating the freedom of expression and causing bloodshed in the South instead of offering a realistic solution to the Southern problem.

In this context it is interesting to note that the SCP, which had a very clear view regarding the South since 1953, had little to say regarding this problem during 'Abbūd's rule. Even the appearance of the *Anya-Nya*, the armed organisation of Southern resistance in September 1963, and the open revolt which flared up in the South a month later, failed to draw the attention of SCP leaders. This was probably due to the harsh and repressive measures of the régime and to the complete pre-occupation of the communists with the organisation of a political strike. Such a strike could only be organised among the workers, peasants and intelligentsia of the Muslim North and hence the South remained neglected.

## THE POPULAR REVOLUTION OF OCTOBER 1964 AND THE SECOND PARLIAMENTARY GOVERNMENT

The events which brought about the downfall of the military and its replacement by civilian government started in August 1964. The deteriorating situation in the South had made the government realise at last the hopelessness of its policy and forced it to set up a commission to study the problem.[47] It invited citizens to express their opinions freely on this matter thus lifting the restriction on the freedom of expression in matters dealing with policy in the South. The students were the first to seize the opportunity and on 9 September a forum was convened at the university where Dr. Ḥasan al-Ṭurabī, a member of the university staff and a leading Muslim Brother, analysed the problem of the South by stating that it was part of the constitutional set-up of the whole country which could not be treated in isolation. Thus, instead of discussing the South the ensuing debate provided an opportunity for far-reaching general criticism of the régime. Further discussions were now banned by the government. Nonetheless, on 21 October, university students, including communists, Muslim Brothers and others, assembled to continue the debate. They were ordered by the police to disperse and, upon refusing, a violent battle ensued in which the police used at first tear gas and later opened fire, killing one of the students and wounding several others. The student's funeral turned into a mass demonstration and a general political strike, advocated by the SCP since 1963, was well on its way. The old Opposition Front was now revived under a new name: The National Front of Political Parties. Together with the leftist National Front of Professionals, it organised the general strike in a most effective way. On 26 October, 'Abbūd announced the dissolution of the Supreme Council of the Armed Forces as well as the Council of Ministers and three days later an agreement was reached whereby the military handed over the reins of government to the new civilian authorities.

What role did the SCP play in these events? In an interview with *Humanité* on 15 May 1965, 'Abd al-Khāliq Maḥjūb stated that in the summer of 1964 the communists had prepared the ground for a general political strike. Knowing from its experience in the Opposition Front that the old traditional parties could not be relied upon, the SCP concentrated its efforts in organising its supporters among the workers, peasants, students and professionals. In the elections to the Trade Union Federation in the summer of 1964, forty-five of the sixty members elected were communists. Similar results were achieved in the elections of the Jazīra Tenants Union where a noted communist was elected president. Among the students and professionals, communist supremacy had been achieved even earlier. Thus, when the October events occured, the SCP decided that the time was ripe for the general political strike it had been preparing. Maḥjūb admitted, however, that the SCP and its allies could not have forced the armed forces to hand over power without the co-operation of the other political parties.

It was generally acknowledged, even by critics of the SCP, that the party played an important role, far exceeding its actual strength, during the October upheaval.[48] Its role in organising the demonstrations and the general strike was predominant, but from then onwards the traditional forces called the tune. The fact that three SCP members became ministers in Sirr al-Khatim al-Khalīfa's first transitional government on 30 October, was the result of the role played by the SCP, the trade unions and the professional organisations during the preceding week.[49] Yet it was clear from the outset that the traditional leaders, both religious and political, would not tolerate the disproportionate representation of the SCP for long and when Sirr al-Khatim al-Khalīfa presented his second government in February 1965, only one communist minister was left. It would therefore be true to state that while the SCP was strong enough to exploit a revolutionary situation, it was too weak to lead the revolution towards the realisation of its own aims. A communist attempt to save the revolution by declaring a general strike and by rushing armed peasants from the Jazīra to Khartoum failed to produce the hoped-for results and proved once again that the SCP was weak even in its so-called strongholds, i.e. the trade unions and the tenants associations.[50] Under these circumstances, the communists' decision to participate in the May 1965 elections was probably prompted by a desire to test their strength rather than by their belief that the majority of their candidates stood any real chance of being elected. The results of the elections could therefore be regarded as a relative communist success. Out of fifteen special graduates' constituencies,[51] communist-supported candidates gained eleven seats in the new assembly, including the first woman MP ever to be elected in the Sudan.[52] However, no communist candidate was elected in the regular constituencies.

According to communist sources, their victory was even greater, as communist-supported candidates received 73,103 votes or 17.3 per cent of all the votes cast.[53] This result was mainly due to the fact that the elections were boycotted by the Khatmiyya-supported PDP and also to the prominent role played by the communists in the October 1964 revolution.[54]

The reaction of the other parties to the communist success became clear on the morrow of the elections. In an interview with the Lebanese press, al-Ṣādiq al-Mahdī, a graduate of Oxford and the new leader of the Umma, stated that his party would refuse to co-operate with the communists in the future. He defined the differences of opinion between the communists and other political parties in the Sudan as embracing both foreign policy and internal affairs. His main criticisms were directed against communist attempts to politicise the trade unions, and against their attitude towards Islam.[55] The special link between politics and religion in the Sudan was, however, regarded by al-Ṣādiq as an effective barrier against communist success.[56]

It was, indeed religion that provided the pretext for one of the biggest anti-communist drives, which started a few months later. On 8 November 1965, the Muslim Brothers organised a mass demonstration against the SCP and its affiliated organisations, and petitioned the government to declare communism illegal. The immediate reason for the upheaval was a speech in Omdurman by a Syrian communist who declared that belief in God and the Prophet was an anachronistic superstition.[57] Despite denials by the central committee of the SCP, which protested that the Syrian student was not a member of the communist party, the Supreme Sharī'a Court devoted a special session to a discussion of the case. It then issued a statement to the people of the Sudan, stressing the dangers of communism to Islam and requesting a full scale investigation of communist propaganda and study courses in the Sudan.[58] The political leaders followed suit and both the Umma and the NUP demanded a ban on communist activities.[59] On 15 November 1965, several MPs proposed that the Constituent Assembly urge the government to outlaw the SCP and to confiscate all its property. The proposal was passed by 161 votes against 12, with 9 abstentions. While the debate in the House went on, thousands demonstrated outside under anti-communist slogans.[60] Sayyid 'Alī al-Mīrghanī, head of the Khatmiyya, took the opportunity to propose an Islamic state based on the *sharī'a* which he regarded as the only effective antidote to communism.[61]

On 24 November the Constituent Assembly passed an amendment to the constitution outlawing any communist or atheist propaganda in the Sudan.[62] At the second reading of the amendment, in December 1965, it was further decided that no communists might remain members of the assembly and that the SCP would henceforth be dissolved and its property confiscated.[63] The government was quick to act: it confiscated the passports of leading communists and forbade them to undertake any political activities.[64] The reason for the anti-communist drive was clearly political and the anti-religious utterances of the Syrian student had only provided the convenient pretext. Al-Ṣādiq al-Mahdī's statement, made in a radio and television press conference shortly after the event, expressed the opinion of his religio-political fellow-leaders. He stressed the two dangers confronting the Sudan: first, factionalism or, in other words, the problem of the South which might affect other regions such as Dārfūr in the West, the Nuba mountains in Kordofan or the Beja tribes of the Red Sea Hills; second, the danger of communism which, as al-Ṣādiq pointed out, was rejected by the Sudanese because of 'its contradiction of the belief in the existence of God, its binding of Sudan sovereignty with an international creed and tie and its dependence on the basis of a class dictatorship which would undoubtedly supply the need for the establishment of other political movements and groupings.'[65] The fear therefore was not that communism would become a major political force but rather of its potential danger as a dividing factor within Sudanese society, and that it would exploit the problem of the South and of sectarian politics in order to enhance its own prestige.

The communists tried to fight back and on 24 December 1965 the hearing of their case against the government and the constituent assembly started in the Supreme Court. After endless postponements, lasting a whole year, the court finally decided that the government's action was illegal and that the SCP had a right to function as any other political party.[66] In the meantime, however, leading communists had been imprisoned, the SCP and its front organisations disbanded, communists expelled from the army and dismissed from the railways and other vital public services.[67] The government was therefore in no mood to give in, and a day after the Supreme Court announced its verdict in December 1966, the constituent assembly decided to uphold its former decision, thereby overruling the decision of the Supreme Court.[68]

Prior to the Court's decision, in October 1966, the SCP and its supporters had led an anti-government demonstration of some 30,000 participants through the streets of Khartoum.[69] In the following December, the government hit back by accusing the SCP of having been behind an abortive military coup of Lieutenant Khālid Ḥusayn 'Uthmān. The coup provided the pretext for the arrest of 'Abd al-Khāliq Maḥjūb and of several other leading communists, although no substantial link between the two groups was ever proved.[70]

While the SCP was re-grouping for clandestine activities under the banner of its newly founded Socialist Party, the fight between the government and the judiciary continued throughout 1967. The Supreme Court decided once again that outlawing the SCP had been illegal and that communist deputies were entitled to keep their seats in the Constituent Assembly.[71] The Government, however, reiterated its former decision, stressing once again that the communists did not fight for democracy but against Islam.[72] At the same time, the Constituent Assembly denied the right of the Supreme Court to interfere in the interpretation of the constitution.[73]

It is hard to deny that the long constitutional crisis was tantamount to a victory for the SCP. All the major political parties were united in their attempt to outlaw communism and yet the communists succeeded in fighting back without being isolated. The judiciary, substantial sections of the intelligentsia, the professionals, the trade unions, as well as several tenants organisations, were fighting under the banner of democracy in order to legalise communism. The long constitutional battle, culminating in the resignation of Chief Justice Bābikr 'Awaḍallāh, was one of the factors leading to the government crisis in May 1967 and prompted the realignment of political forces in the Sudan in the following period.[74]

Matters came to a head during the general elections campaign in 1968. The new election law proposed that communists and members of other illegal organisations should not be allowed to fight the elections.[75] But there were additional ways of keeping the communists out, such as cancelling the special Graduates constituences, where the communists had gained their seats in the previous elections. Another proviso, favoured by other parties, especially the Umma, was to allocate more seats in the new parliament to the provinces and thus to strengthen the traditionalist and tribal elements.[76]

The merger between al-Azharī's NUP and the PDP, establishing the Democratic Unionist Party (DUP), in December 1967, created a new political situation in the Sudan. For the first time, since the 1953 elections, al-Azharī stood a chance of winning the elections single-handed. The new alignment re-established the authority of popular Islamic leadership in Sudanese politics. It merged all the pro-Khatmiyya elements into one political party and thus made it quite clear that the Anṣār would lose their leading role in the political arena as long as the Umma, which in the summer of 1966 had split into two factions (that of al-Hādī al-Mahdī and that of his nephew al-Ṣādiq) remained divided.[77]

The communists and their left-wing allies had in the meantime not been idle, and on 21 January 1967, the founding of the Socialist Party of the Sudan was announced in Khartoum. Its central preparatory committee comprised sixty members, representing workers, peasants and 'national intellectuals'. They announced their adherence to 'scientific socialism' and stressed their respect for religion as a dominant factor in Sudanese society.[78] Nearly a year passed before the first congress of the new party took place in Khartoum just in time for the coming elections. The party's leadership included such well-known communists as Amīn Muḥammad al-Amīn, representing the Jazīra tenants, al-Shafi' Aḥmad al-Shaykh of the trade unions, and Amīn al-Shiblī, a prominent member of the lawyers association.[79]

When the last general elections before the Numeiri coup were held in April 1968, sectarianism was as strong in the Sudan as during the pre-independence elections of 1953. Of the 218 seats in parliament, the DUP and the two factions of the Umma won 167, thus proving once again the predominance of popular Islam and enabling Muḥammad Aḥmad Maḥjūb, leader of the Umma, to head a sectarian based government. The southern parties, SANU and the Southern Front, won 15 and 10 seats, respectively. Five MP's represented the Beja and Nuba tribes in the new parliament and 3 represented the Islamic Charter Front (mainly Muslim Brothers), thus bringing the number of MP's representing traditional forces to 200 and leaving less than 20 seats to the Independents and others; included in the latter was the sole representative of the 'Socialist Front' – 'Abd al-Khāliq Maḥjūb. If the communists ever had any illusions regarding their political prospects in a democratic Sudan, they must have lost them after these results.

The ensuing student demonstrations in Khartoum and other towns, during November 1968, were reminiscent of the pre-October 1964 coup. Again one of the demonstrators was killed, and Molotov cocktails were thrown at the House of Parliament. Ismā'īl al-Azharī asked the constituent assembly to expel 'Abd al-Khāliq Maḥjūb, accusing the communists of trying to bring about the downfall of Muḥammad Aḥmad Maḥjūb's government.[81]

## THE MILITARY RULE AGAIN, 1969–1971

On 25 May 1969, the second parliamentary phase which had started in October 1964 was brought to an abrupt end and the Sudanese army was once again at the helm. However, unlike their military predecessors of the 'Abbūd period, the 'Free Officers', headed by Colonel Ja'far al-Numayrī (Numeiri), regarded themselves as revolutionaries and anti-sectarianists whose aim was to realise the ideals set by the October 1964 revolution.

Three major internal problems confronted the new rulers as they assumed power, and not suprisingly they were the same problems that had beset every government in the Sudan since it became independent. First, the political structure and especially the impact of the Anṣār and the Khatmiyya on the political scene and the sectarian nature of Sudanese politics resulting therefrom. The régime intended to crush sectarianism and, as broadcast in its first public statement, to establish in the Sudan a single revolutionary party, on the Egyptian model, and consisting of workers, peasants, soldiers, the national bourgeoisie, and the progressive intelligentsia. Second, in the economic field, the dwindling foreign currency reserves, the declining standard of living and, most important, the dependence on cotton as the prime source of income, were all viewed by the new régime as requiring immediate attention. The new rulers defined their economic aim as the development of national capital through close economic ties with the new Arab states and the Socialist bloc. The third major problem was that of the South where the solution offered was regional autonomy within a united Sudan. In the sphere of foreign relations the régime defined its aims as the forging of close links with progressive Arab régimes and the Socialist bloc, on the one hand, and the support of national liberation movements, especially that of the Palestinians on the other.

But a sweeping change in the internal political structure was the most urgent task of the new régime and this, according to its rulers, would mark the beginning of a new chapter in the Sudan's political history. Whereas the military government headed by 'Abbūd was but an extension of the traditional civilian rule of the first parliamentary period, Numeiri and his colleagues patterned their so-called revolution on the Egyptian mould.[82] They sought to align the Sudan to the so-called progressive-revolutionary régimes of the Arab states, thereby hoping to overcome once and for all the sectarian and factional political power system, based on the Anṣār and the Khatmiyya, which had defeated the October 1964 revolution within four months after its inception. Instead of seeking the blessings of the leaders of popular Islam, as 'Abbūd had done prior to his coup, Numeiri sought to destroy their political power. While the Khatmiyya and its leaders were quite willing to withdraw from the political scene as they had done under 'Abbūd, the Anṣār, whose raison d'être was political as much as religious, were prepared to fight back rather than succumb to Numeiri. The uprising of the Anṣār on Abā Island in March 1970 was the direct result of Numeiri's plan to exclude them from active politics. The blood-bath that followed diminished the power of the Anṣār considerably and at the same time enabled Numeiri to weaken his previous reliance on the SCP.

The communists had stated their opposition to a military coup in March 1969 and had even reiterated their reservations on the day Numeiri assumed power. However, the SCP was willing to cooperate with Numeiri on both ideological and practical grounds. Ideologically, the SCP regarded the coup as petty-bourgeois, but believed that with communist guidance it might be led along the true path of revolution. In practical terms, the communists knew that the régime needed them at least as long as its main enemy, the Anṣār, was not overcome. In turn, Numeiri's motives in forging an alliance with the SCP were purely pragmatic. He needed popular support against the traditionalist forces, and believed that the SCP, with its strong following among workers, peasants, professionals and students, would be able and willing to provide it. He also knew that the communists had infiltrated the armed forces, including the 'Free Officers', and therefore had to be accommodated in order not to create disunity among the military themselves.[83] To a lesser degree, Numeiri required the organisational skills of the SCP which had been demonstrated during the civilian uprising of October 1964 and again during the mass demonstrations in 1967. True, the 'Free Officers' regarded their own organisation as superior and more efficient than any other, but nonetheless needed a civilian partner at least during the first few crucial months of their régime. Lastly, Numeiri was well aware of the split within the SCP and hoped that through cooperation with the anti-Maḥjūb faction he would assist opposition within the SCP – which had favoured his coup – to become the majority within the party or alternatively, to weaken the party through a split.[84]

Numeiri appointed four communists to his cabinet. However, they were selected by Numeiri himself as 'loyal nationalists', and without consultation with the SCP.[85] More important, three of the communist ministers, Fārūq Abū 'Isā, Makkāwī Musṭafā and Maḥjūb 'Uthmān, belonged to the anti-Maḥjūb faction. Numeiri thereby hoped to strengthen their position within the party. The fourth, Joseph Garrang, appointed on 19 June to fill the post of Minister for Southern Affairs, was probably included, despite his loyalty to Maḥjūb, because of his Southern background which Numeiri began to exploit in his plan for regional autonomy of the South.[86] There were also three pro-communist officers in the Revolutionary Command Council (RCC): Hāshim Muḥammad al-'Aṭā, Fārūq 'Uthmān Ḥamdallāh and Bābikr al-Nūr 'Uthmān, all of whom had at one time or another been associated with the SCP.[87] The reason for their inclusion in the RCC was first and foremost the prominent role they had played in the 'Free Officers' organisation, prior to the coup, and the belief of non-communists, such as Numeiri himself, that communist influence within the armed forces was considerable.[88]

Friction between the régime and the SCP leadership emerged almost immediately after the coup. Numeiri's decision to disband the 'Free Officers' in which the communists were strong, was condemned by Maḥjūb as anti-democratic. The SCP leaders resented even more the appointment of communists to cabinet positions without consultation with the party. This was interpreted by Maḥjūb as intended to undermine the authority of the central committee. Moreover, participation in a government dominated by the military, which opposed political organisations and had announced the dissolution of all political parties, would, according to Maḥjūb, be interpreted as communist acquiescence in these anti-democratic measures. Numeiri's proposals to change the SCP's name and to turn it into a broad popular front embracing all progressive elements in the country, were also rejected by Maḥjūb and his supporters. However, Numeiri made sure that all his proposals were acceptable to the anti-Maḥjūb faction of the SCP and did in fact strengthen their position within the party.[89]

Another important stage in the strife between the military and the SCP was reached in October 1969 and was preceded by several significant events. A statement was attributed to Prime Minister Bābikr 'Awaḍallāh, on a visit to East Germany, where he asserted that the Sudanese revolution could not progress without the active support of the Sudanese communists.[90] This statement aroused strong reaction in the Sudan and immediately on 'Awaḍallāh's return to Khartoum, a joint session of the government and the RCC was held in order to iron out the differences.[91] Sudanese leaders who so firmly reacted to 'Awaḍallāh's statement were probably motivated or, at least, encouraged by several anti-communist demonstrations which had taken place in 'Aṭbarā and Khartoum in July and October, respectively.[92] Consequently, another reshuffle of the government took place, probably prompted by the above mentioned events. Numeiri became Prime Minister instead of 'Awaḍallāh, while the latter became Deputy Prime Minister and Minister of Justice while retaining his Foreign Office portfolio. Important additions to the government were Aḥmad Sulaymān, a leading member of the anti-Maḥjūb faction within the SCP, as Minister of Economics and Foreign Commerce, and Hāshim al-'Aṭā', one of the communist officers in the RCC; as Minister of Animal

Resources.[93] A more detailed look at the portfolios in the new government shows a relative neutralisation of Bābikr 'Awaḍallāh, and a further strengthening of the hold of the military over the government. A significant move in this direction – as future events were to prove – was the appointment of RCC member Khālid Ḥasan 'Abbās to the Ministry of Defence. Nevertheless, a thorough analysis of the political inclinations of the higher echelons of power at this stage, including of course the RCC and the government, leads to the conclusion that Numeirī's circle, though fully aware of communist tactics, estimated at the time that the main potential danger to its power still lay with the traditionalist – not the leftist – forces.

The period between October 1969 and November 1970 was marked by a growing tension between Maḥjūb's faction within the SCP and Numeiri's régime. This tension was a natural outcome of the basic factors mentioned above, and was nourished by substantial differences regarding both internal and external policy. For a variety of reasons, Maḥjūb's faction strongly objected to the Sudan's joining the proposed federation of Arab Republics, together with Egypt and Libya, which was announced in Tripoli on 27 December 1969 (the so-called Tripoli Charter). Their opposition was due primarily to the well-known anti-communist views and actions of Presidents Nasser and Qadhāfi. They knew that a federation implied '... the setting up [of] the political organisation within whose ambit should be incorporated all of the forces of the Revolution ...'[94] Within such a political organisation the SCP could play a role only if it was willing to lose its identity and give up its claims of leadership. This Maḥjūb and his comrades were unwilling to do. They also viewed the proposed federation as detrimental with regard to a peaceful settlement of the problem of the South as it was well known that the Southerners viewed the close link between the Sudan and its Arab neighbours with growing distrust.[95]

During the Anṣārs' uprising on Abā Island, relations between the SCP and the régime were strained even further. The communists opposed the use of arms against the Anṣār claiming that through political measures the reactionary leadership of the Anṣār could be removed, while the mass of ignorant followers of the sect could be brought over to join the democratic front. When Numeiri decided to use the army against the Anṣār, the SCP supported him, but only reluctantly.[96] It was therefore rather symbolic that Maḥjūb was exiled to Egypt shortly after the Anṣār uprising, in company with al-Ṣādiq al-Mahdī, the surviving leader of the Anṣār. Yet despite the arrest of their secretary-general, the communist ministers continued to serve in Numeiri's government and the position of the anti-Maḥjub faction was strengthened even further.[97] This, however, had only marginal effect on the balance of power within the official bodies of the SCP.

In August 1970, the SCP held a special conference to discuss the RCC's demand for the dispersal of the communist party and its merger with other progressive forces into the government-sponsored Sudanese Socialist Union (SSU). The party decided, by an overwhelming majority of more than 80 per cent, not to liquidate itself but to press instead for the formation of a National Front which would include the independent SCP alongside other progressive and anti-imperialist organisations.[98]

Numeiri's next step was the dismissal of the three pro-communist officers from the RCC on 16 November 1970. The three, Lt. Colonel Bābikr al-Nūr 'Uthmān, Major Hāshim al-'Aṭā' and Major Fārūq 'Uthmān Ḥamdallāh, later became the main actors in the abortive coup of July 1971. Explaining the reasons for their dismissal, Numeiri stated that they had cooperated with elements who pretended to be progressive but in fact stood in the way of the revolution and tried to weaken it.[99] On a later occasion he said that 'they did not adhere to one collective decision of the RCC but were operating outside the framework of the RCC and fighting against the council's decisions ... I regret to say that these ideas were inspired and schemed by 'Abd al-Khāliq Maḥjūb ... who won them over, indoctrinated them with his subversive ideas, and fed them his intentions. Their first and last aim was to reach power ...'[100] Numeiri's action was prompted by the continued opposition of the SCP to its dissolution and to the proposed Arab Federation. It was made possible by a combination of two important factors: first, the reassurance Numeiri had gained in the relatively long period which had lapsed from the Abā affair and during which the Anṣār had shown no signs of recovery from the blow dealt to them, and second, the growing pressure of anti-communist circles within the RCC.

The official explanation published by the SCP on the dismissals of 16 November is enlightening as it stated, for the first time, the main points of divergence between the party and the RCC.[101] Politically, the SCP charged Numeiri with attempting to liquidate the Sudanese revolutionary forces. In this, they claimed, he was aided by reactionary tendencies in the Arab world and particularly by Egypt, whose intelligence service in the Sudan was 'exercising its black methods in sabotaging the revolutionary movement ...'. The proposed federation with Egypt and Libya was part of this policy 'which helped to create the belief of the masses that a plot is in process of being hatched, and a serious danger threatens the Sudanese revolution and its democratic movement ...'[102] In the field of economics, the SCP charged that it had constantly warned the RCC of the deterioration in the management and administration of the nationalised industries and confiscated corporations. It had also submitted memoranda on the impact of the economic recession on the masses who were suffering from the constant rise of the cost of living. Instead of heeding these warnings, Numeiri had in fact played into the hands of the counter-revolutionary forces who were making 'use of the discontent of the masses in achieving their aims ...' Again, in the South, the SCP claimed that 'the revolutionary forces have mobilised all their resources in an effort to create a democratic movement in that part of the country, capable of having a firm grip of regional autonomy ...' Yet the 'rightist and bureaucratic elements' within the state machine in the South constantly tried to sabotage a democratic solution.

Numeiri's anti-communist measures were therefore described by the SCP as anti-revolutionary: 'It is an open invitation to the traditional forces to continue their activities overtly or covertly against the Communist Party ...' In taking these measures, Numeiri was, according to the SCP, aiming at the liquidation of all democratic revolutionary forces in the RCC and in the armed forces and especially in the SCP itself, thus ensuring the absolute power of the State. Apart from the support he received from Egypt and the traditional forces in the Sudan, the SCP maintained that Numeiri's anti-communist drive was facilitated by a new and valuable ally: the group which had split from the SCP in September 1970 and had since been disseminating lies and false accusations against the party and its leadership: 'These elements, which are being employed in the national security organs, do not even shrink from taking part in the registering of the names of communists as a step toward arresting them ...' The central committee of the SCP concluded its very frank exposure of the reactionary tendencies of the Sudanese régime with a direct appeal to the people to save the revolution. Stating explicitly that mass demonstrations had helped to strengthen the revolution on 2 June 1969, and 30 March 1970, the SCP called upon the people to show their force and 'to block the way against the relapse to which the recently taken measures have left the door wide open ...'

In a lengthy interview published in the Egyptian leftist journal *al-Ṭalīʿa*, Numeiri, not surprisingly, claimed that during its first eighteen months of existence the revolution had already achieved many of its most important goals.[103] Firstly, the reactionary forces headed by the Anṣār had been crushed. Secondly, the nationalisation of banks and foreign firms and the five-year programme, both of which were decreed on the first anniversary of the revolution, had rid the country of its dependence on imperialism and its local feudal agents, and opened the way for socialism and economic independence.[104] Thus, Numeiri claimed, the revolution was ready for the next stage of its development, namely the foundation of the popular-revolutionary movement which would assume full responsibility for the government once it was strong enough. Sudanese socialism, as envisaged by Numeiri, was scientific socialism adjusted to the realities of the Sudan, to its history, civilisation and traditions. This socialism had, in the opinion of the President, many enemies not only among the right-wing reactionaries who had been defeated on Abā Island in March 1970.[105] With regard to the South, Numeiri blamed imperialism, and especially the US, West Germany and Israel, for his failure to reach an acceptable solution. He maintained, however, that progress towards regional autonomy had been made and that development plans were beginning to have an impact on the political stability in that region. In the sphere of foreign relations Numeiri emphasised the Sudan's close cooperation with the communist bloc which through its assistance had enabled the country to free itself from imperialist exploitation. In the Arab world, Numeiri stressed the importance of unity in the fight against Zionism and imperialism and promised that the Sudan as part of the Arab homeland would take part in that battle. The President concluded by emphasising the special role of the Sudan as a bridge between the Arab and the African revolutions.

The next major clash between Numeiri and the SCP occurred in February 1971 during a state visit to the Sudan of Joseph Mobutu, President of Congo-Kinshasa. During their tour of Wād-Madanī, the SCP distributed leaflets, condemning the two presidents. Numeiri retaliated immediately and on 12 February announced his intention to fight and destroy the SCP. Listing the 'crimes' of the communists he said:

> They regard anyone outside the party as unworthy of responsibility and a reactionary ... To attain power they would trample upon all our people's values and morals, which are the morals of free citizens ... They oppose any noble cause so long as it was not initiated by them. For instance, they opposed government programmes on education and drought and also the Tripoli state charter ... They sabotaged government work by turning trade unions against government action in ministries, departments, and establishments ... They exercised personality cults just like the reactionaries ... They have been traitors at this critical stage when our people are fighting imperialism by printing intriguing, venomous, false, and rancorous statements and dropping these outside the embassies so the latter can convey the contents to their countries. They also send hostile reports and leaflets to some embassies and governments abroad giving the impression that the situation in Sudan is disturbed and that these governments should freeze all interests and agreements with Sudan ...

He added that there was no room for the communists in the Sudanese revolution and warned:

> I repeat today that the revolution is for all the masses of the people. Anyone who opposes it will be immediately isolated ... It is your responsibility to destroy anyone who claims there is a Sudanese Communist Party.[106]

The communist party reacted promptly both against Numeiri's accusations and his measures. In a statement published on 12 February, immediately after Numeiri's speech, the SCP openly accused him of betrayal.[107] It claimed that without communist support 'the régime would never have been able to last ...' It further accused Numeiri that by trying to monopolise the revolution and by purging all his one-time allies he had in fact become the leader of the reactionary forces. The communists claimed that there could be no revolution in the Sudan without their active participation, and that Numeiri by his 'rightist somersault' had 'closed the door forever on the possibility of an alliance and cooperation ...' With regard to Numeiri's declared intention to destroy the communist party, the SCP stated mockingly that he was 'living in a day-dream ...' and that no matter how many communists would be arrested, communism would continue to exist for ever. 'A Government that could claim the ability to 'solve" the question of the C.P. and completely abolish it had never and will never be created in the Sudan ...' The SCP again repeated its accusation against the 'renegades' who had left the party in order to gain ministerial posts. Having lost their battle within the party they had then asked Numeiri and the 'reactionary forces' to help them destroy the SCP. But behind it all, claimed the authors of the declaration, was the bankruptcy of the revolution and its inability to solve the political and economic problems of the Sudan. Those who would benefit were the Muslim Brothers and other reactionaries, who were again preaching in the mosques and demonstrating in the streets under the slogan 'no Communism, no Atheism'. The only way to save the Sudanese revolution was, according to the SCP, not through Numeiri and his RCC but through the establishment of a national democratic front. This front, supported by the masses, would be able to abolish the government's anti-revolutionary measures; fight against its destructive economic policies; defeat its reactionary conspiracy in the South; and uphold the national sovereignty of the Sudan against the proposed Tripoli Charter.

Following these open accusations and expressions of hostility there was a state of permanent conflict between the erstwhile allies. The SCP, with most of its ranking leaders in prison, was fighting for survival and hence opposed the régime as a matter of principle even on issues which might have warranted communist support.[108] Numeiri retaliated in words and deeds. Upon his return from Cairo, on 20 April where he had announced that the Sudan would not at present be joining the tripartite federation, he launched an all out attack against the SCP and dissolved the communist-dominated students', women's and youth organisations.[109] This was followed by a major speech, delivered by

Numeiri on 25 May during the celebrations of the second anniversary of the Revolution. He announced officially the setting up of the Sudanese Socialist Union (SSU) as the sole political organisation in the Sudan. Moreover, he emphasised that, in the interest of national unity, the whole political and constitutional structure of the Sudan would be reviewed, and an overall reform of the trade unions leading to their democratisation would be introduced.[110] This as well as the arrest of several more communists prepared the ground for the final denouncement of Numeiri by the SCP. On 30 May the central committee published what amounted to a declaration of war against Numeiri and his supporters. The party claimed that all Numeiri's anti-revolutionary measures had only come about in order to cover his failures in solving any of the pressing economic and political problems facing the Sudan. In setting up the so-called SSU, Numeiri was, according to the SCP, guided by his desire to turn the Sudan into a police-state and to silence all opposition. The sole aim of the SSU was alleged to be the destruction of the true representatives of socialism in the Sudan which included the trade unions, the tenants' organisation and the youth, women and students unions which the government had disbanded by decree. The SCP therefore called upon the people to fight against the military dictatorship and to replace it with a National Democratic Front.[111]

On 29 June Maḥjūb escaped from prison, probably with the aid of 'Uthmān al-Hajj Ḥusayn, the commander of the guard of the republican castle and one of Numeiri's confidants. The hunt for communists and leftists was now in full swing and was intensified in mid-July following a warning by Aḥmad Sulaymān, one of the leaders of the pro-Numeiri communists, that the communists in the army were planning to overthrow the régime.[112]

## THE FAILURE OF THE JULY 1971 COUP AND NUMEIRI'S RESUMPTION OF POWER

Major Hāshim al-'Aṭā' acted before Numeiri's orders to arrest him had been executed, and on the morning of 19 July 1971, he and his collaborators managed to capture the presidential palace and to put Numeiri and his colleagues under arrest.[113] In his first decree, al-'Aṭā' declared the Sudan an independent democratic republic and announced the abrogation of the laws promulgated by Numeiri's régime and the dissolution of the organisations it had established. The programme of the new régime included the establishment of a 'democratic political system' based on mass participation, in which all popular organisations would be represented; regional autonomy would be granted to the South; an 'industrial and agricultural revolution' would take place and 'pursue a non-capital path for development, which approaches the horizon of socialism'. In the sphere of international relations the programme advocated support of the Palestinian cause and of national liberation movements and a struggle against colonialism and neo-colonialism together with the third world and with the friendly socialist countries headed by the Soviet Union.[114]

Of the three leaders of the coup, only al-'Aṭā' was in the Sudan on 19 July. His two colleagues, Bābikr al-Nūr 'Uthmān and Fārūq 'Uthmān Ḥamdallāh, were at the time in London which tends to prove that the coup was executed in a hurry – probably as a result of Numeiri's actions. The three leaders were among the founders of the 'Free Officers' movement and had served both on the RCC and in the government until they were ousted in Numeiri's anti-communist purge in November 1970. Their communist leanings in the past were well known and freely admitted but it is questionable whether they retained their loyalty to the party and followed the dictates of its leadership in later years. However, it is beyond doubt that following the coup, al-'Aṭā' approached the SCP to help him draft the policies of the new régime and organise the popular support it needed. But despite the aid of the SCP, the trade unions, the students and other professional associations, the new régime did not survive for more than seventy-two hours.

This was probably the result of lack of preparation of the coup which in turn led to some fatal mistakes in its execution. First, while al-'Aṭā' had gained the support of the troops in the capital, he neglected to induce those in the provinces to come to his side. Second, the two other leaders of the coup were arrested by the Libyans when the latter intercepted the BOAC aircraft which carried them back to Khartoum. Thus, al-'Aṭā' was left to deal with the situation single-handed.[115] Third, the pronounced pro-communist views of the new régime were bound to arouse suspicions and fear among many Sudanese, including the army.

Last, al-'Aṭā' did not fully realise that despite his promises of continued friendship with Egypt, President Sādāt would not be pleased with the deposal of Numeiri and instead do his utmost to help him regain power. In fact Sādāt acted wisely. He sent two representatives to negotiate with al-'Aṭā', but at the same time ordered the Egyptian troops at Jabal Awliya to move on Khartoum, a distance of some forty miles, and help overthrow the new régime. Instead of mobilising the army against the Egyptian threat, al-'Aṭā' was occupied with matters of government in Khartoum.[116]

Thus, on 22 July, the seventy-two hour coup came to an abrupt end, and Numeiri was once again returned to power. Since then, several journalists and analysts have attempted to decide who stood behind the 19 July coup and whether the SCP was really involved in its planning and execution. The main evidence put forward by Numeiri's régime, claiming communist responsibility, consists of the following: firstly, the communist party declaration of 30 May 1971 had called for Numeiri's overthrow and for the establishment of a National Democratic Front to rule the Sudan; secondly, the leaders of the 19 July coup were SCP members, who despite the severance of their official ties with the party had been in constant contact with Maḥjūb and complied with his orders. Thirdly, Hāshim al-'Aṭā' 's first act after the coup was the release of all communists from prison and the legalising of all the pro-communist organisations which had been disbanded by Numeiri.

All this is circumstantial evidence which can be otherwise interpreted. Similar accusations could be made against Numeiri himself who also released communist prisoners after his coup in May 1969 and who included several communists both in the RCC and in the Cabinet. And it is well known that Maḥjūb had opposed the Numeiri coup prior to its execution just as he claimed to have opposed an anti-Numeiri coup two years later.

Of a more significant nature are three documents, published by Numeiri's Ministry of Information, in order to present direct evidence of communist complicity. The first is a handwritten version of al-'Aṭā' 's first announcement after the coup, consisting of seventeen pages, and written, according to the authorities, by al-Tījānī al-Ṭayyib, one of the founders of the SCP and a member of its central committee. The second document consists of three handwritten pages containing suggestions about the composition of the new government and a list of communist officers who had been expelled from the army by Numeiri and who should be reinstated. These pages, according to the authorities, were written by ‘Abd al-Khāliq Maḥjūb. A third document, put forward as evidence by Numeiri's Minister of the Interior, consisted of the SCP's declaration of support for al-‘Aṭā’, published on 20 July. In it the SCP called upon the ‘revolutionary masses’ to support the officers who performed the historical task of founding a progressive democratic Sudan.[117]

Even if the authenticity of these documents was proved beyond doubt, they cannot prove communist complicity in the coup itself but rather communist support immediately after al-‘Aṭā’ had assumed power. One is reminded again of the immediate aftermath of Numeiri's coup when the news-media all over the world announced that Numeiri's coming to power was in reality a leftist-communist take-over. The SCP was in an unenviable position on both occasions. Many of its leaders had been in prison on the eve of the Numeiri coup and again during the first half of 1971. Thus the party had nothing to lose from the accession of the new régime and could only gain by supporting it. And yet on both occasions the SCP opposed the coup on principle and only came out in its support after it had seized power. Even the list of ministers, which, according to the Prosecutor, was prepared by Maḥjūb, contained only four SCP members, the same number that had served under Numeiri. Once again Maḥjūb could have prepared the list, as he freely admitted during his trial, after the coup had succeeded, either at al-‘Aṭā’ 's request or in order to bargain with him about the composition of the Cabinet. The fact that the Cabinet was not yet formed when Numeiri resumed power three days later would tend to support this theory.[118]

Another argument against the SCP's complicity in the coup was its very poor organisation and execution which hardly corresponded with the SCP's record of performance on other occasions. A major tactical mistake was the long period which elapsed between the first announcement on Radio Omdurman that al-‘Aṭā’ would broadcast to the nation and his actual speech, some five hours later.[119] These long hours in turn would have been more than sufficient to enable al-Tījānī to prepare the speech without having been involved in the coup prior to its execution.

The SCP's own description of its role in the 19 July coup was given some six months after the events and tends to corroborate previous impressions. It suggests that while the planning and time-table were decided upon by Hāshim al-'Aṭā' and his colleagues without consulting the SCP, the latter supported it actively and helped in planning the steps which were to follow it.[120]

Whatever verdict history will pass on communist complicity in the coup, the SCP paid dearly for its support of al-'Aṭā' and his colleagues. Three of the most prominent leaders of the SCP, 'Abd al-Khāliq Maḥjūb, al-Shafi' Aḥmad al-Shaykh and Joseph Garrang were executed after a brief, mostly secret, trial. All known communists who could be found, were arrested and some of them were shot in the streets.[121] Even the anti-Maḥjūb faction, which had supported Numeiri throughout the events did not reap the benefits of its loyalty. In the government reshuffle on 3 August 1971, Mu'āwiya Ibrāhīm and Fārūq Abū 'Īsā, both of whom had been imprisoned during al-'Aṭā' 's brief rule, lost their ministerial posts and Aḥmad Sulaymān remained the sole communist minister.[122] Their dismissal was apparently caused by Numeiri's desire to strengthen his political and economic ties with the West.[123]

How did the Soviet Union react during the al-'Aṭā' coup and more importantly during its aftermath? Both Tass and *Novoe Vremia* greeted the new leadership of the Sudanese revolution, on 20 and 21 July respectively. Tass also relayed al-'Aṭā' 's message that 'the coup was necessitated because of the suppression of democratic freedoms by the former Sudanese leaders ...' Anatoli Nikolaev, Soviet Ambassador in Khartoum, visited al-'Aṭā' as early as 21 July, to pay his respects. However, this was 'Aṭā''s last day in office and from 22 July, the day Numeiri resumed power, until 27 July there were no official communications from Moscow. On that day, Tass condemned the harsh measures taken by the Numeiri régime against communist and other Sudanese patriots and emphasised the danger inherent in the present situation for the very destinies of the Sudanese national democratic revolution. *Izvestia*, in an article signed 'Observer', which was published on 30 July, accused Numeiri of attempting to liquidate the SCP, its leadership, and rank and file communists.

'Observer' went even further when he stated quite openly that the 'Soviet people are not indifferent to the destinies of the fighters against imperialism ...' On 26 July the Soviet leaders sent a message to Numeiri emphasising that they had no intention of interfering in what they regarded as an internal Sudanese affair. All they asked was that acts of hostility against Soviet advisers and property be stopped in order not to upset the very friendly relations between the peoples of the Sudan and the Soviet Union. True, the Soviets expressed concern about the fate of Maḥjūb and his colleagues, but they were very careful in phrasing their anxiety in an unobtrusive manner.[124] However, in an interview he gave to *al-Siyāsa* on 28 Dec. 1976, Anwar al-Sādāt, the president of Egypt, stated that he had known about the intended coup prior to its execution and that he had evidence that the Soviet Union was attempting to regain in the Sudan the ground they had lost in Egypt with the deposition of 'Alī Ṣabrī and their other allies. Sādāt tried to warn Numeiri but the warning came too late.

Other communist states adopted a similar line while Yugoslavia and China refrained from any criticism at all. The most outspoken criticism of Maḥjūb and his leadership came from Mr. Bilak, secretary for International Relations of the CP of Czechoslovakia, on 21 October 1971. During a speech on the CCP's relations with other communist parties, Bilak stated that Maḥjūb and his faction had developed sectarian tendencies and had therefore failed to appreciate the revolutionary potential of Numeiri's régime. They had erred in giving up their positions in the régime and had alienated public support through their opposition to the proposed Federation of Arab Republics. Moreover, Bilak accused Maḥjūb of preparing the coup with his army accomplices, without even consulting other members of the central committee. The coup had allegedly enjoyed neither the backing of the people nor of the army itself and therefore, deservedly failed. Bilak also stated that neither the CCP nor other communist parties had any prior information regarding the coup.[125]

Despite the harsh measures employed by Numeiri and the lack of support they received from outside the Sudan, the SCP managed to survive. Only two weeks after Maḥjūb's execution, it elected its new secretary-general, Muḥammad Ibrāhīm Nuqud, a leading ideological theoretician and a member of the central committee since 1960.[126] The central committee devoted its September-November 1971 session to an assessment of the '19th July Movement' and attempted to draw conclusions from its defeat. It stated in its report that Numeiri's victory would not have been possible without outside assistance which consisted of direct military aid granted primarily by the Egyptian forces stationed in the Sudan.[127] It also stressed the role played by Libya in hijacking the BOAC plane which carried two of the coup's leaders back to the Sudan. But more important were the SCP's charges that the leaders of the 19 July coup were too lenient toward their adversaries and under-estimated the preparedness of the 'counter-revolutionary forces' to liquidate the 'revolution'. Numeiri's counter-coup was, according to the SCP, a return to the old power-structure of the Sudan. With the communists and progressives out of the way, Numeiri had to rely on 'the traditional anti-communist forces which are opposed to social progress and democracy ... since the dawn of independence ...'[128]

The communists diagnosed their own shortcomings not as a local occurrence, but rather as part of 'an all-out victory for the political line of the forces of the right ...' The fact that this counter-revolutionary policy was carried out by so-called revolutionaries such as Sādāt in Egypt, Qadhāfi in Libya, or Numeiri in the Sudan, was according to communist views irrelevant: 'The experience of the Sudan has proved – at least for us – that opposing colonialism ... and the advance along the road of social progress cannot be taken genuinely unless they are identified within the country with the fulfillment of the tasks of democratic revolution ...' The military seizure of power by a 'fragment of the petty-bourgeois' forces and the creation of a state-party with an imposed ideology were counter-revolutionary in essence even when their slogans seemed progressive.[129]

The report of the central committee's session in September-November 1971 is a clear proof of the party's weakness. It is a lengthy, poorly phrased, ill-defined and repetitive document. The main concern is with Numeiri's evil deeds and with his 'reactionary allies'. But it contains very little about the communists' own shortcomings in the past and about what they seek to accomplish in the future. Under the heading 'The Future and the Horizons of the Development of the Sudanese Revolution', the authors stated: 'We are re-organising and regrouping our forces under new political conditions which demand new methods of leadership, new methods of work, new methods of protection and security of party cadres and apparatus and new methods of resistence [*sic.*] We are facing a long and strenuous battle for which we should get prepared now, and not in the future, by every serious and firm step we take ...'[130]

Understandably, the SCP leadership had little to offer as to the ways and means by which the party should prepare itself or as to the methods it was to adopt. Only the few last pages of the report deal with practical issues such as rebuilding the party and planning for meaningful activities. But even in these passages, the sense of lack of leadership is acute. The new central committee dealt with matters of organisation and activities, probably in the same way as Maḥjūb, al-Shafi' and others had dealt with them in the late 1940s. The defeated SCP was undergoing a 'second childhood.' It had to rebuild both its cadres and its branches, to renew its links with students, workers, peasants and women's organisations, all of which had been extensively weakened since Numeiri's comeback.

In December 1971, the central committee of the SCP came out with yet another declaration against Numeiri's dictatorship. The occasion was the fifteenth anniversary of Sudanese independence. The message to the people was to fight for unity in order to consolidate independence and achieve democracy through 'the overthrow of the bloody rightist and retrogressive military dictatorship ...'[131] Numeiri was defined as 'a blood-thirsty, insanely angry maniac, manipulated by the Egyptians and Arab nationalists, as a puppet in the 25th May coup ...' His policies, according to the SCP, had made the Sudan easy prey for neo-colonialists from the surrounding countries and the US. So much so that 'never before had the Sudan been made so ignominious and the pride of her people so belittled since the breakdown of the Funj Sultanate and the downfall of the Mahdi's state ...'[132] The fate of Numeiri and his collaborators would, according to the SCP, be at the hands of 'popular revenge ... The ropes that strangled Abdel Khalig, El Shafie and Garang, shall surround their filthy necks; and the bullets which the cowards maliciously fired at Hashim and his comrades shall rest in those chests which contain neither soldierly bravery nor manhood ...'

One year after the counter-coup, the SCP was still criticising all of Numeiri's policies even in such spheres where his actions largely corresponded with their own views. The Addis Ababa agreement regarding the Southern Sudan was labelled by the SCP as a 'drastic crime that ... endangers the passage of progress and revolution not only in the Sudan, North and South, but also in all parts of the Nile Valley as well as in the Arabic [*sic*] area ...'[133] But even more important, the SCP resented the newly founded SSU because it had attracted many of the erstwhile supporters of the SCP especially from among the intelligentsia, who had been disappointed by the SCP's performance and its lack of leadership during the July coup and had hitched their wagon to the SSU. The SCP now described them as 'corrupt opportunists' and as 'enemies of the Sudanese revolution and imperialist puppets on the Arab and African arena ...'[134]

From his return to power in July 1971, Numeiri's policy can be defined best as following an independent Sudanese line. Its most outstanding achievement was the Addis Ababa agreement, signed in February 1972, which brought peace to the Southern Sudan after some seventeen years of civil war. While this could be described as a realisation of the regional autonomy offered by Numeiri to the Southerners ever since he came to power, in other instances the post 1971 policy was a reversal of Numeiri's previous principles. A gradual withdrawal from the Arab political scene manifested itself both in the Sudan's refusal to join the Federation of Arab Republics and in the resignation of such noted pan-Arabists as Vice-presidents Bābikr 'Awaḍallāh and Khālid Ḥasan 'Abbās.[135] The Sudan's growing interest and involvement in the African continent was a direct result of this new policy. Another result was the political weakening of the so-called Arab socialists, whose ascendancy was one of the most notable outcomes of the SCP's decline after the July coup. The founding of the SSU in January 1972 seemed to herald the supremacy in Sudanese politics of the Arab Socialists and the pan-Arabists in general. So indeed it seemed to the SCP who had opposed the founding of the SSU even before 1971. Aware of the Egyptian experience, where the CP had been forced to vanish from the political scene following the establishment in 1961 of the Arab Socialist Union (ASU), the SCP vigorously opposed a similar fate for itself. While supporting the merger of the Egyptian CP with the ASU, Maḥjūb and his comrades had claimed that the strength of sectarianism in the Sudan dictated a different road to socialism. Socialism, so they stated, could be achieved by establishing a broad National Democratic Front, which would embrace all the progressive forces such as trade unions and other professional organisations as well as the SCP itself, while each would be allowed to preserve its organisational and ideological independence. This 'dogmatic and sectarian concept of development', as it was defined by a leading Yugoslav commentator, was defeated after the July coup.[136] In January 1972 the SSU held its first national congress and has since then become an important factor in supplying the popular support for Numeiri's policies. However, the SSU opposed any federal ties between the Sudan and other Arab states and likewise turned down a suggestion to establish an organisational link with the ASU or similar political movements. It supported Numeiri to the hilt in his settling the conflict with the South and has, since February 1972, been instrumental in making the agreement work. On the whole, ideologies notwithstanding, the SSU has been pragmatic in its approach to political problems and despite criticism of certain aspects of the régime, has on the whole lived up to Numeiri's expectations. [137] While some of the more outspoken exponents of Arab Socialism and unity have therefore resigned, the majority continued to serve Numeiri in one capacity or another in spite of the apparent ideological gap between them and the régime.[138]

Another instance in which Numeiri has reversed his previous policy is his relation to the Soviet and Western blocs. Following the July 1971 coup, when Numeiri expelled Soviet military and technical experts from the Sudan, trade with the Soviet bloc came to a virtual standstill. The Sudanese claimed that the prices of Soviet goods sold to the Sudan were some 30 per cent above prices on the world market and that the Sudan had lost between £25 million and £30 million for every £100 million worth of trade.[139] The two notable exceptions in this sweeping accusation against the Sudan's trading partners were China and Yugoslavia. Both have increased their trade with the Sudan since 1971 and have also undertaken some of the technical assistance previously supplied by the Russians. However, the main trend in economic-foreign relations has been the attempt to gain economic and financial aid from the West, notably from the United States, Great

Britain, and West Germany. In September 1972 Numeiri announced that an Anglo-American consortium would finance $600 million worth of development projects in the Sudan.[140] This trend culminated in the re-establishment of diplomatic relations with the United States after an interval of some six years.

CHAPTER 4

# Four Aspects of Sudanese Communist Ideology and Practice

## EGYPT, ARAB UNITY AND THE ARAB ISRAELI CONFLICT

Between 1953, when the SCP first formulated its relations towards Egypt, and 1956 when the party called upon the Sudanese people to mobilize and come to Egypt's help during the Suez Campaign, the SCP's attitude towards Nasser's regime moved from one extreme to the other. The agreement between General Neguib and the representatives of the Sudan's political parties in January 1953, and the Anglo-Egyptian agreement regarding the Sudan a month later, both of which determined the future of the Sudan, were condemned by the SCP as imperialist acts. Moreover, the SCP regarded the 'unity of the Nile Valley', which had been the dominant trend in Egypt's policy toward the Sudan since 1919, as clear proof of Egypt's imperialist designs.[1] If additional proof was needed it was amply provided, according to the SCP, by the Egyptian Wafd Cabinet, headed by Naḥḥās Pasha, when it signed the Anglo-Egyptian Agreement in 1936.[2]

The first clear proof of a change in the SCP's attitude towards Egypt came in 1956, when the SCP called upon the new Sudanese government to support the progressive bloc within the Arab League headed by Egypt.[3] This was followed by a much stronger declaration of support for Nasser, when the latter announced the nationalisation of the Suez Canal in July 1956. Lastly the SCP was the first party in the Sudan to favour a treaty of friendship with Egypt during the Suez Campaign in October of that year. It demanded an immediate severance of diplomatic relations with France and Great Britain, a request which was turned down not only by the Sudanese government but also by the opposition. Moreover, the SCP and the trade unions organised volunteers to come to Egypt's aid, headed by the AIF's secretary general and including such well-known communist leaders as al-Tījānī al-Ṭayyib, Aḥmad Sulaymān and al-Shafī' Aḥmad al-Shaykh.[4]

The abrupt change in the SCP's attitude towards Nasser's Egypt is all the more surprising if one takes into account the crucial events of 1955. During February of that year Nasser had first launched his anti-imperialist attack against the Baghdad pact. In April he went to the Bandung Conference from which he emerged as the strongest leader of the Arab progressive camp supporting positive neutrality. Finally, in June, he opened the Middle East to the Soviet bloc by signing the first arms deal with a communist state. And yet throughout these events, which brought Nasser's Egypt closer to the Soviet bloc than any other Arab state, the SCP remained hostile to Egypt and regarded it, alongside England, as the Sudan's most dangerous imperialist enemy.[5]

One crucial event may perhaps help to explain this seemingly illogical stand of the SCP: the fight for Sudanese independence throughout 1955. Until the Sudan was finally and irrevocably declared an independent sovereign state on 31 December 1955, Egypt presented the main danger regardless of its so-called progressive posture elsewhere. With Sudanese independence guaranteed this danger was removed and the SCP was free to modify its former policies and to reverse its attitude towards Egypt.

On the eve of the 1958 elections the SCP announced its plan for gradual unity between Egypt and the Sudan and 'Abd al-Khāliq Maḥjūb tried to explain the party's new policy in a lengthy interview with *al-Mīdān*.[6] The SCP proposed that the Sudan and Egypt should co-ordinate their foreign policies, defence, economies and cultural programmes, by establishing permanent Egyptian-Sudanese advisory boards. Maḥjūb explained that the historical ties between Egypt and the Sudan, going back to the times of the Pharaohs, made the special relations between the two countries in the political, economic and cultural fields a source of strength not to be ignored. This was particularly so in the modern era as the Sudan's struggle for independence led by the Sudanese national movement was connected with its Egyptian counterpart.

But even more important, Maḥjūb contended, were the

political-economic realities of the two countries. The close relations and the co-ordination of Sudanese-Egyptian policies, were dictated by the need to preserve Sudanese independence. Thus the fact that both the Sudan and Egypt were dependent on the Nile for their livelihood and that the growing and export of cotton provided their main source for economic development, made a common and co-ordinated policy essential. This, according to Maḥjūb, was where the Sudanese interests clashed with interests of the surrounding imperialist powers. The Sudan was still economically tied to imperialist markets and thus was at a disadvantage both in its exports and imports. Moreover, as long as this dependence continued, there could be no pretence of real Sudanese independence. The only truly independent country bordering on the Sudan and capable of helping it to liberate itself from the surrounding imperialist interests was Egypt, and hence the necessity of co-ordination in the field of defence and foreign relations.

When asked whether the SCP's programme would eventually lead to unity between Egypt and Sudan, Maḥjūb replied in the affirmative. However, he tried to explain this shift in communist positions by stressing the difference between the conditions prevailing in the Sudan before independence and present-day realities: the SCP sought to unite two independent republics on a basis of equality. Moreover, ever since 1956, when the Sudan became officially independent, its struggle to secure this independence coincided with that of Egypt. Thus, the Sudanese fought against the Baghdad pact and against similar pacts in Africa alongside their Egyptian brethren and later forced their reactionary government not to join the Eisenhower doctrine. The present AIF programme therefore aimed at bringing about Sudanese-Egyptian unity not only on a popular basis but to make it an officially binding agreement.

From 1956 until 1969 the SCP's support for Nasser and his policies remained consistent despite periods of tension between Egypt and the Soviet Union. The party gave its enthusiastic support to the union between Egypt and Syria when the United Arab Republic was founded in February 1958. This was viewed by the SCP as an historical victory for independent Arab nationalism, and it was hoped that the Sudan would become part of that union in the near future.[7] If one takes into account the opposition of the Syrian CP to the union and the fact that many communists were imprisoned on Nasser's orders, the SCP's all-out support is surprising.

But the SCP went even further when it supported the 'self-dissolution' of the Egyptian CP in April 1965. This decision was bitterly opposed by many Egyptian communists, mainly in exile, as well as by communist leaders in the Arab world, notably the Syrian leader Khālid Bakdash. And yet the SCP supported Nasser on this as it had on other issues, claiming that the dissolution was justified by the special conditions prevailing in Egypt.[8]

The SCP shifted its ground again after the Numeiri coup, when it opposed the proposed federation between the Sudan, Egypt and Libya, which was announced on 27 December 1969. The SCP's opposition was probably prompted both by internal and external developments. On the internal front, Numeiri had not yet started his anti-communist drive, but the SCP was already suspicious of his intentions, especially his support for the anti-Maḥjūb faction. Externally, both Nasser and Qadhāfi had declared their outright opposition to communism on several occasions and the latter's fundamentalistic-Islamic views were anathema to the SCP. Lastly, the party claimed that by joining any union with Arab countries the Sudan was consciously undermining the prospects of settling the conflict in the South within a united Sudan.[9] Both Maḥjūb and other communist leaders emphasized that while the SCP supported Arab unity on principle it was opposed to unity which was forced by Arab rulers whose only aim was to stabilise their régimes. Such a unity could not succeed as it ignored the basic conditions necessary for its survival and thus could only serve the interests of the reactionary forces.[10]

The most detailed treatment of the SCP's views on Arab unity was that of Maḥjūb in his report presented to the fourth party congress in Khartoum in October 1967.[11] Maḥjūb stated that Arab unity could only be put into effect through social revolution and a long and arduous struggle and could therefore not be achieved through political declarations. Hence, the first task of Arab nationalism was to rid itself of the old traditional ruling class, whose factional pro-imperialistic policies were diametrically opposed to socialism and national unity. This was proved, in Maḥjūb's opinion, when the Egyptian-Syrian union came to its end in 1961. It then became clear that real unity could only be brought about through socialism. Therefore, Maḥjūb stated, the real test of Arab unity would only come when progressive socialist governments would rule the Arab states. Such governments would be prepared to forego their factional and egoistic interests as well as their chauvinism. This in turn would pave the way for the union of the Arab revolutionary movements whose selfless devotion to the cause of Arab nationalism was the only guarantee for its success. Only then would the time come when the united Arab revolution would be prepared for its final struggle against the Zionist-imperialist danger. Therefore, Maḥjūb concluded, all attempts at national conciliation between progressive and reactionary Arab regimes in order to fight Israel, the common enemy, were playing into the hands of the imperialists. The latter's true aim was to turn Israel's military victory into a political one by destroying the Arab revolution and installing their own agents, the reactionary revisionists, instead.

The SCP's attitude towards Israel was another issue on which the party pursued a line independent from Moscow. While the Soviet Union opposed Israeli 'aggression' and demanded a return to the borders decided by the United Nations in 1947, including a just settlement of the Palestinian problem, it never questioned Israel's right to statehood. A similar line was adopted by most of the communist parties in the Arab world, an attitude which did not add to their popularity, especially among the intelligentsia. The SCP, on the other hand, despite its remoteness from the Arab-Israeli conflict, adopted the Arab nationalist view which denied Israel's right to exist. Maḥjūb's view, even before the June 1967 war, was that Israel would have to vanish and be replaced by a democratic Arab republic.[12] After the war, the SCP became even more outspoken in denouncing Israel. It opposed the Security Council's Resolution No. 242, and in a lengthy declaration titled 'The Current Situation of the Arabs', it specified what it regarded as the only solution of the Arab-Israeli conflict.[13] Its main premise was that the Jews were not a nation and hence had no right to self-determination. The Zionist state, set up as it was with the aid of imperialism, was therefore not an expression of national self-determination but an anti-revolutionary act aimed against the Arab national liberation movement. The solution consequently was the destruction of the Zionist régime and the '... establishment of a progressive democratic Palestinian state on its ruins ...'[14] The struggle was, according to the SCP, not between Israel and the Arabs but between imperialism, Zionism and their reactionary feudal Arab allies on the one hand and the Arab national liberation movement on the other. The latter included not only the workers, peasants and the progressive elements within the middle class, but also the Palestinian revolution. Moreover, they had their allies in the socialist bloc and in the working class all over the world.

The Arab-Israeli war was, according to the SCP, not the only battle which confronted the Arabs, as in many other cases they had to rid themselves of their own reactionary régimes before they could fight against Zionism. The June 1967 war was aimed against the progressive Arab régimes in Egypt and Syria and it was only through Soviet aid that the Arabs could save these régimes and thus defeat the purpose of imperialist aggression. On the other hand, the 1967 war brought about an upsurge of anti-imperialist feelings in the Arab world which paved the way for the overthrow of the reactionary régimes in the Sudan and Libya.[15] The SCP therefore proposed the following plan for the continuation of the Arab-Israeli conflict: first, reversing the Zionist conquests through the employment of both political and military means; second, unifying the Arab revolutionary forces; and third, supporting the Palestinian revolution in order to turn Palestine into a democratic progressive state. With this in mind the SCP weighed the pros and cons of the Security Council's resolution. Its advantages lay in the prospect that the conquered territories would be returned to their rightful owners, thus strengthening the progressive régimes of Egypt and Syria and enabling the Palestinian revolution to pursue its war against Zionism from the liberated West Bank of the Jordan. However, the Security Council's resolution demanded a recognition of the State of Israel, a demand totally unacceptable to the SCP. This would be tantamount to granting Israel a prize for its aggression and weaken the Palestinians' chances by enabling the reactionaries in Jordan and Lebanon to fight against the Palestinian organisations under the cover of the Security Council's resolution. The SCP therefore proposed not to recognise Israel and rather to remember that behind the Security Council's resolution stood the United States, the first and most persistent enemy of the Arab liberation movement.

### ISLAM AND POLITICS IN THE SOCIAL SETTING OF THE SUDAN

The Sudanese are first and foremost a religious society. Their loyalty to sectarian or even tribal leaders is based on tradition rather than on ideology. This is true not only with regard to the more primitive sectors of the population such as the tribes of Dārfūr, Kordofan or the Red Sea Mountains but also as regards the more sophisticated social groups. Three such groups which emerged in the Sudan, especially since World War II, were affected by what may be loosely defined as modernisation. These groups were the Jazīra tenants, the railway workers, and the educated class.[16]

The first represented the only sector where modern methods of cultivation were introduced in Sudanese agriculture on a large scale. The cultivation of cash-crops depending on prices of the world market combined with the unique partnership between the tenants and the government, helped to weaken traditional loyalties and to create a new class of peasants fighting against their partner, the government, for an increased share in the profits like any industrial workers' union. Moreover, being the biggest employer in the Sudan and controlling by far the most important branch in the country's economy, the tenants' union became one of the most important pressure groups in the Sudan.[17]

The second group consisted of industrial workers and primarily of the railway workers whose union was since its foundation the strongest and most militant one in the Sudan. This resulted both from the importance of communications in a country stretching over roughly one million square miles, and from the relative weakness of industries and hence of industrial workers. Moreover, the creation of the modernised railway centre at 'Aṭbarā, bringing together people of different tribal and sectarian backgrounds, helped to undermine traditional loyalties and to replace them, at least partly, with loyalty to the trade union in its fight for better working conditions. Commanding the most important centre of communications, the railway workers were in a position to embarrass the authorities and to utilise their power whenever possible in order to achieve their aims.

The third group was that of the graduates and students who may be defined as the Sudanese intelligentsia. Modernisation affected this sector through education and through their occupational skills. The university, and to a certain extent the high schools, tore their students away from their traditional surroundings and implanted in them, at least partly, new patterns of behaviour and new loyalties. However, a close observer of the graduates' scene defined the intelligentsia as a 'cross-breed of strong traditionalism and romantic militancy' and implied that they exhibited 'all the characteristics of a split personality'.[18] This may be one of the explanations of the fact that the students were torn between two such divergent ideologies as those of the Muslim Brothers and the communists.[19] Being a relatively small group, the intelligentsia was nonetheless conscious of its importance in a society where the bulk of the adult population was practically illiterate. The graduates, since they first emerged as a political force in the years 1938/42, regarded themselves as the only legitimate spokesmen of Sudanese nationalism. The special graduates' constituences were institutionalised, ever since the first general elections in 1953, in order to legitimise the intelligentsia's special standing in Sudanese society.

These three groups, despite their importance, accounted for less than ten per cent of the population. The vast majority of Sudanese remained loyal to their traditional leaders and sects and were hardly affected by so-called modern concepts of society and politics.

The SCP was well aware of the socio-economic realities of the Sudan and adopted therefore very early in its existence a rather flexible attitude towards ideology and religion. Unlike other more doctrinaire communist parties, the SCP did not reject Islam. On the contrary, it emphasised that in many respects the two movements, communism and Islam, were indeed allies. This view was first explained by Maḥjūb in a long article titled: 'How did I become a Communist'.[20] The only enemy of communism according to Maḥjūb was imperialism, while believers, be they Muslims or Christians, who were willing to fight against imperialism, were the communists' natural allies. Furthermore, communism sought to harness human knowledge and scientific achievements and to exploit them for the benefit of society. Here again, Maḥjūb asserts, communism and Islam were striving to achieve identical aims.

The SCP in fact boasted that it had several Muslim leaders on its central committee who did not find any contradiction between their duties as teachers of religion and their communist beliefs.[21] The leaders of Islam reciprocated and in most cases adopted a much more tolerant attitude towards communism than in other Muslim states. Thus, for instance, Sayyid 'Abd al-Raḥmān al-Mahdī welcomed the communists when they wanted to join in the battle against the proposed union with Egypt in 1954.[22] Moreover, when in October 1954 the SCP was accused of rejecting Islam and spreading anti-Islamic propaganda, the Sayyid warned the Anṣār that the accusations were false and motivated by the political opponents of the SCP.[23] Conversely, it is important to note that whenever the issue of communism and its legality were discussed in public the issue was communism vis-à-vis Islam rather than the political, economic, or social aspects of communist ideology.

However, in the religious-political structure of the Sudan, the attitude towards the Khatmiyya and the Anṣār and the identification with either were not less important than the attitude towards Islam itself. While the SCP was fully aware of these realities it was in no position to compromise politically with sectarian divisions. To announce that individual religious beliefs did not contradict communism was one thing, while the admission of the central political role of Islamic sects was quite another. Moreover, in the more practical realm, communism in the Sudan could only hope to appeal to those sections of the population which had either rejected sectarian politics altogether or whose sectarian loyalties had been weakened and to whom the SCP could present an alternative. In consequence, the SCP rejected the political role of the religious sects on principle while in practice it tried not to antagonize their religious leaders and at times even admitted their importance in the political realm. Historically, the SCP defined the 19th century Mahdi as 'the patriotic (*waṭanī*) commander' who led the struggle 'against the Turkish Empire and British penetration'.[24] Politically, the party blessed the two leaders of popular Islam when they announced their agreement in October 1955 to work together for Sudanese independence.[25] Further, they recognised the leading political role of Sayyid Ṣiddīq al-Mahdī in the fight against 'Abbūd's military régime, and expressed their appreciation of his deeds on more than one occasion. At the same time the SCP denied the political role of the sects on principle. It stated that the prevailing sectarian divisions were weakening the nationalist anti-imperialist struggle of the Sudanese people. Therefore the only basis for political action was an agreed platform on which both sectarian and non-sectarian parties could co-operate.[26]

Under these conditions the SCP, or any other non-sectarian party, had little chance of penetrating into the strongholds of the Anṣār or the Khatmiyya. Yet it could hope to gain a foothold within the three sectors of society mentioned above, whose sectarian loyalties had been undermined through the economic, social or cultural impact of modernisation. While the appeal of Marxist-Leninist ideology to members of the intelligentsia is easy to comprehend, especially in a primitive society, it is rather more complex with regard to workers and especially peasants whose education, if any, was purely traditional. While both workers and peasants welcomed communist backing in their struggle to overcome economic grievances, they were less inclined to accept alien doctrines of which they had little understanding. Yet these so-called 'illiterate marxists' were among the most important supporters of the SCP.[27]

The question whether the SCP ought to be flexible in order to attract prospective members of the peasant class and to what extent it should be prepared to compromise became one of the first ideological battles within the SCP in the years 1951–1955. One group, headed by the then secretary-general of the party demanded an orthodox interpretation of Marxism and opposed any compromise on such matters as religion. According to Maḥjūb, who led the battle against these so-called revisionists, they consisted mainly of the middle class intelligentsia who failed to recognise that unless Marxism was adapted to the unique conditions of the Sudan, communism had no chance to succeed.[28] Thus, for example, the 'revisionists' claimed that there was no point in creating a national front which included the peasants, as the latter had first to be taught the principles of Marxism. But, asked Maḥjūb, could the study of Marxism lead to agrarian reform or further the anti-imperialist struggle? The battle against this group lasted for well over four years, but by the time when they were finally expelled from the party, in 1956, the party's line towards the workers and peasants was firmly established. In its programme, *Sabīl al-Sūdān* (The Sudan's path), adopted at the third congress in 1956, the SCP gave priority to organising the workers and peasants and consolidating the pact between them and the intelligentsia. This would provide the party with a sound basis and at the same time give the national movement a democratic character.

The very fact that the SCP, alone among the Communist parties in the Arab world, regarded the peasants as potentially important allies, is noteworthy. In a way Maḥjūb, in propagating this line, may be defined as a pioneer of what later became known as 'Maoism'. There is no evidence of any direct influence of the Chinese Communist ideology on the SCP and it seems more likely that Maḥjūb formulated his ideological-political ideas independently, based on the realities of Sudanese society and without external influence.

Communist propaganda among the peasant class, including illiterates, now became a major part of the SCP's activities, but was, at the same time, practically divorced from the theories of Marxism-Leninism.[29] In March 1955 the party led the struggle in parliament on behalf of the Jazīra tenants who demanded a greater share in the profits as well as representation in the project's management. This struggle, which lasted more than a year, enabled the communists to become deeply involved in the affairs of the tenants' union and to capture its leadership. Al-Amīn Muḥammad al-Amīn, president of the tenants' union both at that time and in later periods, became a prominent leader of the SCP and helped to turn his union into one of the strongholds of the party.[30] Thus, while the poorer peasants and the landless agricultural workers were neglected by the SCP, the more privileged 'gentlemen farmers' of the Jazīra became the party's allies. The importance of these peasants for the SCP became evident in the wake of the civilian uprising in October 1964 when al-Amīn Muḥammad al-Amīn became Minister in the transitional government alongside al-Shafī' Aḥmad al-Shaykh, representing the federation of trade unions and two other communist ministers. The problem facing the SCP was whether it could rely on peasant support in its forthcoming battle against the traditionalist parties who were trying to regain control of the government. In his report to the party's central committee, 'Abd al-Khāliq Maḥjūb devoted a special section to the prospects of securing the active participation of the peasants in the revolutionary movement. While the party felt quite secure of its hold over the tenants' union leadership, it was apparently aware that the mass of the peasants was likely to follow their traditional religious leadership in all matters not pertaining to their professional demands. Therefore, the SCP had better, as Maḥjūb advised it, convince the peasants that their only chance for a brighter future lay in a socialist, non-capitalist, society:

> '... How to talk to the peasant masses and how to organise them are highly important questions. The peasant masses openly strive for independence, wishing to take their destiny into their own hands. This will deliver a crushing blow at the reactionary elements, who have for many years enjoyed the peasants' support secured by fraud and economic pressure. We should pay special attention to this question. We must tackle the problem of ensuring the independence of the bulk of the peasantry if we want our country to develop along the road of national democracy. It has become clear now that the reactionaries can no longer deceive the peasants into submission. Hence their resort to religious customs and prejudices, their attempts to present progress as the enemy of religion and in this way to retain their influence on the peasants. It is therefore essential for the Communists to find a correct approach to the peasants, to respect their religious views. The Communists should always know the needs of the people, both material and spiritual. To overlook these needs means to hamper progress. There is nothing hypocritical in our attitude to religion for we know that no religion can give people more than socialism gives them. To leave the field of activity among the religious masses in the reactionaries' hands would be inexcusable ...'[31]

The emphasis was once again on religion, because Maḥjūb knew only too well that, economic grievances notwithstanding, the bulk of the peasantry would vote for the traditionalist parties in the forthcoming elections. Indeed, in the general elections of May 1965, even the Jazīra tenants supported the Anṣār-dominated Umma party rather than the SCP although the latter included their own president al-Amīn Muḥammad al-Amīn as a candidate.

After 1965 the SCP's fortunes among the tenants seem to have declined. This may have been caused at least in part by the split within the Anṣār, to whom most of the Jazīra tenants still belonged. With al-Ṣādiq al-Mahdī and his uncle al-Hādī al-Mahdī both fighting for the tenants' support, the SCP stood little chance. This may also have been one of the reasons why the tenants' president Muḥammad al-Amīn, after many years of loyalty to

Maḥjūb, joined the dissidents within the party and advocated a military coup as the only means to break the traditional stronghold in the Jazīra and elsewhere.

According to ʻAlī ʻAbd al-Raḥmān al-Amīn, leader of the PDP, the SCP never really enjoyed the confidence of the Jazīra tenants or of any other section of Sudanese society. Farmers, workers, teachers or students, supported the SCP at times, because of the militant support the latter afforded to their professional grievances. However, they never supported communist ideology which they regarded as a '... creed which is in conflict with their religion, tradition and morals ...'[32]

### THE PROBLEM OF THE SOUTH AND ITS SOLUTION

The problem of the Southern Sudan was one of the major and most difficult ones facing the Sudan since the eve of independence. It had of course existed long before and been in fact part of the geo-political reality of the Sudan ever since the Egyptians conquered the upper regions of the Nile in the 1860s and annexed them to the then Turco-Egyptian Sudan. Under British rule, the three southern provinces, comprising about 250,000 square miles and inhabited by a multitude of Nilotic and Negroid tribes, became a separate administrative unit. The British authorities viewed the blacks of the South, whose religion and culture were different from those of the Arab Muslims of the North, as requiring a different administration which could best be conducted by British officials. Moreover, they forbade the use of Arabic in the South and introduced English instead as the region's official language. In the religious sphere the authorities stopped all attempts to Islamise the pagans of the South while they encouraged Christian missionary activities, especially in the field of education. The Southerners even had their own army, the Equatorial Battalions, while the Arab-Muslim Sudan Defence Force was barred from entering the region. Only in 1947, when it became clear that the Sudan was on its road to independence and that the future of the South lay in a united Sudan, did the British modify their policy. They began introducing economic and educational development plans into the South in order to bring it up to par with the more developed and sophisticated North. But these plans came too late and thus achieved only moderate results.

On the eve of independence, in August 1955, following numerous blunders made by the newly-appointed northern Arab politicians and administrators in the South, the Equatorial Battalion rebelled. A general revolt, which was to rage through the Southern Sudan until February 1972, was well under way.[33]

What the Southerners basically demanded was a federal solution. They argued that a state divided by racial, religious and cultural differences into two distinct regions, could only remain united if it recognised these realities and introduced decentralised government. However, no Sudanese government, whether civilian or military, was willing to accept a federal solution. The most important reason for this objection was probably northern Muslim fear that federation would only be a first step towards complete secession. In addition, the Northerners realised that by compromising with Southern demands they might be compelled to grant similar rights to other regions in the North itself, such as Dārfūr or the Nuba Mountains, both of which had expressed their support of decentralised government. The principal political parties also feared that by giving in to such demands they might lose their public support in the North, where these claims were generally resented. Lastly the problem of the South was largely viewed as a legacy of British imperialism whose aim it had been to separate the South from the Sudan and to annex it to British-ruled East Africa. Once independence was achieved, Northern politicians regarded the separatist tendencies of the South as signs of renewed imperialist attempts to destroy the independent united Sudan from within.

Until October 1964, the situation in the South went from bad to worse. 'Abbūd's military régime had tried to solve the problem by the use of force and as a result thousands of Southerners fled to neighbouring countries while others were killed or took refuge in the interior. The *Anya-Nya*, the military arm of Southern resistance, was founded in 1963 and did its utmost to make the life of Northerners in the South as hazardous as possible. Southern politicians set up their own governments in exile and talked openly about Southern independence and sovereignty. The only serious attempt to negotiate a peaceful settlement was undertaken in March 1965 by the care-taker government which ruled the Sudan in the wake of the October 1964 civilian uprising. A round-table conference of Northern and Southern politicians tried to hammer out an agreed solution of the problem. But after serious discussions, all it could agree upon was setting up of a twelve-men committee. This committee, after long deliberations, reported in September 1966 that a centralised unitary government would not serve the Sudan's national interests. However, it failed to agree on any specific solution or to suggest what degree of decentralisation was desirable.

In the period that followed until Numeiri's coup, mass killings in the South were resumed which together with the growing militancy and power of the *Anya-Nya* made a peaceful solution completely unrealistic. The situation remained unchanged throughout the second parliamentary period and when Numeiri assumed power and announced his plan for regional autonomy it seemed that only a miracle could bring the civil war to an end.

The SCP was the first and only party to propose regional autonomy for the South as early as 1954 and had stood firmly behind this plan ever since it was first formulated. In a declaration published in *al-Ṣarāḥa* on 28 September, 1954 the AIF spelt out its views on the problem.[34] There, the party stated that unless its views on Southern autonomy were accepted and executed the unity of the country might be endangered. Moreover, the SCP viewed the matter as only one of several regional problems confronting the Sudan and suggested that these too should be solved on a similar basis. Like India, the Soviet Union and China, the Sudan, being a multi-national state, should realise that some sort of local government or regional autonomy was the only solution suitable under present conditions. This autonomy would, as stated by the SCP, not weaken the united Sudan, because the various regions would remain under one constitution, one parliament and one government. As long as this was not realised by the Northern parties, the South would continue to present an insoluble problem only to be exploited by imperialist powers.

In the field of economy, the SCP demanded rapid development projects in the South in order to close the rift between it and the North as soon as possible. It also requested higher wages for workers and government officials there, who at the time were paid less than their northern counterparts.[35] In the educational sphere, the SCP urged the government to allocate a greater proportion of its budget to the South in order to bridge the gap between the two parts of the Sudan. On the other hand, the party opposed the use of missionaries for education in the South and demanded an immediate plan for Sudanising the teaching personnel in all schools.[36]

After the first uprising in the South in August 1955, the SCP reiterated its previous warnings. While stating explicitly that the bloodshed was caused by British imperialist intervention, the party warned the government that only rapid development under regional autonomy could solve the problem. The SCP also suggested to close the borders with Uganda and Kenya and to expel all foreign missionaries from the South.[37]

The party's outspoken and courageous stand regarding the South had, however, as little impact on Northern politicians as it had in other spheres. The newly independent state had too many problems to overcome and was too preoccupied with internal intrigues and power games to become concerned about the South. Therefore, on the eve of 'Abbūd's military coup, the Northern-dominated committee on constitution decided to turn down Southern requests for federation and to propose instead the establishment of a united Muslim Sudan.

Under 'Abbūd, the SCP suffered repression and did not concern itself publicly with the South. It was only after the October 1964 civilian uprising and especially in connection with the round-table conference, that the SCP again came forth with its plans for the South. In February 1965, Maḥjūb reiterated communist support for national-regional autonomy.[38] This was followed by active communist participation in the round-table conference itself where a three-member delegation of the SCP, led by Maḥjūb, presented the party's programme to the delegates.[39] As analysed by the SCP, the roots of the problem were to be found in racial and geographical differences which, in turn, were exploited by imperialist interests and increased through northern negligence. The party also blamed Southern politicians for the dependence on foreign aid and influence and for their lack of a coherent political programme to solve their problem. Federation, stated the SCP, implied economic independence of the South, and this, because of the inherent weakness of the Southern economy, could only lead to renewed imperialist intervention. The solution therefore lay in regional autonomy which would include '... the setting up of a representative democratic council for the South ... and an executive council under its surveillance to run local affairs such as education, health, roads etc ...'[40] All other matters, such as finance, economic planning, foreign affairs and security, would remain the prerogative of the central government of the united Sudan. The SCP concluded by asking all the participants to unite around its programme which alone was capable of solving the impasse. It proposed to set up a National Development Board dealing with economic planning and at the same time establishing in the South an institute of higher learning in order to train Southern Sudanese for their future roles.

As mentioned, the round-table conference did not arrive at a unanimous decision. However, the proposals put forward by all northern parties were largely based on what the SCP had propagated ever since 1954.[41] In the end, the conference adjourned without reaching a decision, while the promise to convene another meeting after three months was soon forgotten. When the general elections of May 1965 brought the old traditional parties back to power, the prospect of a settlement became even more remote. The SCP was in the meantime fighting for its own legal status and could hardly concern itself with the problem of the South until the Numeiri coup in May 1969.

Numeiri's plan for regional autonomy for the South was announced on 9 June 1969. For the first time since independence, the Sudanese government adopted a definite plan for the solution of the issue.

The plan was based on the recommendations of the 1965 round-table conference and similar in many respects to the views propagated by the SCP.[42] Significantly, a Southern communist, Joseph Garrang, was appointed Minister of State for Southern Affairs and entrusted with executing the plan of regional autonomy. Among the steps suggested in order to put the programme into effect were: the training of Southern personnel for service in the South and for central government positions; the speedy execution of economic, social and cultural development projects in the South; and lastly, an amnesty to all Southern rebels who were urged 'to come home and participate in the execution of the whole programme'.[43] To implement these plans, the sum of £S2.7 million was budgeted in 1969/70 for special development in the South, mainly for agricultural projects. A regional economic planning board was set up at Juba, in the South, and several schools which had been destroyed during the civil war were being rebuilt. Already during its first year in office, Numeiri's government prided itself on promoting many Southerners to leading positions in the administration, the police, and the army, something that had never happened before.[44] But even Garrang had to admit that progress was slower than anticipated. This was due to lack of funds, low standards of performance and mainly to foreign intervention. Garrang singled out Israel, the United States, West Germany and the Catholic Church as the major culprits who smuggled large quantities of modern arms to the hands of the *Anya-Nya* in order to 'create another Biafra in the Sudan and, if possible, to transform the Southern question into an Afro-Arab conflict on a continental scale.'[45]

At the same time, both Garrang and Abel Alier, the Southern Minister of Supply and Internal Trade, tried to make contact with Southern leaders in exile in order to convince them to return to the Sudan and to take part in the establishment of regional autonomy. These attempts failed and both ministers reached the conclusion 'that the rebel leaders had no common platform. Some of them insist on secession and demand that a conference be held with Khartoum to work out practical measures leading to that goal. Others go further and say that they must shoot their way to the independence of the Southern Sudan and threaten to destroy any economic or social projects carried out in the South ...' In these circumstances, the government decided '... to go ahead with the execution of its Southern programme while keeping the door open for the rebels ...'[46]

While there was certainly no unity among Southern politicians, there seems to have been general agreement that Numeiri's plan for regional autonomy was another 'northern bluff'. In an interview with the BBC correspondent in Kampala, on March 19, 1970, B. A. Wanji, a leading Southern politician, stated that with 750,000 Southerners killed and 500,000 in exile, there could be no confidence in the sincerity of northern politicians. In fact, he stated, Numeiri only wanted '... to buy time and mislead African public opinion for committing more atrocities ...' Some Southern circles even accused Numeiri of planning a genocide of the Southerners with Soviet and Arab aid.[47]

Under Numeiri, the SCP's views on regional autonomy in the South had thus become official policy, while a leading member of the party's central committee had been given ministerial rank in order to execute it. The party was therefore in a unique position, for the first time in its history, to enact one of its major political programmes. The central committee decided to devote a special session of its meeting on October 8, 1970, to the matter.[48] Aside from the customary accusations against imperialism and its African and Sudanese agents, the central committee also criticised the execution of regional autonomy and offered what it regarded as constructive suggestions as to how its shortcomings might be overcome. Most important was the SCP's assertion that the government had not yet defined what regional autonomy really implied. More than a year had passed since the government had officially adopted regional autonomy as its solution for the South and yet nobody knew in what spheres the Southerners would be autonomous and how regional government would be institutionalised. Worse, no timetable had been set for effectuating the government's platform. '... It is quite obvious,' reported the central committee, 'that Southern confidence cannot be gained without a clear plan of action and a well-defined time-table.'[49] The SCP further criticised the inadequate funds allocated to development projects in the South and stated that even those were completed too slowly. Each ministry had certain responsibilities in the South and these were, as alleged by the central committee, always the last on their list of priorities. The budget for and supervision of Southern development projects should be concentrated under the Ministry for Southern Affairs. But the central committee also accused the government of attempting to slow down the fulfilment of its promises on purpose. The officer-politicians were said to be prisoners of their petit-bourgeois background which, combined with their chauvinism, made them view legitimate steps towards autonomy as leading to separatism. Moreover, having accepted the communist programme and having appointed a communist leader to put it into practice, the government now feared that a successful regional autonomy would only strengthen communism in the South. The SCP claimed in effect that certain reactionary elements, hiding behind the name *al-Qawmiyūn al-'Arab* (the Arab nationalists), were doing everything in their power to undermine the democratic movement in the South, with the active co-operation of Southern opportunist elements. The central committee ended its session with a number of resolutions aimed at overcoming the obstacles mentioned above. Most dealt with increased propaganda, both in the North and the South, for a better understanding of regional autonomy, whereas others specified measures to be undertaken by the SCP in order to strengthen 'revolutionary democrats' and trade unions in the Southern regions.

The anti-communist measures which Numeiri applied with increasing force after November 1970, brought about a much stronger criticism of his Southern policy by the SCP. In fact, the South became one of the major issues in the so-called communist coup of July 1971. Hāshim al-'Aṭā' accused Numeiri's régime of failing to bring about regional autonomy in the South and denounced the government for its ambiguous attitude towards it. But, in reality, negotiations between Numeiri's government and Southern politicians, including *Anya-Nya* leaders, started already in August 1971, and by January 1972 agreement was well under way.[50] On February 28, 1972 the 'Addis-Ababa Agreement on the problem of South Sudan' was signed, and on March 3, 1972 Numeiri was able to broadcast his success over Radio Omdurmān.

## THE COMMUNISTS AND THE MILITARY

The political and ideological strife within the SCP which came into the open in 1969 and brought about the party's split in the following year, had its origins in the period following the October 1964 civilian uprising. The communist hey-day which had started with the October revolution and had reached its abrupt end in February 1965, forced the SCP to take stock and to try to assess the causes of its declining fortunes. Moreover, the legal status which the SCP had enjoyed in 1964/65, for the first time since its foundation, was probably partly responsible for a general loosening in the party's discipline and the decreasing authority of its historical leadership, most notably that of 'Abd al-Khāliq Maḥjūb. This leadership therefore initiated a thorough debate in which it proposed a number of questions the replies to which were in a way detrimental to the SCP's future. Most important among them was the entire future course of communism in the Sudan and whether or not its prospects depended on co-operation with the 'revolutionary forces' within the army.

In part, these questions were already treated in January 1965 in 'Abd al-Khāliq Maḥjūb's report to the central committee where he emphasised the following points:[51]

a) The revolutionary movement was unarmed and had no close contacts with the revolutionary forces within the army. Consequently, the army was in a position to use its strength and to force the entrance of the traditionalist and reactionary forces into the government, as it actually did in February 1965.
b) Since there was no unity among the democratic forces during the revolution, the working class was unable to provide the essential revolutionary centre.
c) The revolutionary forces were not admitted into the constituent assembly and had failed to force a change in the old electorial system. The SCP's demand of increased representation of 'the advanced sections of the people (the workers, organised peasants, progressive-minded intellectuals) ...' was disregarded. Thereby the traditionalist reactionary forces made sure that they would secure a majority in the forthcoming elections.

In general, however, Maḥjūb's report sounded optimistic. He believed in the SCP's chances to rally the broad masses of workers and peasants to its flag. He proposed new ways for organising the peasants, stating that the SCP should pay special attention to the religious beliefs of the rural population and, especially, the Anṣār, in order not to alienate them.

By February 1965, however, it had become abundantly clear that the SCP, had no chance of forcing a revision of the election law or of postponing the elections. It therefore branded the elections as anti-democratic and in its memorandum of 18 February, 1965, the central committee stated '... that elections should not be viewed as an aim in itself, but as a means of developing democracy ...' The 1965 elections were, as described by the SCP, both anti-democratic and opposed to the nationalist interests of the country. Their sole objective was allegedly the defeat of the revolutionary forces, thereby reversing the country to the pre-1958 period when a minority of imperialist agents ruled the Sudan through its traditionalist parties.[52]

What could one conclude from the set-back suffered by the SCP, between October 1964 and May 1965? The major conclusion drawn by those who later led the anti-Maḥjūb faction was that a successful revolution in the Sudan could only take place with the active and decisive participation of the army. This was based on the central committee's reasoning, as stated in Maḥjūb's report quoted above, that the senior army officers had forced the re-entrance of the traditional-reactionary forces into the political arena.[53] Yet Maḥjūb himself, while admitting the importance of the progressive sections of the army within the revolutionary camp, declined to give them a leading role and viewed an army-led revolution as just another military coup. When asked about the prospects of socialism in the Sudan, Maḥjūb stated that they depended on '... gradually transforming the people's social conditions. The people should take an increasing part in government. The state machinery should be democratised and all working people united ...'[54] According to his opponents within the SCP, Maḥjūb in fact betrayed the communist cause when he supported Nasser's liquidating the Egyptian CP in 1965. They claimed that while Maḥjūb believed in a broad front of socialist forces, he was in fact preparing the ground for the liquidation of the SCP as proved by the foundation of the Socialist party in January 1967. A statement issued on January 16, 1968 by the 'Revolutionary Trend' of the SCP accused Maḥjūb of collaborating with semi-feudal elements and of advocating national unity instead of class struggle as a peaceful way for achieving socialism.[55] In line with these principles Maḥjūb accepted the government's decision to dissolve the SCP and even went as far as to form an alliance with al-Ṣādiq al-Mahdī in 1968, promising him the full support of the SCP should al-Ṣādiq succeed in his struggle against the Umma-NUP coalition.[56] In order to strengthen this new partnership, Maḥjūb, so his opponents claimed, closed down the SCP's Marxist printing shop, disbanded the Communist Women's League and did everything possible in order not to antagonise his traditionalist friends.[57]

It would be interesting to know whether the so-called 'Revolutionary trend' was an extension of the pro-Chinese 'Revolutionary leadership' which was expelled from the SCP in 1964–65 and appeared soon after at the 5th Congress of the Albanian Workers' Party as 'The Communist Revolutionary Party of the Sudan'. There is, however, a definite similarity in the charges made by both groups against the SCP, branding it as a 'revisionist' movement.

Most of these charges seem to be either exaggerated or malicious. Maḥjūb, throughout the second parliamentary period in the years 1964/69, attempted to build the broad popular front in which he believed and to reconcile religious and traditional elements in order to succeed. One cannot discern, however, any sign pointing toward his willingness to liquidate the SCP. It is true that again and again Maḥjūb and his supporters advocated associating with workers, farmers, intellectuals and the nationalist anti-imperialist bourgeoisie, only in order to advance the cause of socialism. Yet he always regarded an independent SCP as the essential revolutionary centre without which the partnership would be unable to function.[58]

It would probably be true to conclude that the most important issue to cause the split of the SCP since 1966 was the role of the army within the revolutionary forces. While the opposition inside the central committee was ready to grant the 'revolutionary forces' within the army a leading role in the forthcoming struggle, Maḥjūb and the majority of the SCP leadership opposed this view and would grant the army a subsidiary role only in the revolution which would be led by the working class.

What were the chances of communism in these conditions? Maḥjūb's opponents maintained that his doctrinaire views led him to revisionism. His concept of a communist-led national-democratic revolution seemed unrealistic to them in the conditions prevailing in the Sudan in the 1960s. Yet instead of relying on the revolutionary potential of the 'Free Officers' movement, Maḥjūb, according to his critics, opted for the Anṣār who, he believed, could be disengaged from their traditional leaders. His close relations with al-Ṣādiq al-Mahdī between 1965–1968 were based on this conception. He regarded the Oxford-educated al-Ṣādiq as heralding a more progressive trend within his sect, despite his pronounced anti-communist declarations. The opposition viewed this policy as being responsible for the weakening of the party in all its traditional strongholds, so much so that in 1971 it was no stronger than it had been on the eve of independence.[59]

The events of 1969 proved to be crucial in the SCP's stand vis-à-vis the army and consequently brought about the party's final split. In April of that year, when the Umma party re-united, the hopes Maḥjūb had pinned on the more progressive elements within the Anṣār had vanished. At the gathering of communist leaders in Moscow, which was called in 1969 to deal with the Sino-Soviet conflict, Maḥjūb stressed that without military backing and the support of the socialist camp, no revolution could succeed in the Sudan. His thesis was based on the following three premises: first, the dominance of western imperialism in the Sudan's economy; second, the enormous strength of the traditionalist counter-revolutionary forces; and third, the factional divisions between North and South, East and West, which were exploited both by the imperialists and their Sudanese reactionary agents. Therefore, a successful revolution depended first and foremost on a strong organisation of the democratic-revolutionary forces, who, with the backing of the revolutionary elements within the army as well as those of the socialist camp, could overcome the existing economic and social obstacles. To start a revolution with only the army ready to act would be a guaranteed failure.[60]

Matters came to a head during the March 1969 meeting of the central committee, only two months before the Numeiri coup. The discussion centred around the political situation in the Sudan and whether the country was ripe for revolution. Maḥjūb and the majority of the central committee believed that a popular revolution was at that stage impossible. If the 'Free Officers' should try to seize power their action would amount to no more than a military coup which would only serve the interests of the middle class. Even on 25 May 1969, the very day Numeiri assumed power, the SCP explained to its members that the military coup was not the revolution the party had been working for. The new rulers belonged to the petty bourgeoisie and the SCP would support them only in order to help them develop their movement into a popular revolution.[61]

Maḥjūb expressed similar views when he addressed the SCP's cadres conference in February 1970. He insisted that neither the 'Free Officers' coup in Egypt in 1952 nor that of the Sudan seventeen years later were revolutions. The fact that the leaders of these coups had progressive views and declared their revolutionary intentions could not transform these coups into revolutions. Moreover, Maḥjūb insisted that the army did not constitute a social class and for that reason its progressive sections could join the democratic forces individually but not as a distinct group.[62] These views were adopted by the SCP's central committee on 8 October 1970, and were from then onwards binding on all sections of the party. The fact that Numeiri's régime was not revolutionary and consisted only of the progressive section of the lower middle class was again underlined. Hence the SCP, while stressing the transitory nature of the régime, was called upon to use its full impact in order to guide the present rulers along the revolutionary path. It would present the military with a plan for a democratic revolution and at the same time deepen the revolutionary consciousness among the masses of toilers who alone could lead the country from the present stage towards real revolution.[63] The military rulers were accepted as a progressive and essential ally, but were not 'allowed' any leading role.

It is therefore rather understandable why Numeiri, backed by the anti-Maḥjūb faction which had left the SCP following the October session of the central committee, launched his first all-out attack against the communists in November 1970, one month after the central committee had decided to back Maḥjūb. It is also abundantly clear that the split within the SCP, including its leadership, had become final and that the pro-Numeiri faction had decided to back the régime in its actions against Maḥjūb and his supporters. By October 1970, the split within the party had been institutionalised by the anti-Maḥjūb faction. The leaders of this faction held several meetings in Khartoum and started to collect party dues from its supporters. They even printed anti-SCP propaganda on circulars and distributed them throughout the country.[64] On 10 October 1970 twelve members of the central committee published a declaration accusing Maḥjūb of dictatorship and of adopting a revisionist line. They demanded that Maḥjūb be replaced and a specially elected preparatory committee be set up for the party's fifth conference. The signatories included 'Umar Muṣṭafā al-Makkī, Mu'āwiya Ibrāhīm, Aḥmad Sulaymān and notably al-Amīn Muḥammad al-Amīn, president of the Jazīra tenants' union. Thus the year which had started with an attempt to oust Maḥjūb from his position as secretary-general, ended with his victory and with the de facto existence of two communist parties in the Sudan.

## FUTURE PROSPECTS

The preceding study indicates that while communism never succeeded in becoming a major force in the Sudan, its impact on Sudanese politics was nonetheless considerable especially during periods of crisis. This was due to three main reasons. Firstly, the penetration of the SCP into the most important sectors of Sudanese society: the cotton growers, the railway workers and the intelligentsia, enabled the party to become an effective pressure group despite its relatively small numbers. Secondly, the SCP provided the only consistent alternative to the sectarian and factional divisions which harassed Sudanese politics ever since independence. Consequently many of the intelligentsia joined the SCP in order to express their opposition to sectarianism rather than out of ideological convictions. Lastly, the leadership of the SCP, since 'Abd al-Khāliq Maḥjūb became secretary-general, was probably the most capable leadership of any communist party in the region. Its flexible attitude towards religion, nationalism, Arab unity, etc., enabled the party to retain its freedom of action, at least partly, during the long periods in which it was illegal. Yet, despite this flexibility, which at times bordered on opportunism, the party remained consistent in its fight against sectarian politics and factional splits and was the only political force which advocated regional autonomy for the South ever since independence. Moreover, the party's attempts to become part of a broader national-democratic front were never allowed to threaten its independence.

The final split between Maḥjūb and some of his erstwhile colleagues in 1970 was caused by the latters' belief that the SCP could play a leading role within the Sudanese Socialist Union, even if it had to forego its organisational independence. It was on this issue that the ever flexible Maḥjūb was unwilling to compromise. He regarded the party's continued independent existence, providing the revolutionary centre, as the sole guarantee for the future of communism in the Sudan. For this both Maḥjūb and some of his colleagues paid with their lives and the SCP suffered a severe setback. But judging by the virtual disappearance from the political scene of those communist leaders who had opposed Maḥjūb and supported Numeiri, one would probably be justified in concluding that Maḥjūb was right in opposing what he regarded as the voluntary suicide of the SCP.

While it is true to state that the SCP suffered a severe setback in the wake of the July 1971 coup, it would be premature to draw any definite conclusions regarding its prospects in the future. The emergence of a new communist leadership and its activities since 1971, despite severe repression, tend to prove that Numeiri has so far failed to realize his aim of annihilating the SCP. Communist fortunes will be largely determined by the continuation of military rule and by the measure of the régime's success. Should Numeiri remain in power until the politicians of the old guard disappear, the Anṣār and the Khatmiyya may be politically weakened to such an extent that sectarianism will not be able to re-appear on the political scene as a major force. This in turn might weaken the chances of communism as many of those who supported it in the past were anti-sectarianists whose only reason for joining the SCP was its consistent fight against the dominant position of the Anṣār and the Khatmiyya.

The same may apply to the accommodation which Numeiri has reached with the South. Many of the erstwhile supporters of the SCP, from within the intelligentsia, were drawn to the party because of its Southern policy. Should regional autonomy lead to permanent peace between North and South within a united Sudan, the SCP might lose another section of its supporters.

Two major problems will however continue to beset the Sudan in the foreseeable future: its economic weakness and its geopolitical position. Since 1971 Numeiri has made a major effort in order to attract Western capital to the Sudan. This policy is beginning to bear fruit and may lead to strong economic and political ties between the Sudan, Western Europe and the United States. In due course this may enable the SCP to regain some of its influence both within the new industrial workers and the modernised section of Sudanese farmers. Furthermore, the rapidly growing intelligentsia which under military rule has practically no political power, might seek communist support in order to further its political aims.

In conclusion the prospects of communism in the Sudan do not seem too bright. It appears that at the very best the SCP may hope to regain its previous strength. A more balanced view, however, might claim that the hey-day of communism in the Sudan has passed and that another few years of military rule will strengthen the one-party-system and thus spoil the chances of communism in the foreseeable future.

CHAPTER 5

# Documents Published by the Sudanese Communist Party

## A. Announcement of the Political Bureau of the Sudanese C.P. regarding the 'Current Situation of the Arabs'*.

1. ... The Zionist state, which has been established through the aid and support of imperialist forces, does not express the Jewish right of self-determination, because the Jews are not a nationality which expresses itself through the foundation of a separate state. Moreover, the establishment of a Zionist state, based on a wrong interpretation of the right of self-determination, has caused damage to the revolutionary front, which opposes world imperialism. The actions of that state have been aimed against the development of the Arab national liberation movement, which has played an important role among the toiling peoples opposing world imperialism. At the same time that [Zionist] state is undermining the African national liberation movement. To this, one should add the damage caused by world Zionism to the international movement of the working class and to the Socialist bloc.

Hence, the victory of the Arab national liberation movement over that state and the establishment of a democratic, progressive state in Palestine on the ruins of the Zionist class-régime [*sic.*], should be regarded as a victory of the revolutionary-front which is opposed to world imperialism. Based on this class-position [*sic.*] we call for a struggle against the Zionist state and for the self-determination of the toiling masses of Palestinians whose aim it is

* Published on August 18, 1970; translated from Maṭar, pp. 186–90. The Announcement was made following the acceptance of the Rogers Plan by Egypt and Jordan.

to establish a democratic progressive state. We bear this aim in our minds as we confront the problems faced by the Arab revolutionary movement, including the American proposals and the security council resolution [242].

2. The Arab-Israeli conflict is in reality a struggle between the Arab national liberation movement and the Imperialist-Zionist front. Based on that assumption one should define accurately [both] the forces of that Arab movement and of its enemies.

The forces of the Arab national liberation movement consist, largely, of the masses of peasants and the working class, the progressive-nationalist sections of the petite-bourgeoisie and all other elements who oppose imperialism and strive for progress. While the enemies of that movement are represented by world imperialism, Zionism and the forces of feudalism and the bourgeoisie who tend towards imperialism.

The forces of the Palestinian revolution, who seriously fight against the Zionist state, the ally of world imperialism, are part of those sections and social groups which make up the Arab national liberation movement.

The Arab national liberation movement, including the Palestinian revolution, is part and parcel of the world national liberation movement. Based on that understanding, the permanent and loyal allies of that movement are the Socialist camp and the international movement of the working class. The more numerous and cumbersome the problems facing the Arab national liberation movement become, the more absurd it is to solve these problems, in a way favourable to the Arab peoples, without the solid alliance of the Socialist-camp and the international movement of the working class.

3. The [Arab] national liberation movement is fighting its enemies on several fronts and not on one front. Parts of the Arab masses are still struggling for their national independence, others are fighting against reactionary régimes who are secretly cooperating with imperialism, while a third group is struggling for a non-imperialist path of development and the successful completion of the democratic revolution etc ... [*sic.*]. The Arab peoples are called upon to struggle resolutely on all fronts and every victory achieved in one front strengthens these peoples and weakens the positions of the enemies of the Arab revolution.

In this struggle, which has been going on for many years, this movement has selected its battle weapons, upon the efficiency of which the future of the movement depends. There exist the Arab progressive régimes which confront imperialism in the region; there is the working-class movement in the Arab states and its communist organisations; there are the democratic-revolutionary organisations which play an important role in the struggle against imperialism and for progress; there are the armed forces of the Palestinian revolution etc ... [*sic*.]. The forging of these weapons and the increase of their efficiency are of importance in the struggle of the Arab peoples for a solution of the various problems confronting them.

4. In June 1967 the Arab national liberation movement faced a new situation as a result of the Zionist-Imperialist victory. The Zionist state expanded its borders on the territories of two progressive Arab states namely Syria and the United Arab Republic, and succeeded in conquering all the Palestinian territories. This situation weakened these two states [Syria and the UAR] militarily, politically and economically and in turn affected the whole Arab national liberation movement.

Thus a new burden was cast upon the movement of the Arab peoples and that is the liberation of the Arab territories which were conquered by the Zionist state as a result of its military victory in June 1967. The liberation of these territories from the conquest will help to strengthen the progressive régimes in both Syria and Egypt and will also abolish the conquest of Palestinian Arab land [*sic*.].

5. The Arab peoples, with the active support of the Socialist camp and especially of the Soviet Union, have succeeded in avoiding the downfall of the progressive nationalist régimes, which was the aim of the aggression. This affected the Arab revolutionary movement favourably. At the same time a wave of anger passed among the Arab masses against American imperialism whose true aims became clear to these masses, and in turn brought about important changes in the temperament of the Arab revolutionary masses. Hence, it was no accident that the reactionary régimes of both the Sudan and Libya were overthrown and that the People's Republic of Yemen continued its development along the revolutionary democratic path, despite the obstacles. Simultaneously, there developed mutual links between large sections of the [Arab] national liberation movement

and the Socialist-camp, which put the proposal of an alliance between them on the agenda.

These developments, which cannot be stopped by American imperialism as long as it supports the Israeli position, herald the strengthening of the Arab revolutionary forces and at the same time threaten the repugnant American exploitation, from which the masses suffer, especially in the oil-producing regions.

The American imperialists are putting forward the Rogers Plan for the execution of the Security Council Resolution of November 1967, in order to stop these developments and to prevent them from reaching their ultimate goal.

6. Our position regarding the Rogers Plan for the execution of the Security Council resolution is determined by the general interests of the Arab national liberation movement. To begin with, we adhere to the resolutions of the fourth congress of our party regarding solutions through peaceful and military means. As the fourth congress determined three principles regarding our struggle within the Arab-Israel conflict:

(a) Elimination of the Zionist conquest of Arab territories resulting from the June 1967 war, through all political and military means.

(b) Strengthening the progressive Arab régimes and uniting the forces of the Arab revolution.

(c) Supporting the Palestinian revolution and strengthening it, for the return of the Palestinian land [and the establishment of] a progressive democratic state.

Hence, we do not oppose negotiations regarding the Security Council resolution and we do not oppose political and diplomatic action.

On the other hand, we view the Security Council resolution as harmful to two important principles of the Arab revolution. First, the fact that Israel has conquered some of the territories of the progressive régimes, in addition to her conquest of the Palestinian land [the West Bank]; and second, the fact that the aims of the Palestinian revolution cannot be achieved only through the liberation of the territories conquered after June 1967, but also must contain the right of self-determination of the Palestinian people through the establishment of a progressive democratic Palestinian state on the ruins of the Zionist state.

The Security Council resolution regarding Israeli withdrawal from the territories conquered in June 1967 will certainly strengthen the Arab national liberation movement: firstly, it strengthens the position of two progressive Arab states and enables the development of these two régimes and the correction of certain negative aspects from which they suffer. The Zionist conquest without doubt affects negatively the economic development and prevents the toiling masses from enjoying the fruits of their labour and efforts. It also stops any struggle leading to fundamental reforms within these régimes which would tend to push them forwards towards the decisive completion of their democratic revolutionary stage. The introduction of these reforms has become an urgent matter for the development of the revolution in these countries and for the current struggle against world imperialism and Zionism. Secondly, it helps liberate the West Bank, which is Palestinian land, and enables the forces of the Palestinian revolution to gain from it politically and militarily in its struggle for the achievement of its aims. Thirdly, it places the problem of the Arab refugee nation [*sic.*] in a position from which the Palestinian revolution can benefit and from which it can broaden the framework of its struggle in order to weaken the Zionist class entity [*sic.*].

But when the Security Council resolution provides for the recognition of the State of Israel:

(a) It recognises the principle of benefiting through aggression and enables the artificial Zionist state concerned to gain profits.

(b) It weakens the ability of the Palestinian revolution to move and act freely in order to realise its just aims. And the most dangerous aspect in this respect is that it enables the reactionary forces in Jordan to benefit from the Security Council resolution by crushing the Palestinian revolutionary organisations. Similarly, these [reactionary] forces in Lebanon will be able to do the same.

We therefore reject Israel's right to benefit through its aggression and that it ought to be granted recognition, thereby obstructing the development of the forces of the Palestinian revolution.

In order that this will not happen, it is important in the present circumstances for all the forces of the Arab revolution to unite and take up a unanimous position aiming at:

(a) Strengthening the Palestinian revolutionary organisations and protecting them, by means of a 'fortified wall' [*sic.*], from any reactionary attack and helping them, in a fraternal manner, in order to strengthen their ties with the Arab masses so as not to be isolated from them during this important change in the Arab revolutionary movement.
(b) Non-recognition of Israel because of the damage that such recognition would cause the Palestinian revolution and the bulk of the Arab national liberation movement.
(c) A firm stand against reactionary attempts to adorn American imperialism in our region and to sabotage the mass-movement which is fighting it stubbornly and unyieldingly. For American imperialism is the first and most consistent enemy of the Arab national liberation movement.

The disunity amongst these forces [of the Arab revolution], based on the struggle between the régimes and the progressive organisations in the region, is a major disaster to the movement of the Arab peoples. For the victory of the Palestinian revolution or the liberation of the territories conquered since June 1967, cannot be achieved through the destruction of one progressive Arab régime or another. It will not be won on the ruins of the United Arab Republic or of the Arab Syrian Republic. For the progressive Arab régimes, despite their deficiencies and negative aspects, are the tools of the Arab masses in their battle against imperialism and Zionism.

The revolutionary movement in our country is called upon to play a sublime role in all the complicated problems which confront us and especially regarding the problem of uniting the forces of the Arab revolution so that American imperialist activities will not disband them and weaken them. By means of our ideological clarity and our ability to act among the masses, together with all the progressive trends which oppose imperialism in the Arab region, we shall be able to play this role successfully.

## B. When The Arab Nationalists Become Active.*

... The South is, as is known, the weakest link of our revolutionary defence. We are in competition with world imperialism especially since Abā† when the South became the main focus of world imperialism and Zionism. Since September 1969, the imperialists and the Israelis have started to pour in arms via the frontiers of Ethiopia and Uganda. The bulk of these arms arrive by air ... These weapons are of various kinds and include Soviet-made small anti-aircraft guns arriving from Israel, automatic machine guns and other guns from Britain, as well as arms produced in America and Western Germany ...

The *Anya-Nya*‡ has started since the beginning of this year to increase its activity on the east bank of the Nile in the Equatorial province, it has also spread towards the west bank on the Ethiopian borders. There are also Israeli officers and white mercenaries to train the rebels. The *Anya-Nya* has blown up several vehicles by the use of mines and has started to attack distant regions and police stations as well as blowing up bridges with dynamite and [other] explosives (TNT).

In the sphere of propaganda, the imperialists have launched a major offensive, both in Europe and Africa, by means of the press, radio and television. In this propaganda they emphasise three things: firstly, they describe the southern problem as a racial war, with the aim of gaining African support for the *Anya-Nya*, so as to turn the problem into a struggle between the Arabs and black Africa. To achieve this aim they spread the rebels' publications claiming that Egyptian and Libyan forces are participating in the bombing of Southern villages from Russian-made Migs. Secondly, they describe the rebels as if they were a large organised force having its own government and conducting schools in the South. Their aim in this is to prepare world public opinion to agree to recognise this government officially.

* From the deliberations of the Central Committee of the SCP, Khartoum, October 8 1970; translated from Maṭar, pp. 169–75.

† Refers to March 1970, when an uprising of the Anṣār on Abā Island was crushed by government troops. Government sources claimed Imperialist and Zionist involvement in the revolt.

‡ The *Anya-Nya*, the military arm of the Southern rebellion, started its operations in September 1963.

Thirdly, they describe the Southern citizens as being neglected and suffering from hunger.

It should be noted that this propaganda embraces the whole of Western Europe, while the centres of activity are in London, Italy, Western Germany and the Scandinavian states, and the rebels have opened their offices in these centres.

As far as Africa is concerned, Ethiopia is the secret centre for arms supply, while Uganda provides the centre for the rebels' political activities. It should be added that not a single African government or organisation has declared its official support for the Sudan in its struggle for unity, the reason being that the real state of affairs in our country is unclear to them or that they secretly support the rebels. It is also noteworthy that Uganda's position differs from that of other Central African states, in that she received the political delegation sent to her with pronounced coldness.

As far as the rebels are concerned it seems that they have united their ranks through disbanding their governments and setting up the so-called national forces of the *Anya-Nya* under the command of the ex-army officers: Lago, Abu John and Tafnek.

From this situation we may draw the following conclusions:

1. The imperialists attempt to create a second Biafra in the South with the aim of overthrowing the revolutionary régime which exists in the state.
2. They hope to help the situation develop into an Arab-African conflict by creating enormous pressure on the government in the South, which will force it to seek the assistance of the friendly Arab states, which in turn might provoke the African states and make them join the side opposing us.
3. There exists the possibility that the imperialists will create such pressure in the South that it will lead to the abandonment of the announced programme [of regional autonomy] or to its indefinite postponement.

This situation should be dealt with in various ways, the most important of which is the introduction of a new diplomacy which will make the African states, bordering on us, have a vested interest in our unity. It is also important to increase the efforts aimed at strengthening the anti-imperialist forces in the South.

But above all, there is no escape from increasing the genuine efforts to execute the announced programme.

There are three problems that ought to be discussed, which are:

1. The political aspect of regional-autonomous government.
2. The aspect of political and social development.
3. The democratic movement.

The Southerners ought to know, in general terms, the form of regional-autonomous government which they are about to achieve and it is also important that they learn the target date on which the organs of this government will start functioning. Our party feels that the government should set up a committee consisting [of members] of the Southern intelligentsia and the democratic organisations, in order to deliberate the type of regional-autonomous government most suitable, and fixing the minimum [time?] required, for the institutions of that Government [to be set up?]. Following these deliberations the government should be in a position to provide an agreed plan of action based on a definite time-table.

Our point of view was accepted by a special ministerial committee which was set up, for this purpose, in December 1969. However, despite this, no steps have been taken to execute what was agreed upon. It is self-evident that the full confidence of the Southerners cannot be gained except by means of a clear plan of action and a well-defined time-table. On the other hand, to leave these matters without definition will only create a bad atmosphere and lack of confidence and this will strengthen the separatist forces.

In addition, our party is facing important theoretical problems, which require attention, the first of which is an examination of the development of the enterprises in the South and their usefulness in the future.

This problem is the central issue in the solution of the Southern problem. A lot of attention has already been drawn to it through the June 1970 declaration. This declaration put forward the proposal of allocating a special budget for the South and the establishment of a planning committee. It also brought up the question of training cadres of Southerners. But despite this, the problem has not received the same attention in its execution as it had in the June declaration. No special development budget for the South was proposed, which means that the planning committee which has been set up is limited in its activities as it is unable to finance the enterprises which it proposes. The allocation of funds to the South remains a prerogative of the various ministries who generally put it at the bottom of their lists of proposals.

As a result of these factors, the South has received not more than £2.7 million namely, some eight per cent of the 1969/70 budget, and in the current development plan the Southern share is still eight per cent of the whole plan (£S12m.).

In addition, the major problem is that of execution which is shared by numerous authorities and ministries without any coordination or inspection. Owing to this terrible weakness of the executive power, the execution of the majority of enterprises in the South will remain as at present, unless they are put under one authority which will coordinate them and inspect their execution. The party's proposal in this connection is to grant the Minister of Southern Affairs full executive powers by placing under his authority the main spheres of production and of the services. These are: agriculture, forestry, animal husbandry, cooperatives [?], health, public works and education. Only in this way will it be possible to coordinate between the various decisions and to enforce them. Those heading the different units will be able to determine their budgets and to receive the required capital at once. Only in this way will the so-called 'special development budget' have any real meaning.

The attempts to realise this request have failed, as the government regards the concentration of authority, to such a degree, as leading to separation [between South and North]. Thus a compromise was reached whereby the coordinating council for the South was set up. But this step, despite its importance, is insufficient as this council has no authority over the other ministries and it cannot force them to act. Nonetheless, should the council be given full authority over the regional officials who belong to the departments and ministries from which it is composed, and if it [the council] would be granted full authority over the development budget in the South, this would constitute a big step forward ...

*The obstacles which confront the execution of the programme of the South*

In order to overcome the main obstacles that confront the execution of the programme for the South it is important that we agree upon the analysis of the circumstances in which the programme is to be executed. For if we will not clarify these circumstances and explain them to our comrades in the South they are bound to despair. What then are these circumstances?

1. The democratic programme for the South is being executed under different conditions from those we had hoped for, in that it is not being carried through under the rule of the working class but under the rule of elements of the revolutionary democrats belonging to the petit-bourgeoisie.

These elements, despite the fact that they have accepted the democratic programme for the solution of the problem of the South, are hesitant in executing it because they have not grasped the historical necessity for this solution. Hence we see these elements imprisoned by their class consciousness which expresses itself in exaggerated patriotism and makes them see the danger of separation in everything, as a result of that exaggeration. This fear of separation, from which these elements suffer, is further strengthened through the external-reactionary pressure of the bureaucracy and the right-wing of the officers. This is the only explanation for their refusal to grant the executive powers to the Ministry of the South, which are required for speeding up the establishment of the enterprises decided upon for the South. This also explains the hesitation regarding the recommendation of the Council of Ministers which had called for the establishment of a council which will deliberate the structure and contents of regional autonomic rule and decide upon a time-table for its execution.

2. The intensive class struggle in the country is an additional negative aspect which is being manifested through the anti-communist trend of the ruling right-wing revolutionary democrats. The aim of this trend is to cause the failure of the democratic and communist ministers. Based on this assumption we see that they [the ruling right wing] fear the role of the Minister of State for Southern Affairs*, and the general situation

* The Southern communist leader, Joseph Garrang.

which the communists will face in the South should the Minister succeed in his task. But primarily these groups fear the growth of the democratic movements in the South and therefore we can observe them as they are seeking a foothold within that movement. Lately the so-called Arab Nationalists (*al-Qaummiyyūn al-'Arab*) have initiated the establishment of a political base of activities among the Southerners. They have started cautiously and quietly to found an alliance between themselves and certain opportunist elements belonging to the Southern intelligentsia, as well as with known separatist elements from among the students of the University of Khartoum. The aim in all this is to set up an alternative mass-movement in order to force the retreat of the democratic movement. These right-wing elements are exploiting the unprincipled methods which have become part of the internal struggle within our party, such as the leaking out of reports of the political bureau, the central committee and other institutions of the party.

3. Similarly, the democratic programme for the solution of the Southern problem is being executed under conditions which are different from those which we had anticipated with regard to the development of the democratic movement. It is being executed, contrary to our expectations, in conditions of general weakness of the democratic movement. This is a negative factor of importance as, so far, we have not succeeded in mobilising the Southern masses for active participation in the execution of the programme, or for playing an active role in isolating the movement of the revolt [the *Anya-Nya*], or for denouncing the imperialist intervention. [Had we succeeded] this could have brought about the lessening of the fears of the revolutionary democrats ... and would have helped them overcome their uncertainty and their uneasiness.

The weakness of the democratic movement in the South means the continued existence of the chauvinistic trend in that region aiming to found a small nation (*umma*) in the South ... We also see that the petit-bourgeois intelligentsia in the South views regional autonomic rule in its liberal sense limiting it to constitutional forms and to [the filling of] top positions, etc ... [*sic*]. Therefore, we can see that they are playing a negative role in that they spread among the masses the urge for speed and the lack of patience, understanding and interest, which in turn strengthen the position of the separatist trends and of the imperialist conspiracies

and brings about additional suspicion and hesitance on the part of the government in the execution [of the Southern programme].
4. The fourth negative factor is the opposition of the bureaucracy to autonomous government. It is known that the local-government bureaucracy was opposed to democracy throughout its history. Today it opposes the programme of the South and though it pretends to play a paternal role within the democratic movement in effect it attempts to slow down its development. The same is true with regard to the bureaucracy of the police and the Ministry of Information which play a negative or even a reactionary role. So that the problem of the bureaucracy is a general one throughout the country.

It is self-evident that each one of these hazards can be overcome. Similarly, it is likely that the revolutionary democrats will accept our point of view if we shall continue our discussions with them and especially if the democratic movement in the South will be able to resist imperialism and separatism.

## PROPOSALS OF THE CENTRAL COMMITTEE FOR THE SOUTH

During the discussions about this report the central committee has adopted numerous proposals aimed at increasing the activities in the South under present circumstances:

1. The holding of broad discussions about the execution of the programme of the South, by means of seminars and of the press, as well as symposia of the intelligentsia, which might put forward proposals for action.
2. The immediate preparation of the conference of the South which will denounce the imperialist penetration and the activities of the *Anya-Nya*.
3. The holding of internal discussions between the party leadership and the revolutionary democrats.
4. The trade unions will aid the good elements within their membership to move to the South.
5. In addition to our task with regard to holding a conference in the South … we shall also hold a conference in the capital in which we will attempt to have active Southern participants and in which we will try to convince Northern masses about the importance of the programme for the democratic solution of the problem of the South.

6. Our members will make efforts in order to increase the interest taken by the democratic organisations in activities in the South. This [they will do] by defining responsibilities within these organisations for the achievement of this aim.
7. The trade unions will fulfil their duty in improving the working conditions and increasing the wages of the Southern workers ... and will continue the struggle for their equality with the northern workers.
8. The creation of conditions suitable for the defeat of the revolt by means of actions against the increasing imperialist conspiracies and the movements of the reactionaries in Africa. This depends on our African policy: our political and diplomatic activities in the African countries. We require the mobilisation of our diplomatic corps, its strengthening and the selection of the very best elements for service in our missions there.

It is also the duty of the democratic organisations to play their role in this sphere by means of their contacts with the democratic and progressive forces in the African countries as well as on the international arena in Europe and elsewhere, in order to counter the propaganda of both the imperialists and the *Anya-Nya*.

It is the duty of the respective organisations of our party, and especially of those who have immediate roles to play, to start executing these proposals and decisions of the Central Committee, and to prepare the necessary and suitable plans ...

The Central Committee of the Sudanese
Communist Party

October 8, 1970.

## C. To the Masses of the Sudanese People*

In the early morning of Monday, 16th November 1970, and after the declaration of a state of general alertness in the Armed Forces, a meeting of the Officers in Command of all Commands was held at Khartoum, and Siwa Nimeiri, [Numeiri] President of the Revolutionary Command Council (RCC) and Prime Minister summoned Lt. Col. Babiker El Nur, Major Farouk Osman Hamadalla and Major Hashim Mohd. El Atta. He conveyed to them the decision of the RCC on the relieving of them of their responsibilities, and their removal from their military and civil offices. A meeting of the Council of Ministers was then held at the HQ of the Armed Forces, and Siwa Nimeiri informed the Ministers of the decision of the RCC with regard to the dismissal of the three of its members, and the intention of initiating a purge within the Armed Forces, the Civil Service, and of the arrest of Sayed Abdel Khalig Mahgoub [Maḥjūb].

A communiqué of the RCC was broadcast, in which it was alleged that the decisions mentioned above were taken for the following reasons:

(1) Some elements who claim to be progressive are against the revolution and are creating doubts about the ability of the revolutionary vanguard i.e., the RCC to affect the necessary changes.

(2) The three dismissed members of the RCC have fallen under the influence of these destructive elements, and through these elements the secrets of the RCC have been made public.

(3) The removal of these three members is necessary at this stage where the Revolution intends to give to the people a full constitutional system.

The Central Committee does not think that these measures are so simple as the communiqué of the RCC attempts to portray. They are neither accidental nor sudden. They are in effect a crowning of the efforts of the rightist tendency which continued to exercise itself consistently in order to stop the advance of the

* Declaration of the Central Committee of the Sudanese Communist Party on the events of 16th November 1970; issued in Khartoum on November 16, 1970. (This document has been reprinted verbatim from the authorised translation, including names which have in many cases been misspelt.)

Sudanese revolution, which entered on a new stage after the 25th May, and to confine it to a reformist movement, instead of transforming it towards a wide, popular revolution, capable of completing the tasks of national democracy at this stage and to open the way towards a socialist future for our people.

These decisions are not 'regretted' events, as they are depicted in the communiqué of the RCC, but they are a continuation of the methods of putsch, which usually resorts to such methods in order to resolve differences between revolutionary sections, and in order to effect the liquidation of revolutionary elements within the armed forces. Such measures have led to terrible and disastrous results as can be learned from the experiences of many Arab and African countries, as well as from the experiences of many countries of the Third World bloc – the experiences of Syria and Iraq are manifold evidence of this fact.

These decisions were taken at the present time when the Arab revolution was suffering from an intensified imperialist and reactionary conspiratorial activity through the whole region and especially in the Southern part of our country. They were made at this time when all circumstances demonstrate that the attack launched in Jordan to liquidate the Palestine Resistance had as its aim to destroy the national revolutionary régimes in the area.

As to what was happening within our country, a large part of our people were anxiously considering the pact of Triple Alliance, which was not submitted to popular discussion so that the masses might express their will. The matter was made more obscure as a result of the official statements and those of the press, which helped to strengthen the belief of the masses that a plot is in process of being hatched, and a serious danger threatens the march of the Sudanese revolution and its democratic movement.

As far as the economic field is concerned, the revolutionary movement, in the vanguard of which is the Communist Party, has been exerting serious effort in cooperation with the Authority to improve the state of performance of the nationalised and confiscated corporations, which have been suffering from many drawbacks such as the faulty organisation and the weak administration which constitute a threat to their future. These corporations are in need of a reorganisation so as to ensure a better performance and a higher return to the benefit of the national income. The Communist Party and all the revolutionary forces have put the question of the 5 Years Plan at the head of the daily and urgent tasks, and a wide mass movement has been stirred up among the workers for this purpose.

Our people have not ceased to show their concern and anxiety as to the future of the revolution as a result of the high cost of living, the failure of the administrative methods taken to solve problems, the instability of prices and the anarchy of the market which led to the increased tightness of the financial situation. The Party, in cooperation with the trade union movement, continued to raise their practical proposals to the Authority for overcoming these difficulties and for depriving of strength the counter-revolutionary forces which are enhancing their activities from the chance to make use of the discontent of the masses in achieving their aims.

As a measure against the dangers of imperialist conspiracy in the South, the revolutionary forces have mobilised all their resources in an effort to create a democratic movement in that part of the country capable of having a firm grip on regional autonomy, maintaining the unity of the country, and shouldering part of the burden carried by the armed forces. The revolutionary forces have been and still are shouldering this task despite the difficulties created by the rightist and bureaucratic elements within the state machine in the South. These elements have never believed in the usefulness of the democratic solution of the Southern problem, but the Communist Party and revolutionary movement were capable of overcoming all those difficulties to assist the state power in the development of the revolution there.

It is at such times that the RCC has had to resort to the measures mentioned above, which mean only the weakening of an important part of the forces of the revolution. It is impossible for the state power to protect itself against the attacks of reaction and imperialism and to safeguard the forward march of the revolution without the support of these formidable revolutionary battalions. The description of the Communist Party and its honest leadership, which has been loyal to its country and its people, as 'destructive' can be met by the Party only by a flat rejection. It is a slander against our clear and long standing struggles in the service of the Sudanese revolution and in the service of our working people. It is an open invitation to the traditional forces to continue their activities overtly or covertly against the Communist Party. It is a stepping up of the spirit of anti-communism, which, as our people very well know, can be intelligently exploited by the imperialists and their accomplices to attack and liquidate national revolutions. Our people know very well the efforts exerted by the Communist Party to protect and strengthen the new régime by advocating, and organising the masses for the development of the revolution. Our people likewise know that the criticism levelled by the Communists against mistakes and negative aspects is made from a standpoint which has great concern for the interests of our country and people, a standpoint with great concern for the development of the revolution and the protection of the progressive state power.

The RCC knows of the serious studies submitted by the Communist Party to the state power on the nationalisation of banks and foreign trade, on the radical agrarian reform, on the liquidation of the tribal administration, on the indicators to the 5 Year Plan, etc. During the last few months the leadership of the Communist Party continued to submit numerous memoranda with a view to aiding the state power to march forward along the road of democratic revolution. Properly studied memoranda were submitted dealing with the question of safeguarding state power and the tasks and responsibilities of the state and the people in this respect. A memo on the situation in the South and the means of solving the problems which obstruct the implementation of the democratic solution there, a memorandum on the deterioration of the economic situation as manifested by the sufferings of the masses from the high cost of living due to the high prices and non-availability of some of the necessary commodities (were also submitted). A further manifestation of the deteriorating economic situation is the increase of the government debt to the central bank. Another memo was submitted dealing with our views on the National Charter and the problem of building the national democratic front. A memo giving our views and our objective criticism of the Triple Union, was submitted by us. It was customary to hand all these memos to each member of the RCC without exception, and the Secretary General of the Party, the staunch fighter Abdel Khalig Mahgoub, used to play a leading role in the preparation of these memos and handing of them to the RCC, and through all this he used to show absolute responsibility and great concern as to the future of the revolution, the people and the country.

Is it not strange that the RCC should accuse us of sabotage, arrest the General Secretary of our Party, and dismiss three members of the RCC whose role in the Free Officers Movement and in the existing régime is well known to our people? Is it not strange that the purging process should be extended to include the army officers who were fired from the service and imprisoned by the past reactionary régimes, while the rightist elements in the army who have been and still are trying to weaken the unity of the armed forces and to isolate them from the people are being retained to use their offices to exert more pressure on the state power time and again with the aim of arresting the progress of the revolution and transforming the armed forces into a privileged group. Evidence to support these statements is plentiful. It is sufficient to mention here what occurred in October 1969, just after Babker Awad Alla had delivered his speech in Berlin and the subsequent developments; what occurred at the celebration of the armed forces and President Nimeiri's address of 6th July, to the people; what occurred in the armoured car fleet force leading to the arrest and dismissal from service of a group of soldiers who contributed with the members of the RCC to the success of the military operation on the dawn of May 25th, 1969. What is happening today is a continuation of the rightist political line by the conservative elements which stand in opposition to the progress of the revolution and will not stop at this point but will continue to exert pressure sooner or later to bring about an absolute right-wing coup d'etat which will deprive our people not only of the victories achieved since 25th May 1969, but also of all the victories achieved since the attainment of independence and a reign of terror and oppression will be set up.

Our people have been regarding with concern and distrust the mounting activity of the Egyptian official organs in the Sudan, especially their Intelligence Service, which aims at strengthening the rightist trend and exercising its black methods in sabotaging the revolutionary movement in our country under the pretext of checking the communist influence. The unity of the National Security Organs and the reconsideration of the question of the mass organisations in the three countries are included in the Pact of the Triple Union.

The measures taken by the RCC are aimed at the liquidation of the left-trend and especially the Communist Party, aimed at the liquidation of the group of Free Officers in the Armed Forces, aimed at effecting changes in the leadership of the democratic organisations by expelling the Communists and seasoned democratic elements under the charge of sabotage so as to transform these organisations to mere appendages of the state power and its future national organisation, depriving them of their identity and their popular democratic features.

In taking these measures the state power was aided by the splitting elements which left the CP since last September 1970. It is these elements which continued to instigate the authority to take measures against the Communist Party under the allegation that the Party is hostile to the state power. The splitters went on disseminating their poison against the leadership of the Party and its General Secretary. They did not scruple to voice accusations and lies for the purpose of concealing the essence of the political struggle which took place in the Party since 25th May on the nature of the existing régime and the role of the CP and the revolutionary movement in strengthening it and the method to do this so as to transform the military victory of 25th May to a popular revolution, a revolution blessed with the organised and conscious support of the masses to safeguard it against the dangers of coup d'etats and liquidations which exhaust the revolutionary forces and leave the door wide open to the triumph of reaction.

These splitting elements are continuing to conduct their hostile activity and propaganda against the Party. They do not bother to conceal their hatred (of it) after the rejection by the majority of the CP of their ideas, ideas which are aimed at the liquidation of the Party and its transformation into an appendage of the state power. They did not conceal during the past few weeks their knowledge of the decisions taken by the RCC, but exploited them to threaten and to blackmail – justifying their behaviour by their allegations that the Party is pursuing a conservative extremist line which obstructs the progress of the revolution. These elements, which are being employed in the national security organs, do not even shrink from taking part in the registering of the names of communists as a step towards arresting them.

Valiant people of our country – the Sudanese revolution is

faced with serious internal and external dangers, and the measures taken by the RCC are nothing but an indication of the pursuit of a line of bringing the revolution under check and opening the door for the triumph of reaction.

These measures taken by the RCC are a result of a strenuous struggle which has taken place inside our country, and is reflected in the RCC. The problems involved in this struggle are: which line should the new régime pursue, which methods should it use in solving the numerous problems facing us, which measures should it take to overcome the numerous difficulties facing the progressive decisions already taken; struggle on the forms of the new democracy, struggle against the signs of favouritism, corruption, and misuse of office, struggle on the forms best suited to the unity of the revolutionary forces and the building of the national democratic front, struggle on ideas and notions without respect to the Arab unity and the relations between progressive régimes, struggle on the suitable measures for solving the economic problems facing us, struggle on the role of the armed forces, and the national security organs and their future, etc ...

The measures taken by the RCC are a victory to the conservative rightist line, which has been finding support from the rightist elements inside and outside the state power, exploiting to achieve this end and to acquire new grounds all opportunities afforded to it (this is obscure in the original MSS.RB).* The Central Committee Sudanese Communist Party revealed to the masses in April this year, after the arrest of the staunch fighter Abdel Khalig Mahgoub and his deportation to Egypt, the emphasis laid by imperialism upon the Sudan, and how these circles make use of any mistakes made by the state power and any blows dealt to the forces of the left or any split in their ranks. We called for vigilance and increased pressure to put right that mistake, and we exposed at the same time the failure of the political balance of force theory (equilibrium theory? RB), which advocates cooperation with the left to destroy the right and afterwards the dealing of blows against the left before it gets stronger.

This theory does not succeed in the Sudan and the present experience proves that the measures taken have not led to the liquidation of the left but are leading to the liquidation of the

* RB probably represents the initials of the translator.

revolution. There is no alternative to the peaceful solution of differences amongst the revolutionary groups within the broad unity of those forces. To resort to the state power to intimidate the revolutionary groups with a different point of view is not an alternative and is not correct.

The measures taken by the RCC under the pretext of the intention to give to the people an integrated constitutional system clearly indicates that the struggle is being prepared for the concentration of all powers in the hands of the President of State. Such action threatens all principles of the new democracy for which our people are longing. It has been the endeavour of certain vicious political circles within the state power and outside it to achieve this end. As a result of this the role of the RCC became weak, the Council of Ministers was struck by paralysis, and the power became concentrated in the hands of a small group of the members of the RCC which decides everything, till we reached the stage at which everything comes to a standstill when the President of the RCC is not in the country.

Valiant people of our country! It is not an easy matter to protect and develop the revolutionary-democratic achievements such as the nationalisation and confiscation of foreign capital, the 5 Years Development Plan, the liquidation of tribal administration, the Declaration of the democratic solution of the Southern Problem, the strengthening of friendship and cooperation with the socialist countries headed by the USSR, the active and independent role of the Sudan with respect to the Arab and African revolutionary movement, etc. These are complicated problems which require the collective effort of all who have the interests of our country at heart, to help in solving them. These achievements have been attained through numerous objective and subjective difficulties.

The Communist Party has thrown in all its forces to face these difficulties and has been calling on the masses to participate actively in solving them, submitting at the same time its proposals to the RCC and the state power for the development of the revolution.

The RCC has chosen to take a different line without taking into account its consequences and effects on the progress of the revolution, and in so doing it has committed grave mistakes towards the revolution and the people. The RCC, instead of boldly facing these problems, which are not difficult to lend themselves to proper solutions, has quitted the field of battle, and dealt these blows to their faithful allies and their comrades in arms, under the influence of erroneous notions which serve nothing but the right and the enemies of the revolution.

We appeal to the masses of our people to save the revolution from these dangers which threaten its future, by exerting all efforts to realise:

(1) The cancellation of all the measures taken and the re-instatement of the expelled members of the RCC in their previous offices, in addition to putting to discussion all the disputable problems for the Free Officers, the true defenders of the revolution, to have their say on them.

(2) The re-instatement in service of the Free Officers.

(3) The release of the staunch fighter Abdel Khalig Mahgoub.

Valiant people of our country!

Your unity and vigour, which were clearly illustrated in the 2nd June and 30th March demonstrations for strengthening the revolution, your revolutionary enthusiasm in backing the nationalisation decisions and the 5 Years Development Plan, are called upon now more than ever to block the way against the relapse to which the recently taken measures have left the door wide open.

## D. Declaration to the People of Sudan on the Declarations made by President Nimieri on 12th February 1971*

The revolutionary Government of the Sudan has retreated when faced with the enormous difficulties of social change and with the problem of carrying out the slogans they announced on the day of the May 25 coup, work that was above their mental and physical capabilities. They tried to kid the people about the real cause and real reasons for the crisis in the Sudan and the real cause of the worsening financial situation, they tried to kid them about the economic crisis worsening every day. They tried to do this by attacking and slandering the Sudanese Communist Party, by repeating all the sorts of accusations used by our rulers since colonial times by which they thought they could deceive the Sudanese people. But let them remember that all those rulers and Governments have long since gone but the Sudanese Communist Party has remained and still remains at the heart of the revolutionary movement, the movement that is trusted by the people of the Sudan to guard the sovereignty of the Sudan and which is heading the Sudanese people's fight for victory, for socialism.

The policy followed by the régime since its birth of having one and only one revolutionary force monopolising the revolutionary forces of the country and refusing the idea of a national democratic alliance with the partners concerned, by solving all the various problems and differing political points of view within the cadre of the alliance. It is this which has led the régime to its present crisis and has alienated the régime from the rest of the people.

The Sudanese Communist Party has always held that no single force, no body just on its own can succeed and solve the various tasks of the national democratic revolution. The régime has failed to follow the path of the revolution and has tried to give reasons for this by throwing the whole blame on the Sudanese Communist Party, attacking the Party as subversive and an obstacle to the revolution. It forgets that the masses know very well that but for the support of the Communist Party the régime would never have

* Statement issued by the Communist Party of Sudan on February 12, 1971 (reprinted verbatim from the authorised translation, including some misspelt names).

been able to last until today when it now asks the people to have the Communist Party crushed and destroyed. This is simple ingratuity [*sic.*] and the rejection of the simplest cores of morals in political work. The régime has retreated and pulled down the banners of revolution, it has destroyed the principles of the democratic revolutionary forces. The Sudanese revolution cannot go ahead and fulfil its aims without having before it two aims by which we mean the revolutionary alliance of all the revolutionary forces and the democratic revolution.

The Communist Party has been steadily fighting for this for years and years but the Government has always refused to put this into practice and in fact went on its own way to its present rightist summersault [*sic.*] which began on 16 November last year, and which closed the door forever on the possibility of an alliance and cooperation. But if the régime believes that it has smashed and destroyed the Communist Party because some or even all of its leaders have been arrested, because they have called on the reactionary forces to destroy the Party, they are only living in a day dream, in a vacuum. The Communist Party does not disappear just because a Government asks it to. The CP will always exist in our country as long as there is a working class and toiling masses fighting capitalist exploitation and looking towards a socialist future. The CP will continue to exist as long as there are in our country broad democratic masses determined to defend our sovereignty against fake unions. The Communist Party will remain to defend day and night the real democratic rights of the people against any kind of dictatorship, any kind of police state and of the devious methods of the intelligence services. The Communist Party will remain among the many sections of our nation to forge a real national democratic alliance and build the authority of the régime of the national democratic front instead of on just one faction in the national democratic alliance which is insisting on taking all power into its hands yet is incapable of advancing the revolution. We believe that this group draws its ideas from experiences that are alienated from the revolutionary traditions of the country. The régime's claim that it will crush and destroy the Communist Party and that it will wage open war against it is a very dangerous step, dangerous even for the very existence of the régime. But the régime has adopted this step because it has failed to face up to and solve the problems blocking the path of further development for the revolution and has given a cold shoulder to the progressive programme issued at the start of the revolution going along instead with the rightist and revisionist ideas.

The régime will from now on be solely responsible for what happens. A Government that could claim the ability to 'solve' the question of the Communist Party and completely abolish it has never and will never be created in the Sudan. The Communist Party is no fairy story. The régime would do better to get on with its duties to the people and the country instead of entering into such a forlorn battle. They thought at one time that they had destroyed the Party when they took sides with the renegades who said that they could win the fight against the Party. We would like to say that those people have left the Communist Party and have left the honest struggle for Socialism and Communism in favour of jobs in ministries or elsewhere and for the cheap price they can get out of the revolution. The renegades have put the Government in a dilemma which forced the Government to go ahead into a political action. When it became clear to the renegades that they could not destroy the Communist Party they went to the Government apparatus to arrest and try to stop the activity of the Communist Party, even stooping to an alliance with the reactionary forces asking them to destroy the Communist Party.

The problem is not one of the Communist Party as the authorities declare rather it is one of the inability of the régime to face the economic crisis and get on with the 5 Year Plan to develop the economy via the advance of the public sector of the nationalised and confiscated firms and to stand firmly on the position of revolutionary development. Or again the problem that the régime is being pushed down by international pressure from those who want as a condition for loans the dissolution of the Communist Party and the declaration of the unity of the forces under the tripartite Tripoli agreement. They have accepted this being under the influence of the various pressures of the Egyptian secret services which do not accept the presence of any democratic movement in the Sudan and which failed despite its attempt at creating economic links with the International Banks, Kuweit and the Western world in furtherance of its wrong policies and the rightist ideas of its Minister of Finance. Let the Government find some other excuse than these lies which every single Sudanese knows are quite fallacious. The RCC's President's speech describes us as treasonous, says we crush under foot all moral values to reach our goal of power. What a lie! How power can blind people! This accusation comes from the President of the RCC, who if he just thought back to the 24th of May 1969 when he sat with the delegation of the Party and when they explained their point of view and asked him to explain to his colleagues that the Communist Party would not let them down, would not leave them to be a victim of the counter-revolution would protect their rear, but still the Communist Party was asking for the zero hour to be delayed until such a time as the unity of the various groupings of the Free Officers and others in one good front, and until our national movement could advance to help to create a real broad democratic unity of the people so that what was going to happen would not be a mere coup that could freeze the revolution and make it easy prey for counter coups and attacks from sections in the army. Did our Party members ever auctioneer on that day for jobs or a share in the loot, or betray you? Did they not correct the false estimation of the Party and its degree of alertness given to you by the opportunist Ahmad Suleiman [an ex. CP leader] and despite the fact that you refused the suggestion of the Communist Party it never wavered a minute in supporting the progressive changes that came from the coup of May 25th.

Some of your members know full well the great efforts made that night mainly by our general secretary, Mahgoub, to protect your rear on the eve of the 25th. President, do not try to find treason in the rank and file of our party, but look for it in your Cabinet and Council of Ministers. There you will find those who betrayed you during the October Revolution and who told the authorities about the movements of the Free Officers in the revolution of October 29, 1964. We are again asking the President of the RCC why you have been hurt by slogans of the people who have asked no more than the dissolution of the November 16 decisions and this is a legal revolutionary demand that has been called for by all the various factions of the revolutionary movements of the Sudan. The unemployed graduates of the University have been asking for work, for their right to work, as you said, and they had hope in you which is why they wanted to talk to you. They met you in the University and asked you for jobs. In Wad Medani they only asked you for the release of Mahgoub and [his colleagues?] which is the right thing, and for the freedom of the Communist Party. But in all those meetings you were only impulsive without reason and started to slander these zealous young people who have gathered for you the masses in their thousands who in the first month of the May revolution protected the revolution and the rear of the army during the uprising of the counter revolution. But now they are refusing to approve your rightist decisions taken on the 16th November and your right wing policies which are a retreat from your initial line. Your Government has no right to protest against revolutionary slogans, after it has allowed some rather irresponsible elements to declare through its own radio broadcasting all over the Sudan, statements condemning Mahgoub as a traitor. The revolutionaries of the Sudan will not accept any persecution or contempt and they will pay any one who starts skirmishing them many times over. Despite all this the security apparatus of the Government knows the Communist position very well. Our struggle can never help the reactionary forces. Our daily political and practical ideological work has always and always will lead to the complete destruction of the reactionary forces we fight wherever we find them. But your speech today gave new hope and life to the Muslim Brotherhood who started giving speeches in various mosques and going out into the streets in Omdurman driving in cars with loudspeakers raising high the banner of 'no Communist Party' and starting to put again the slogan of 'no Communism, no atheism'. It is your right wing policy that has hurt the revolution and opened the door wide for the reactionary and right wing forces after you have called on them to cooperate with you in crushing and destroying the Communist Party – a thing they failed to do before. You even made a complete sell out to them when you declared that you had changed your policy and were starting a 'new alliance'. But be sure Mr. President we are going to fight back courageously, in the knowledge of our people's honour its manhood and the tradition of its revolutionary forces we are going to fight in defence of our party and its revolutionary movement against any rash attack by the reactionary forces. We say you had better revise your position before it is too late. What you have done up to now will lead the country to disasters no one will gain from except our people's enemies.

Your charge that we see any Sudanese who is not a member of our party as a reactionary is an accusation we heard so many times before. We know the real motives behind it. We have never before called the RCC reactionary. But we'd declared before the masses to all that there had been a national and progressive takeover of the Government and that this military takeover would not stand in the way of revolutionary work. To have this change to a deep rooted national democratic revolution it is a must that a structure of a revolutionary alliance be created. From the first we refused the idea of having just one faction of the revolutionary movement taking power alone. Since then we have said that revolutionary democracy and the giving of more civil liberties to our people is an imperative element for the development of our revolution. What the RCC is now accusing us with does not tally with their own behaviour and policy. Because they believe that any criticism of mistakes on the part of the RCC is something counter to the régime. You have refused to reorganise the Free Officers as the body to which the Council is responsible and as the basis of an alliance with the popular fronts and to be the political leadership of the armed forces, yet your council opposed this sensible and correct idea and thought this might be the start of preparations to remove some of the RCC members and therefore the RCC moved to a purge of all the Free Officers even those who started the movement. The RCC refused our suggestions for a revision of the Budget and the financial system to serve the interests of the people, to advance the development plan and to cut the high cost of living from which the people are suffering. The RCC believes that this is an attack on the Government aimed at weakening it. The RCC again refused the idea that the revolutionary forces including the Communist Party should from their own independent stands elect their own representatives in this alliance from top to bottom levels. The RCC insists that it and only it becomes the trustee for the whole revolutionary movement and its fate. The RCC again refused the idea we have voiced for a long time that the CP should not alone take up important positions in the Government because in this particular phase of development there must be an equal representation of all the national democratic forces in the various organisations and offices. But Nimieri believes that the self denial on the part of the Communist Party does not stem from this but is a sort of desire for non-cooperation. The RCC refused our idea on the question of nationalisations and confiscations because we said it must be governed by certain legal procedure so as to prevent an economic collapse and a retreat of the national capital from participation in the five year plan. Again the RCC considers this is a kind of attack on and opposition to the question of nationalisation.

When they say we are attacking the armed forces it is a kind of cheap jibe no one will believe. We have said and we repeat it here, that the policy of giving certain privileges to the armed forces is wrong and will create a barrier between them and the people, will prevent the building-up of the armed forces and the development plans needed by the country. We look and still look to the armed forces as one of the parts of the State apparatus that has its definite role in protecting the country and its sovereignty, but we oppose political auctioneering by officers and we oppose trying to push it forward by clashes with the various revolutionary forces.

The question of Arab unity and the common struggle with the Egyptian people and other revolutionary peoples has always been a question well at the top of our list. Before the RCC accuses the CP of opposing Arab unity let it ask itself about the results of its behaviour that destroyed the relations between Egypt and Sudan built up over years of struggle, changing if from a noble relation in the joint struggle for national liberation and socialism into one of state apparatus and intelligence services. We have always said the relations between Egypt, Libya and Sudan must be one of cooperation, one of alliance against imperialism and Zionism and from this angle we saw the positive aspects of the Tripoli agreement of 1969. But we opposed and still oppose the other parts of the pact, we are still against the deal between the four states which does not even tally with the view of the Sudanese delegation to the talks. Today we have to declare loud and clear against a new danger – the appearance of an anti-Communist centre in Libya after this wave had been defeated in our area and localised in Saudi Arabia. This aspect of policy was clear in Gen. Nimeiri's speech when he repeated almost word for word what had been written in the Libyan journal *Al-Thawra* (The Revolution) on the Sudan CP.

Let us leave aside the question of slanders, of unfounded charges. If the RCC does not know the real reason for the shortage of labour for the cotton harvest let them ask anyone who knows the results of the rainy season and the bumper crop of sorghum on those workers in the cotton areas, let him read the declaration of the agricultural director of the Gezira scheme in the papers on the great efforts made by the various branches of the Sudanese youth an action run by the students and others in the cotton picking and the money that was thereby saved. And we ask the RCC who authorised the forces who sent them? Was it the Ministry of Youth? The main youth organisations? Or was it the CP? The same thing applies in our anti-illiteracy [?] campaign in the new system and despite our demands that the anti-illiteracy [?] campaign must be linked part and parcel with the general development plans in the backward areas of our country and despite our proposal that the new education campaign should start by wiping out illiteracy, widening the basis of education linking it to the development plans of the country and with real national syllabuses and not mere copies of those of other countries (i.e. Egypt).

Charges that we steal the victories of others are the results of psychological complexes, the results of which the people know full well. But our advice to the Government was and is, not to raise any slogans for which the conditions are not yet ripe. Our advice was and still is to give political and ideological weight equivalent to the real conditions, Nimeiri should not believe that he is the political and ideological leader of the masses. The best thing for the Sudanese revolutionary movement is the cooperation of all the revolutionary movements and factions with full respect for each of their possibilities, capabilities and independence on the basis of the common aims of the democratic national front. If the RCC wants to go on building a single revolutionary party and sees the destruction of the Communist Party as a necessary prelude for the success of this operation then it is just living in a day dream which the revolution will not accept. It is not imperative for our success that any Egyptian experiences should be applied in the Sudan. The régime has come to the end of the road in trying to free the revolution under the banner of attacking the Communist Party and having a middle stand, but our people know very well that all its life the Communist Party has been the main support for the development of the Sudanese revolution, for protecting the present régime against all reactionary and imperialist conspiracies. They know very well the CP has never raised the idea of toppling this régime, they know the CP is not working for its downfall, but that it is the Government which is retreating and has started to take anti-CP positions. It is the Government that has moved to foster the Rightist elements in a new alliance. It is the Government alone that is responsible for this work.

The Sudanese CP holds that the only way out of this dilemma is through the struggle to unify all the democratic forces and the establishment of a Government of a national democratic front which is the only organ that can carry out successfully the tasks of this stage of the revolution and which can save it from a Rightist relapse.

We call on our people to fight vigorously against the decisions of the Government and its counter revolutionary style of work.

We call on all members of the Communist Party, all in the working class movement and the student movements to stand firmly and courageously against the rightist counter-revolutionary movement and completely defeat it.

We call on the entire working class to fight the economic crisis and the destructive economic policies now being followed, to fight and refuse the freezing of the Unified Labour Act* and to take into its own hands the right to make any changes in it.

We call on our people to be vigilant against any reactionary or imperialist conspiracy against the South.

We call on all national forces to get up and defend revolutionary national sovereignty against the erroneous application of the Cairo agreement and the anti-Communist Party policies we have seen as a result.

Long live the unity of the democratic forces!

Victory to the national democratic front!

* This probably refers to the act limiting trade union activities.

## E. Report of the Central Committee of the Communist Party of Sudan Sept.–Nov. 1971 Session*

*... What are the Weaknesses and Defects that led to the Defeat of the 19th of July Movement?*

The hasty execution of the military operation and the short period lived by the new régime, did not conceal the meaning and content of what has happened – the success of the uprising of the Free Officers and Soldiers and the support given by the democratic movement to this successful uprising; the continuation in power of the 19th of July for four glorious days during which it put forward such programme and policies that were welcomed by the masses. The support of the masses was positive and active from the initial hours of the 19th of July Movement and culminated into the huge mass rally of Thursday, the 22nd of July. The clear and decisive attitude of the 19th of July power towards the safeguard of national independence, the strict preservations of the Rule of law and the liquidation of institutions of terror and espionage had its deep and obvious effect within the people.

An outstanding feature within the movement of mass support was the active role played by the working class and its understanding of the deep changes that took place.

There are now, apparently, obvious reasons and factors that led the Free Officers and Soldiers to give their military readiness top priority when they took the decision to take power. But this alone does not constitute all the defects and shortcomings. Identical to every revolutionary action are defects and shortcomings, but such defects and shortcomings do not alone form a basis for the collapse and failure of such action unless they are utilised by a reactionary force of a considerable weight and influence. Here we note that during those four days no force within the country could move alone at that earlier stage had it not been for the external conspiracy and instigation from the Tripartite Alliance, especially from Egypt and Libya, assisted by the British Intelligence.

Secondly, the military operation took place while three of its principal military and political leaders were outside the country;

* Extracts reprinted verbatim from the authorised translation, including some misspelt names.

Babikar El Nur, Farouk Hamadalla and Mohamed Mahgoub Osman. The main blow rendered by foreign intervention and conspiracy took the form of the hijacking of the plane [*sic.*] which carried El Nur and Farouk back home, in order to cripple the new régime. It was also supposed – as it is known in international law – to be a kind of declaration of war on the new régime; since hijacking and arrest of a head of state can only be considered as such.

Added to all that is the isolation of the old régime, its weakness and deep crisis which made the military victory over it easy and swift, and the popular reaction broad and instantaneous. This created an atmosphere of leniency and non-vigilance with regard to the military situation and the safeguard of the new régime and the preliminary victory achieved. All the possibilities were available to preserve such victory and to deal with the shortcomings by arming battalions of revolutionary masses which learnt through its long experiences the necessity of defending its rear; its movement and actions.

This weakness led to the exposition of the rear-front of the new régime and made the revolutionary movement ignore the fundamental law of revolution, i.e. the law to defend the revolution and to safeguard its preliminary victories without mercy or pity. The Central Committee in its letter No. 11 which was published immediately after the victory of the movement placed this task before all other tasks. The aim was to defend the new régime and to ensure that the mass movement is not threatened by adventurists within the regular army while it is carrying out the revolutionary transformation. The leaders of the 19th of July movement were aware of the movements and readiness of at least two groups within the army which were engineering coups since May this year and that the forces of these two groups were almost ready to launch a coup. (Detailed facts will not be mentioned in this report.)

Under the pressure of events and the hasty take of power [*sic.*] a proper evaluation of the danger of the Tripartite Alliance was not made – not from the well-known general political sides – but from the point of its practical military and political danger of intervention – nor that such intervention can reach the level of conspiracy with the British circles to suppress the movement. (We shall publish the facts in a separate document.) The intervention can be summarised in the following facts.

The role played by the Egyptian Military College in Gabal Awlia and the Egyptian Air base in Wadi-Seidna as well as the role played by the Egyptian military attache.

The plane that arrived from Cairo under the pretext that it carries a message from Sadat – as well as Egyptian personalities known for their good relation with the progressive elements in Sudan.

The cooperation between Egypt, Libya and the British Intelligence Service to hijack the (BOAC) plane.

The sending by Sadat of his Minister of War with Khalid Hassan Abbass to Libya to work out the military plan for the intervention.

The mobilisation of Egyptian paratroopers and the provision and preparation of planes to carry the Sudanese forces in the Suez Canal zone to Sudan.

The permission given to Khalid Hassan Abbass to contact and instigate the Sudanese Forces in the Suez Canal which led to mutiny among its rank and later to the detention of a section of it in Kubar prison after it arrived to Sudan.

The statement made by Khaddafi that he does not recognise the (Communist) régime in Sudan and his readiness to receive Sudanese immigrants.

The speech addressed by Khalid Hassan Abbas inciting the Sudanese Armed Forces for mutiny and promising that he will arrive accompanied by military forces.

The subsequent statements made by Sadat that 'the Tripartite Alliance has been born with its teeth on, as was demonstrated in Sudan'.

The statements of Jallood (Libya) that their forces were alerted for intervention; and so on.

The radio broadcasts of London and America played a clear and essential role in mobilising all the reactionary forces against the 'Communist danger' in Sudan.

The leaders of the July 19th movement took a lenient attitude towards elements of the old régime, especially towards members of the Revolutionary Council. They did not realise that those elements have since November 16th 1970, become a bridge for the right and counter-revolutionary forces and a centre for the grouping together of the anti-progressive and anti-Communist forces and all the forces interested in the liquidation of the revolution i.e. a platform for the counter-revolution which had no other platform to rally around against the 19th of July movement.

If the 19th of July movement came with the aim of correcting previous mistakes, the developments of events revealed that it would not confine itself to that role alone. It gave a new push for the revolution and tipped the balance of forces in favour of the democratic forces. It was a decisive answer to the major question: In which direction will the revolution advance? Towards the non-capitalist way of development or towards the way of dependence and capitalist development? That was the question posed since the 25th May 1969, around which the fight was concentrated until the clique of Arab Nationalists decisively resolved it on the 16th of November 1970 in favour of the right-wing line – the line that represents the freezing of the revolution at a certain point; the crippling of democracy; the advance on the road of the one-party system, the road of dictatorship; the opening of the road for the victory of the right-wing and the counter-revolution; the surrender of our national independence; and the submission to the neo-colonialist circles and the dictates of the petrol producing Arab States.

*The Essence of the 19th of July Movement*

We shall, in this respect, base our analysis on the two statements issued by the Central Committee on the 19th and 20th of July, the documents published by the new régime including its first Policy Statement addressed to the mass rally – the laws, decisions and Republican Orders which drew out the constitutional structure of the state – and the statements and slogans of the popular forces and their organisations. Relying on all these documents we can notice the following features:

Within the process of the Sudanese revolution, the 19th of July movement represents a revolutionary change of political power made by the forces of the National Democratic Front – specifically by the forces of Sudanese revolutionary democrats, both Marxists and democrats – within the Armed Forces represented by the Free Officers Organisation and the Democratic Soldiers Movement. The 19th of July transformed the power and placed it in the hands of the national democratic Alliance – and not in the hands of a single section of it. And for the first time in our history, it clearly stated that the Free Officers Organisation, which executed the military operation is one of the organisations of the National Democratic Front and an instrument of it. This was an obvious diversion from the traditional military coup d'etats, whose leaders generally pose to represent the Armed Forces as a whole and who claim that the Armed Forces are the vanguard of the popular forces; and as such confuse between the function of the Armed Forces as an organ of suppression and state power and the function of the progressive revolutionary vanguard within its ranks.

*The 19th of July Movement* did not confine its principles to public statements and declarations but drafted them in the Republican Orders it issued; thus giving them a constitutional force. It clearly stated that the supreme power of the Democratic Front is the basis of government at all the levels in the Republic of the Sudan.

It clearly specified, on a constitutional level, the principles of new democracy. It conducted negotiations with the democratic organisations and the progressive forces for the formation of the new government and new state organs. It ensured the right of the democratic national forces to establish their organisations and political parties. It repealed the laws and decisions that curtailed the liberties of the national democratic forces. It liquidated the organs of terror, espionage and the police-state that previously existed.

It opened the way before the struggle of the masses to accomplish the task of the democratic revolution. It raised high the banner of the rule of law and the independence and honesty of the Judiciary. It stated the necessity to exercise democracy as political rights, and as a system of government. It specified the nature of the representative system and the executive organs of the State and stated the right of the Masses to elect and recall their representative. It specified the form of applying democracy to the production relationship that exist in the countryside; in order to emancipate the vast majority of the population. It emphasised the necessity of the participation of the working people in the management of production. In this way it provided the practical possibility of abolishing the contradiction that exists between political and economical democracy. It made democracy a prerequisite and a condition for the unity of the country and the solution of the Southern problem.

It raised high the banner of independence and national sovereignty. It specified the place of Sudan and its role in the movement towards unity and in the Arab and African revolutions. It determined the position of Sudan in the anti-colonial and anti-imperialist front as well as its relations with the socialist countries and particularly with the Soviet Union.

The 19th of July movement has proved an important and fundamental fact, that there exists an alternative (a real revolutionary and practical alternative) to the dictatorship of the petty-bourgeois or the dictatorship of a section or a side of it. In this way it directed a strong blow to those theories which justify such dictatorships as a destiny that is historically inevitable, under whom or with whom the working class and the revolutionary movement should submissively live and coexist. Such a theory helped the petty-bourgeois military régimes in general and the Arab Nationalists in particular to follow a rightist line to liquidate the revolution. The experience of Sudan has proved that the submissive attitude towards such régimes in fear of a return of the counter-revolution leads that section of the petty-bourgeois who concentrated the power in its hands, to play the same role of the counter-revolution in suppressing and liquidating the revolutionary movement, in regard to the political and economic fields and in its surrender before the neo-colonialist dictates.

The 19th of July proved that a more progressive alternative existed. And it also proved the necessity to be vigilant not only in safeguarding the revolution against the schemes of imperialism but also against the schemes of the Arab rightist régimes.

The defeat of the 19th of July movement should not minimise its importance, its essence, and the lessons to be drawn from it, whatever great may be the losses. It was destined to be a bulwark for progress in Africa and the Arab world. It was destined to be a rallying centre for the forces of the national liberation movement in Africa, and a step forward from the traditional line of freezing the revolution and terminating its advance which is adopted by the military Arab petty-bourgeois. The 19th of July movement was an original expression of the internationalist character of the Sudanese democratic movement, which launched its initial battles among the masses at the middle of the forties in close relationship with the world-wide movement for progress and socialism.

And this is the secret behind the feverish assault and conspiracy of all the imperialist, reactionary and conservative régimes against the 19th of July movement. They organised foreign military intervention from abroad and instigated the local reactionary gangs inside the country. They made a deliberate distortion of the programme, the essence and origin of the 19th of July movement. They labelled it 'a communist plot', an 'ill-fated coup d'etat', a 'joint venture of the Sudanese Communist Party, the Soviet Union and the Socialist Countries', etc. They finally drowned it in bloodshed.

In fact those forces were terrified at the depth and magnitude of the democratic revolution in Sudan. They were astonished that it exclusively possesses such capacities. They had to console themselves with the allegation of a Soviet intervention as if the over-throw of such isolated régime requires any foreign help let alone the help of the Soviet Union. Even in the future, the revolutionary movement in Sudan will be able to overthrow this régime as it did with many of its predecessors, and will then be richer in experience, wisdom and abilities to maintain its victories. They invented the allegation of Soviet intervention to cover the real intervention committed by the Tripartite Alliance in collaboration with Britain.

The 19th of July movement exposed the apprehension felt by those forces as well as by the petty-bourgeois régimes of Egypt, Libya and Guinea, from the new evolution taking place in the depth of the Arab and African national liberation movement; from the revolutionary transformation taking place within the masses who are aspiring for closer and deeper cooperation with the socialist camp – even in the countries of those nationalist régimes themselves. The 19th of July declared in its programmes – within the framework of a national, democratic and revolutionary platform rather than from a communist platform – a position of alliance with the Soviet Union and the socialist camp as an expression of the realities and requirements of the conditions prevailing in Sudan. Thus it surpassed such vague formulas of cooperation which speak of 'neutrality', 'non-commitments', etc; formulas that were raised by the national bourgeoisie in the middle of the fifties and to which the ruling petty-bourgeoisie now cling with an idea of abandoning it whenever the social revolution acquires deeper character and the popular revolutionary mass movement reaches new horizons.

The Chinese and Yugoslav leaders, each from his position, played a subversive role, a role full of treachery and disloyalty to the principles of proletarian internationalism by giving cheap support to the rightist and counter-revolutionary movement, by condemning the 19th of July movement, and by their implied approval of the execution of communists, democrats and the physical bloody liquidation of the revolutionary movement in Sudan. The Chinese leaders acted in accordance with their basic role of weakening the alliance of the national liberation movement with the world socialist system. They are scrambling for spheres of influence and seeking the liquidation of those communist parties and revolutionary movements which do not approve their political line. The Chinese leaders are driven by their deep-rooted hatred of the Sudanese Communist Party which blocked the road in the face of the opportunist political line they intended to impose on the popular movement in Sudan and defeated all their attempts to build an effective or influential 'Chinese-Communist' organisation.

The Yugoslav leaders adopted a truly miserable and poor stand. They believe that they possess the ability to influence the development of events in Sudan; they believe that they are the ideological and political leadership of those countries which advocate 'positive neutrality'. They believe that the joint communiqués which they sign with Aboud or Azhary or Nimeiri will change the balance of power within the country and will subside in the conscience of the Sudanese people. They believe that they will find in Sudan a refuge after their escape from the revolutionary commitment towards the world socialist system, a refuge that may cover their theory of neutrality between the two social systems – the socialist and the capitalist. They placed themselves in such a ridiculous position where nobody envies them. They would do themselves better to look for a way-out. The counter-revolutionary régime shall undoubtedly collapse much sooner than they anticipate. It is advisable that they do not exaggerate the significance of their role in Sudan, because there is in Sudan influential and effective democratic movement on the threshold of power. They better look for a role to play in a country where the rulers control everything and exclusively decide everything, because the democratic movement in Sudan has, ever since the pre-independence days, made the questions of foreign policy a matter of its everyday activity; and has always had a distinct and independent position on such issues and never relied on the official positions of governments however progressive such positions were.

The position of the Chinese and Yugoslav leaders has exactly coincided with the political line and position taken by the splinter group which lost no time to announce over the radio and in the press its unwarranted support of the counter-revolution, its early condemnation of the communists and revolutionaries who were standing before the tribunals set-up by the counter-revolution; its support of their executions and the bloody liquidation of the revolutionary movement. Members of the splinter groups appeared as prosecution witnesses before the military tribunals, and collaborated with the police in its hunt for the arrest of the communists and revolutionaries. These positions were a logical consequence of their ideological positions, their actual split from the Communist Party and their support for the coup of the 16th of November 1970.

... If we examine the situation during the past period, we find that the state of sudden bewilderment, confusion and paralysis that followed the quick development of events has completely disappeared. The political movement resumed its activities on all fronts, within the trade-unions, the youth, the women, the peasants etc.

Accordingly, we submit the outlines of our programme of actions and its direction. Later we shall deal with its details.

*The Party:*

The basic task is to secure the safe and stable function of its leading centre. This is followed by the reorganisation in the leading central bodies of the provinces, districts, students and other fields of activities, and the establishment of close contact between these centres and the Party's leading organ. We should continue our efforts to reorganise the party branches, to group together the party members in each field and provide them with the necessary minimum conditions for their work. We have to continue our efforts to secure the necessary materials for party work, such as finance, typing machines and similar resources. We have to secure the minimum standard necessary for the Marxist education of the party members. We have to reinforce our relations with the international communist and progressive movement and with our Party branches abroad.

The further security of the party and the protection of its leading cadres is an urgent task that sustains no leniency or relaxation especially when we have started to issue public statements among the masses. We have to economise and cut-down party expenditure to the minimum necessary limits. We have to be highly vigilant against the covert methods of destroying the party by installing subversive elements within its ranks.

*The Mass Activities:*

Here too, we outline our general approach and leave the details of each field of activity for the proper time. We have to examine the best methods of how to submit these outlines to the concerned people. We begin by rallying and mobilising the democratic forces within the working class movement, in every trade-union and in every field of working class activity, around a programme and methods of activities within each trade-union notwithstanding the situation prevailing in the leadership of such trade-union. We have to charter and submit the general and particular workers demands in each field of work. We have to put forward the trade-union rights; to call for the implementation of the Amalgamated Trade Union Act, the application of Social Security Act, and The Workers Vocational Education Act. We have to call for the release of trade-union leaders and an end to their dismissal and persecution. We have to organise a broad movement against the new Act of 'Reorganisation of Trade-Unions' and the interference of the state in the trade-union activities, etc.

We have to submit for discussion with the democrats, proposals as to the best suitable form of uniting and mobilising the democratic forces within the trade-union. Due to the recent nature of the structure of teachers' and government employees' trade unions and due to the unrest prevailing within their ranks, we have no other alternative but to start work from the base, and maintain 'The Teachers' Socialist League'.

Within the organisations of professionals and intellectuals, the socialist and progressive groups have always been united and have contributed a great deal to the activities of these organisations. Initially in all of these organisations we should maintain the existing form of organisation and encourage the participation of the membership in their activities however small and limited these activities are. We have to combat any tendency that rejects the work within these organisations on the ground that they are not completely free or have been dominated by reactionary or opportunist elements. We should also combat the tendency to form parallel trade-unions or parallel associations.

Despite the indiscriminate arrests among the youth, the authorities are still exerting big efforts to win over the youth, to distort its democratic traditions and to impose [El Katayeb] as a youth organisation. Under all conditions, we should maintain the existence of the independent youth union branches. We should, at the same time, expose the provocative misconduct of 'El Katayeb' members among the local inhabitants; their indecent behaviour, their trespass of other peoples' premises and the public nuisance they have caused.

The relationship between the party branches and the democratic fronts within the student movement is distinct and needs no further clarification. Similarly clear are the necessary alliances between the democratic fronts of students and other democratic student organisations which should be achieved, subject to the position of such organisations after the counter-coup and the requirements of the struggle in each educational institution.

The women's movement has been exposed to open subversion and corruption. And despite the facilities rendered by the state, yet the official women's organisation still depends mainly on the cheap propaganda provided by the official mass media and is capitalising on the weaknesses of the democratic women movement. It is therefore necessary that the Sudanese Women Association should continue to function actively and maintain its contacts. Doing so, it shall succeed, in due time, to work out the most suitable forms of reviving the democratic activities within the women movement.

The campaign that was initiated after the split in the party to improve the situation in the peasant areas helped in regrouping and regenerating the democratic forces there.

The 19th of July events have demonstrated the real weight, the integrity and militancy of these democratic forces, as well as the complete isolation of the leading bodies imposed on the Peasant Associations. The existence of the party branches and the unity of the democratic forces, as well as the peasant vanguard organisations around these branches, the submission to the authorities of peasant demands, which were neglected by the present leadership, especially those demands related to the programme of agrarian reform, shall make possible the regeneration of an active movement in the countryside, with greater possibilities of action than those possessed by the movement in the towns at present.

Both in the capital as well as in the other towns all over the Sudan, the tribal leagues and associations played an important role, they could resist their arbitrary dissolution on the 25th of May 1971 and resume their full activities during the 19th of July days. The role played by these leagues in the rural areas is obvious and well known and their cooperative and relief services to members are quite appreciated. Therefore we have to activate these leagues, and help them not to become isolated or lose their membership, having in mind that they have acquired enough experiences to continue their work and maintain their contacts.

The democratic movement in the South has been exposed to successive blows. The freedom of movement and action is exclusively assured for the Southern traditional parties alone. We are still short of securing regular contacts with the South. Yet the democratic groups that were set-up among the Southern students in the North should continue to uphold the programme chartered by the martyr Joseph Garang and should help to expose the régime and the Southern elements collaborating with it. These groups should assist in the transmission of the influence of the democratic movement to the South.

The active work among all these sectors of the national democratic forces; their awareness of the existence and militancy of the Communist Party; their realisation of the huge campaign of international solidarity with our people and the deep crisis of the régime; all these factors will enable the Party to find out new forms of mass action and organisation. The popular movement itself will surely provide unanticipated new forms of organisation. The democratic revolution in Sudan always develops and expands its base in direct proportion to the participation of the masses and their real weight within their existing democratic organisations; in proportion to its ability to create various suitable forms of organisations that serve the interest of and promote the mass movement; in proportion to the progress and development of the stage of the political struggle, as determined by its slogans and forms of actions and under the condition that our political line in comprehensive and proper and conforms with our basic stand to be with the masses, to learn from the masses and lead the masses. Our magnanimous people and their lofty ideals are too great to submit to the rule of such ignorant, conceited and vulgar stooges.

The working class which is the vanguard of the struggle for democracy, national sovereignty and socialism shall not abandon the banners of its independent class entity, its unity and fundamental rights; and shall not betray the revolutionary traditions bequeathed by its leaders and martyrs Abdel Khalig Mahgoub, El Shafia Ahmed El Sheikh and Joseph Garang.

The peasants, and especially the poor peasants and agricultural workers – who, for tens of years, have been cultivating hopes and only harvested poverty, will continue the struggle endeared by the blood of their martyrs in 'Joda' [?] for a radical agrarian reform and for their unalienable right to form their own associations for the realisation of their daily demands and the necessary means of life.

The democratic intellectuals, holders of the torch of knowledge, who never stooped before a despot or a dictator, will not retreat from the march to achieve the freedom of organisation and expression. They shall continue to be loyal to the aspirations of progressive social changes and shall continue to propagate progressive and healthy ideas among the masses in order to launch and promote the cultural revolution, regenerate the cultural heritage of our people and guard it against abuse and vulgarisation.

Among the soldiers and the free officers in the Armed Forces, the national and progressive conscious [sic.] is still beating alive and is loyal to the aspirations of the Sudanese revolution. They continue to respond to our peoples' resistance of the puppet dictatorship and reject the leadership of the puppet clique and its methods of corruption and favouritism. Our Armed Forces have refused and still reject submission and dependence smuggled in under the cloak of 'Arab Unity' which the gang of Arab Nationalists has vulgarised and ridiculed. The Armed Forces consistently reject this road and are ready to defend, in blood, the sovereignty of Sudan and render support to the fraternal Arab and African peoples.

The Sudanese students, who were and still continue to be the initiators of popular indignation against the dictatorship and foreign domination shall remain loyal to their historical role in the battle for democracy and freedom. They will continue their staunch fight for the overthrow of the dictatorship and for the victory of a national democratic régime.

The vanguard groups of the Southern population who learnt through their own experience that democracy and alliance with the democratic movement in the North are indispensable conditions for victory shall not follow the secessionist elements.

The democratic women movement, and its deep-rooted centre, the Association of Sudanese Women with its traditions and close contacts with each Sudanese family shall continue its efforts to protect the Sudanese women emancipation movement against suppression, falsification, careerism, opportunism and cheap glorification of the authorities. Its efforts will undoubtedly bear fruits in the mobilisation of Sudanese women against the terror and for an end to the dictatorship.

Our youth which aspires for progress and which is full of vitality and defiance is surely capable of preserving and defending its youth association; seeking for this purpose various forms and fields of actions. It will continue to play its role both in the North and in the South in order to restore to our people, our country and revolution the banners of progress and social change.

Outside the Sudan, groups of Sudanese students, intellectuals and workers are exerting great efforts for the resistance of the dictatorship, and are mobilising the progressive world public opinion to express solidarity with the democratic forces of Sudan and their revolution. They are consistently beneigning [?] the manoeuvres and moves of the régime abroad, and are exposing its lies.

In the Arab countries, wide campaigns of protests are made not only in condemnation of the bloody terror, but with a deep understanding of the essence of the 19th of July movement and the national democratic revolution. More and more popular circles are rallying around the communist and progressive Arab parties rejecting the tendency to freeze the revolution and the petty-bourgeois military dictatorships.

The campaign of solidarity with the Sudanese people still continues in every country where there is a communist party or a progressive force with the aim of putting an end to the terror and for the release of political prisoners and detainees. All this abundant and rich reserve awaits the action by our party to exploit and transform it into a practical level in the struggle to achieve the final victory of the national democratic forces.

We have to work patiently, wisely and avoid hasty [acts], we have to proceed step by step with full responsibility and deep consciousness to preserve the party and mobilise the popular movement. We shall draw courage from the martyrs of the staunch 19th of July movement, from their fearless challenge of death and their great sacrifices; from the spirit of resistance and defiance of those imprisoned and detained. We shall draw from the aspirations of our people and our working class an unconquerable confidence in the final victory and shall vigorously combat any spirit of defeat or surrender.

Forever loyal to the martyr leaders – founders of our party, who instilled it with an unconquerable spirit of struggle, Abdel Khalig Mahgoub, Shafia Ahmed El Sheikh and Joseph Garang, we shall hold high the unity of the Communist Party, shall conduct a persistent struggle to raise high the banner of the purity of Marxism Leninism within the ranks of the party against deviation and petty-bourgeois mentality. We shall continuously struggle to maintain close relationship with our working class and our popular masses and shall uphold the unity of the International Communist Movement.

Glory and deep respect to the martyrs of the 19th of July and a continuous struggle to uphold the banner they raised high above our country.

Long live the Sudanese Communist Party.

Long live the National Democratic Front.

The Central Committee
of the Sudanese Communist Party
November, 1971.

# Notes

**Introduction** (pp. 1–17)

1. H. A. MacMichael, *A History of the Arabs in the Soudan*, 2nd impression, Cass, London 1967, lists more than fifty tribes who claim to be of Arab origin.
2. For a detailed description of the 'holy families', see P. M. Holt, *Holy Families and Islam in the Sudan*, Princeton Near East Papers, no. 4 (1967); see also P. M. Holt, 'The Sons of Jābir and their Kin: A Clan of Sudanese Religious Notables', *Bulletin of the School of Oriental and African Studies* 30 (1967): 142–57. Islam penetrated Dārfūr from three different directions: West Africa, the Nile Valley, and the Arabian Peninsula. The heads of the 'holy families' played a central role in this process too. For details, see: R. S. O'Fahey, 'Saints and Sultans: The Role of Muslim Holy Men in the Keira Sultanate of Dār Fūr' (Paper presented to the A.S.A.U.K. Conference, School of Oriental and African Studies, University of London, September 1971).
3. R. Hill, *Egypt in the Sudan 1820–1881*, London, 1959, p. 96; P. M. Holt, *A Modern History of the Sudan*, London, 1961, pp. 49–52.
4. For examples relating to the tribes of Kordofan and Dārfūr, see S. M. Nur, 'A Critical Edition of the Memoirs of Yusuf Mikha'il' (Ph.D. diss. University of London, 1963); R. C. Slatin, *Fire and Sword in the Sudan* London, 1896, p. 93.
5. Na'ūm Shuqayr, *Ta'rīkh al-Sūdān al-qadīm wa'l-ḥadīth wajughrafiyatuhu*, Cairo, n.d. [1903] 3: 109–12.
6. See, for example, Talal Asad, *The Kababish Arabs*, London, 1970, pp. 158–60: see also Slatin, pp. 153–6, who tells about the split in the leadership of the Rizayqāt, one of the important Baqqāra tribes in Dārfūr.
7. *Fakī* – a corruption of *faqīh* (jurist); meaning in colloquial Sudanese Arabic both teacher, whether of religion or Ṣufism, as well as healer, holder of religious (usually Ṣūfī) office, and a variety of other functions.
8. Holt, *Holy Families*, pp. 4–5.
9. *Anṣār*, supporters, was the name originally given to the Prophet's supporters at Medina. In the Sudan, the Mahdi called his supporters *anṣār*

when he fled from the Nile to the Nuba Mountains in September 1881. The name was revived by Sayyid 'Abd al-Rāḥmān, the Mahdi's son, when he started to organise his religio-political movement during World War I.

10. Shuqayr, 3:112 'Abd Allāh 'Alī Ibrāhīm, *al-Ṣirā' bayn al-mahdī wa'l-'ulamā'*, Khartoum, 1969, p. 8.
11. Lieutenant Colonel Stewart, *Report on the Soudan*, Khartoum, 9 February, 1883, C.3670.
12. 'Abd Allāh 'Alī Ibrāhīm, pp. 22–43.
13. *Manshūrāt al-imām al-mahdī*, Khartoum, 1964, 2; P. M. Holt, *The Mahdist State in the Sudan, 1881–1898*, London, 1958, pp. 41–2.
14. *Waqā'i' 'Uthmān Dinqa*, Khartoum, 1964.
15. Shuqayr, 3:354.
16. Holt, *The Mahdist State*, pp. 130–1.
17. *Ibid.*, pp. 141–6.
18. *Ibid.*, pp. 135–6.
19. Major F. R. Wingate, D.S.O., A.A.G., *General Military Report on the Egyptian Sudan, 1891*, War Office, London, 1892, compiled from statements made by Father Ohrwalder.
20. *General Report on the Egyptian Soudan, March 1895*, compiled from statements made by Slatin Pasha.

**Chapter 1** (pp. 21–66)

1. For details see my paper 'Religious policy in the northern Sudan: 'Ulamā' and Ṣūfism 1899–1918', *Asian and African Studies*, vol. 7, 1971, pp. 89–119.
2. For details see chapter on tribal policy in G. Warburg, *The Sudan under Wingate*, London, 1971.
3. For details see G. O. Voll, *A History of the Khatmiyyah Tariqah in the Sudan*, unpublished Ph.D. thesis, Harvard University 1969, pp. 605–16.
4. See for example Wingate to Cromer, 24 Feb. 1915, The Sudan Archives at Durham University, Box 194/2.
5. The following details are from Sayyid 'Abd al-Raḥmān's own autobiographical notes compiled by his grandson al-Ṣādiq al-Mahdī, *Jihād fi sabīl al-istiqlāl*, Khartoum, n.d., pp. 1–15 (hereafter *Istiqlāl*).
6. In his biography of the Mahdī, *al-Thā'ir al-awwal* (Khartoum, n. d.), the author, 'Ubayd 'Abd al-Nūr, emphasises the difference between the Mahdī and his son, Sayyid 'Abd al-Raḥmān. While both were, according to the author, nationalist leaders fighting for independence, the Mahdī fought the Turco-Egyptians with weapons, while his son '... fights the imperialists with tolerance and patience ...' (pp. 57–8).
7. E. Kedourie, 'Cairo and Khartoum on the Arab question, 1915–1918', in *The Chatham House Version and other Middle Eastern Studies*, Frank Cass, London, 1970, pp. 13–32.
8. *Istiqlāl*, pp. 19–20.
9. Stack to Wingate, 12 Dec., 1918, FO/371/3711; for a summary of

Egypt's propaganda in the Sudan see Memorandum by Stack, 25 May, 1924, FO/371/10049.

10. Allenby to Foreign Office, 20 April, 1919, FO/371/3715; see also *Sudan Intelligence Report* (hereafter SIR), 298, May 1919.
11. Izzet Pasha to MacDonald, 27 June 1924, transmitting a personal message from Zaghlul, FO/371/10050; J. Murray of the F. O. minuted: '... if Zaghlul really believed ... his message his ignorance of the Sudan is colossal; if he did not his message is an impertinence ...' (ibid).
12. See for instance: Allenby to MacDonald, 6 July, 1924, FO/371/10050; Record of Conference held in Foreign Office on 13 Aug., 1924, FO/371/10051; for further details on the White Flag League, see Muddathir 'Abd al-Raḥīm, *Imperialism and nationalism in the Sudan*, London, 1969, pp. 102–8.
13. Keown-Boyd to Allenby, 14 March, 1920, forwarded by Allenby to Curzon on 24 March, 1920, FO/371/4981.
14. Stack to Allenby (Confidential), 18 Aug. 1924, FO/371/10052.
15. Allenby to MacDonald, 26 July, 1924, FO/371/10051.
16. See also Lloyd to Maffey, 20 March, 1927, FO/141/669. Lloyd asked whether the Wafd's claim to the possession of documents proving that the Egyptian evacuation was decided upon prior to Sir Lee Stack's assassination, could be substantiated. In his reply Maffey stated that evacuation plans were completed on 10 September, 1924, more than two months before Stack's assassination. But as this highly secret document was undated, the Wafd could not use it as proof; Maffey to Lloyd, 11 April, 1927, ibid.
17. Allenby to Curzon, 27 April, 1919, FO/371/3725; for the 'Letters of loyalty' see also: Allenby to F. O., 6 June, 1919, ibid.; Scott to Curzon, 12 October, 1921, FO/371/6306; *SIR*-358, May 1924; The authenticity of these letters was questioned not only by the Egyptian press, but even by certain British MPs who suggested that the letters were induced by the British authorities, see Parliamentary Question by Mr. Swan, 11 May, 1922, FO/371/7759.
18. The Hindiyya was founded in the Jazīra, by Yūsuf al-Hindī at the turn of this century. It never became a big *ṭarīqa* and its adherents usually joined forces with the Anṣār and later the Umma in all political matters. After al-Hindī's death in Dec. 1942 the *ṭarīqa* declined even further; see H. B. Barclay, 'A Sudanese religious brotherhood: al-Tarīqa al-Hindīya', *The Muslim World*, vol. 53, 1963, pp. 127–37; see also *Sudan Political Intelligence Summary*, no. 27, December, 1942, FO/371/35580.
19. *Istiqlāl*, pp. 24–6.
20. Ibid. pp. 21–31; the use of the *rātīb* was allowed following the advice of Shaykh Muṣṭafā al-Marāghī, then Grand *Qāḍī* of the Sudan, that it contained only orthodox prayers and quotations from the Qur'ān. Ibid. p. 28.
21. Ibid. pp. 25–7; see also 'The political situation' by C. A. Willis, Director of Intelligence, Khartoum, 16 June, 1924, FO/371/10050; it is interesting to note that on 6 June, 1924, a meeting of White Flag leaders and Egyptian

officers decided that they needed the support of at least one of the Sayyids in order to succeed, but as '... Sayed Abdel Rahman El Mahdi was simply English, Sherif Yusef El Hindi was too cunning and double faced to be relied upon ... Their only hope was Sayed Ali El Mirghani ...' *SIR*, 359, June 1924, FO/371/10039.

22. Craig to More, 15 September, 1924, FO/141/669 (quoting interview with Sayyid 'Alī al-Mīrghanī).
23. For details see Ja'far M. A. Bakheit, 'Native administration in the Sudan and its significance to Africa', in Yūsuf Faḍl Ḥasan (ed.), *Sudan in Africa*, Khartoum, 1971, especially pp. 256–60.
24. *Political Intelligence Paper*, no. 66, 'Biographical note on Sayed Sir Ali el Marghani [*sic*] Pasha, K.C.M.G., K.C.V.O.' Oct. 1944, FO/371/41363.
25. Interview with Sir Angus Gillan, K.B.E., C.M.G., London, 6 October, 1970. Sir Angus was Civil Secretary of the Sudan government in the years 1934–9.
26. *SIR* – annual report 1923, FO/371/10039; see also T. Hodgkin, 'Mahdism, Messianism and Marxism in the African setting', in Yūsuf Faḍl Ḥasan, p. 117, who writes that '... Mahdist propaganda was thought of at this time as assoicated with Bolshevism, the Third International, Egyptian nationalism, pan-Islamism, and ideas of "world revolution" in general ...'.
27. Stack to MacDonald, 8 Aug., 1924, enclosing memorandum on the 'Possibility of another Mahadia [*sic*] or General Religious Rising of a similar type', FO/371/10052.
28. *SSIR*-3, May 1926; *SSIR*-8, Nov. 1926; *SSIR*-9, Dec. 1926, FO/371/11614, consequently, the relative strength of the Khatmiyya in the SDF and the police, grew out of all proportions; see *Political Intelligence Paper*, no. 66, Oct. 1944, FO/371/41363.
29. 'Mahdism and El Sayed Abdel Rahman El Mahdi K.B.E., C.V.O.', by Public Security Intelligence, Khartoum, 28 April, 1935 (hereafter: Mahdism – 1935), FO/371/19096.
30. Archer to Lloyd, 2 April, 1926, forwarding his letter of resignation and twelve enclosures, FO/371/11609; Lloyd to Chamberlain, 10 April, 1926, ibid.; Chamberlain to Lloyd, 11 May, 1926 (private), FO/800/259. In a reply to a query from Lord Stamfordham whether a command of Arabic was not essential for a Governor-General of the Sudan and hence Maffey's unsuitability, Chamberlain wrote: '... Lord Cromer's ... record in Egypt in effect proves the contrary ...' Chamberlain to Stamfordham, 21 October, 1926, ibid.
31. Note on meeting at the palace, enclosed in Archer to Lloyd, 2 April, 1926, FO/371/11609.
32. Mahdism – 1935, FO/371/19096.
33. Ibid.
34. 'Memorandum on Mahdism and government policy', 22 Feb., 1937 by G. S. S. (Symes) enclosed in Lampson to Eden, 5 March, 1937, FO/371/20870 (hereafter Mahdism – 1937).
35. Ibid.

36. Quoted by Symes in Mahdism – 1935, FO/371/19096; in 1926 the Sayyid had been on the verge of bankruptcy and the government had shown no inclination to come to his aid, due to the political controversy surrounding him.
37. Ibid.; see also *Istiqlāl*, pp. 38–41; the Sayyid states quite openly that he used his relatives in order to acquire new lands in restricted areas. These lands later became part of the Mahdist *dā'ira* (domain).
38. 'Memorandum on the policy of the Sudan Government towards the Mahdist cult' by Reginald Davies, *SSIR*-7, October 1926, FO/371/11613. See also *SSIR*-10, December 1926, FO/371/12374.
39. *Istiqlāl*, pp. 38–41; in denying British charges of exploitation, Sayyid 'Abd al-Raḥmān insisted that it would have been cheaper for him to use hired labour than to provide for the Anṣār.
40. Mahdism – 1935, FO/371/19096.
41. The following information, unless otherwise states was derived from Mahdism – 1935, FO/371/19096; Mahdism – 1937, FO/371/20870; and the *SSIR* series for the years 1926–1931.
42. *Istiqlāl*, pp. 29–30.
43. By 1945 the Sayyid's effort to win the support of other *ṭarīqas* made him invite them to the Ansār's annual marriage festival, where they were allowed, contrary to Mahdist beliefs, to perform their Ṣūfī rituals including the *dhikr*. *Sudan Political Intelligence Summary*, no. 51, July 1945, FO/371/45972.
44. *Istiqlāl*, p. 177.
45. 'A Review of the situation in the spring of 1925', by Davies, Baily and Ewart, encl. in Ewart to Private Secretary, 21 April, 1925, FO/371/10905.
46. *SIR*-359, June 1924, FO/371/10039.
47. Allenby to Chamberlain, 9 May, 1925, FO/371/10879; for details on the government's educational policy during that period, see M. O. Beshir, *Educational development in the Sudan, 1898–1956*, London, 1969.
48. Archer to Allenby, 27 April, 1925, FO/371/10880.
49. Lampson to Campbell, 15 June, 1935, FO/371/19095; James Currie's article 'The educational experiment in the Anglo-Egyptian Sudan' was published in the *Journal of the African Society*, vols. 33–4, 1934–35. Currie was Director of Education in the Sudan in the years 1900–1914.
50. 'Record of Meeting held in the Foreign Office on 13 October, (1936), to discuss Educational Policy in the Sudan', FO/407/219; Symes himself had admitted a year earlier that '... a lacuna of our present administrative system – perhaps an aftermath of the disturbances in 1924–25 – was that it did not afford sufficient opportunities for Sudanese in higher branches of the public service ...'. 'Political Memorandum on the Anglo-Egyptian Sudan' by G. S. Symes, June 1935, FO/371/19095.
51. G. S. Symes, 'A Note on Local Government Policy', May 1939, FO/407/223.
52. *SSIR*-8, Nov. 1926, FO/371/11614.
53. *SSIR*-3, May 1926; *SSIR*-4, June 1926, FO/371/11613.

54. *Istiqlāl*, pp. 177–8.
55. Mahdism-1935, FO/371/19096, reporting on the situation in 1927–8.
56. Minutes of Governor General's Council, 344th Meeting, 19 Feb., 1931; and 352nd meeting, 18–20 May, 1931, FO/867/17.
57. Maffey to Loraine, 27 January, 1932, FO/407/215.
58. Mahdism-1935, FO/371/19096.
59. *Istiqlāl*, p. 178.
60. Mahdism-1935, FO/371/19096; see also Mahgoub Mohamed Salih, 'The Sudanese press', *Sudan Notes and Records*, 46, 1965, p. 6.
61. Interview with Mr. K. D. D. Henderson, C.M.G. September 1972; see also *Sudan Political Intelligence Summary*, no. 22, December 1942, FO/371/35580.
62. Enclosed in Kelly to Eden, 7 November, 1936, FO/407/219.
63. John Voll in his study of the Khatmiyya emphasised that there has also been no ideological development worth mentioning in that *ṭarīqa* during the twentieth century, and that the great variety of Khatmī organisations made the formulation of a well-defined and generally accepted ideology impossible. Voll, pp. 641–5.
64. For details of the *bay'a* and the evolution of Mahdist ideology in the nineteenth century see P. M. Holt, *The Mahdist State in the Sudan*, pp. 103–18; an earlier version of the *bay'a* did not mention the *jihād*; ibid., p. 117.
65. *Istiqlāl*, p. 183; see also p. 190 where he talks of life and its adaptation to present circumstances.
66. Ibid., p. 184; the Mahdī's *dā'ira* (domain) and its wealth was according to Sayyid 'Abd al-Raḥmān a national (*waṭanī*) necessity which helped to pave the way to the Sudan's independence; ibid., p. 189.
67. Ibid., p. 183–4; talking of the accusations made by the British authorities, that the more fanatical western Anṣār were planning a holy war against the government, the author states that this was a misinterpretation. A peaceful *jihād* can accomplish similar results and is therefore a greater *jihād*. Ibid., p. 186.
68. Ibid., pp. 184–6.
69. Ibid., pp. 188–9.
70. Ibid., pp. 185–6.
71. Ibid., pp. 190–91; throughout the book the Sayyid's own role in educating the young generation is emphasised.
72. For a more general analysis of this problem see Muddathir 'Abd al-Raḥīm, 'Arabism, Africanism and self-identification in the Sudan', in Yūsuf Faḍl Ḥassan, pp. 228–38.
73. *Sudan Political Intelligence Summary* (hereafter *SPIS*), no. 46, Jan. 1945, FO/371/45972; according to the author of the report the support for an independent Sudan participating in some form of Arab unity '... received much stimulus from the visit to the Sudan during January of M. Albert Hourani ...' who had served under Toynbee in the Foreign Office International Research Department; see also Clayton to Burrows, 6 April, 1945, ibid.

74. Sir A. Gillan, 'Post-Treaty Egyptian relations', 27 May, 1938, Sir A. Gillan's private papers.
75. On al-Marāghī's dealings with the *ma'had* see Lampson to Oliphant, 12 Feb. 1937, FO/371/20870; Symes to Lampson, 23 March, 1938, FO/371/21998.
76. Symes to Lampson, 16 May, 1939, FO/371/23323.
77. Sir A. Gillan, 'Post-Treaty Egyptian relations', 27 May, 1938; see also Minute by C. S. (A. Gillan) to D. P. S. (Director Public Security), 20 July, 1939, Sir A. Gillan's private papers.
78. See, for instance, Lampson to Simon, 2 March, 1935; Symes to Lampson, 3 March 1935, FO/407/218; Lampson to Eden, 7 July, 1937, FO/407/221. Lampson wrote of the publicity given to Ṣiddīq al-Mahdī, the Sayyid's son, during his visit to Egypt.
79. *Istiqlāl*, p. 36.
80. *Sudan Monthly Intelligence Summary* (hereafter *SMIS*), no. 69, January 1940, FO/371/24633.
81. *SPIS*, no. 1, October–November 1940, FO/371/27382.
82. *SPIS*, no. 35, February 1944, FO/371/41348, reporting on 'Mr. Scrivener's interview with S. A. R. and A. E. M. 27 February, 1944'. Scrivener was at that time head of the Egyptian department at the Foreign Office in London.
83. *SPIS*, no. 6, April–May 1941, FO/371/27382.
84. *SPIS*, no. 25, March 1943, FO/371/35580.
85. *SMIS*, no. 73, Aug.–Sept. 1940, FO/371/24633; following an Italian bombardment of Omdurman, the Khatmiyya leaders spread a rumour that the attack '... was directed against Sayed Abdel Rahman personally, since all the bombs fell in the Abbasia district. The Italians, it was pointed out, would never attack Sayed Alī's quarters ...'; see also *SPIS*, no. 1, Oct.–Nov. 1940, FO/371/27382.
86. *SPIS*, no. 3, January 1941, ibid.
87. *SMIS*, no. 70, February–March 1940, FO/371/24633.
88. *SMIS*, no. 72, May–July 1940; *SMIS*, no. 73, August–September 1940, ibid.; on Sayyid 'Alī's relations with the graduates, see below, pp. 49–52.
89. *SPIS*, no. 41, Aug. 1944; *SPIS*, no. 42, Sept. 1944, FO/371/41348.
90. *Political Intelligence Centre Paper*, no. 66, 'The Sudan and the future', compiled by G. E. R. Sandars, Sudan Agent in Cairo and by K. D. D. Henderson and Samuel Atiyah of the Civil Secretary's Office, Khartoum (n. d. Oct. 1944?), FO/371/41363.
91. The following will deal in detail only with the penetration of sectarianism into the Graduates' General Congress. For other details see K. D. D. Henderson, *The Making of the modern Sudan*, London, 1953, pp. 536–53; Muddathir 'Abd al-Raḥīm, *Imperialism and nationalism in the Sudan*, London, 1969, pp. 124–32.
92. Kelly to Oliphant, 18 February, 38, FO/371/22003.
93. When I interviewed Sir Angus Gillan, K.B.E., C.M.G. and Mr. Reginald Davies, C.M.G., in 1970 I was impressed by their sincere belief in native administration and by their insistence that it was not intended as a

measure to keep the intelligentsia down. At the same time Davies stated that tribal shaykhs were of much higher standing in Sudanese society than the Gordon College graduates and moreover, had more character and intelligence; see also 'Some notes about the Erkowit Study Camp' by Gaitskell (n. d., May 1944?), FO/371/41363; Gaitskell related that he, and most of his British colleagues prior to the 'Erkowit Study Camp' had preferred the tribesmen 'whom they judged as something foreign' to the 'effendia' upon whom they looked down.

94. Henderson, (1953), p. xxvii.
95. Ibid., p. xxix. quoted from the *Arabic and English Newsletter*, Khartoum, 28 March, 1945.
96. Kelly to Oliphant, 2 February, 1938, FO/371/22003.
97. G. N. Sanderson, 'Sudanese nationalism and the independence of the Sudan', paper presented to the Symposium on Islamic North Africa, London, 14 September, 1971.
98. Gillan to Lampson, 5 July, 1938, FO/371/21999.
99. 'Monograph on some outstanding features and general purposes in the administration of the Sudan', by G. S. S. (Symes), May 1938, FO/371/22005.
100. Note on 'The Graduates' Congress', enclosed in Gillan to Lampson, 5 July, 1938, FO/371/21999.
101. *SMIS*, no. 64, June 1939, FO/407/224.
102. Ibid.
103. Intelligence Summary no. 6 (for period ending 28th February, 1940), FO/371/24620; the author of the summary noted that some of the graduates were wearing felt hats, which he regarded as a '... significant sign of independence vis à vis Egypt ... They are at least original in expressing their political views by the hats they wear and not by the shirts.'
104. *SMIS*, no. 70, Feb.–March 1940, FO/371/24633; Māhir's visit was described in detail by Muḥammad Ḥasanayn Makhlūf, who in a book titled *Two weeks with 'Alī Māhir in the Sudan* (in Arabic), claimed that the visit was a turning point in Egyptian-Sudanese relations. The book was probably intended as '... personal propaganda pure and simple ...' for 'Alī Māhir had by that time (March 1941) been dismissed from his post as PM on Lampson's insistence, due to his pro-Nazi sympathies. *SPIS*, no. 5, March 1941, FO/371/27382.
105. *SMIS*, no. 70, February–March 1940, FO/371/24633.
106. Ibid.
107. *SMIS*, no. 69, January 1940, FO/371/24633.
108. *SMIS*, no. 72, May–July 1940, FO/371/24633; it is interesting to note that throughout the war the Sudan, unlike Egypt, Iraq and other Middle Eastern countries, was practically free of Nazi propaganda. The only occasion mentioned in the intelligence reports was 'The Nazi Bill-Posting Incident' in Khartoum in which an Egyptian teacher and three school boys were involved; *SPIS*, no. 9, Aug. 1941, FO/371/27382.
109. *SMIS*, no. 73, Aug.–Sept. 1940, FO/371/24633; Sayyid 'Alī, who was

asked by Congress members to join the National Front, declined the offer. Instead, an article inspired by the Sayyid and published in his *Ṣawt al-Sūdān*, stated that '... there were no "political" leaders in the Sudan and that religious leaders could have nothing to do with the Congress or the National Front ...' Ibid.

110. Ibid.; al-Azharī was at that time still a supporter of Sayyid 'Abd al-Raḥmān.
111. The chief protagonists were Mīrghanī Ḥamza (under an assumed name) for the Khatmiyya, and 'Abdallāh al-Fāḍil and Aḥmad Yūsuf Hāshim, for the Anṣār. The government's censor spent half his time '... trying to rub the poison off the shafts ...' Ibid.
112. *SPIS*, no. 3, January 1941, FO/371/27382.
113. *SPIS*, no. 4, February 1941, ibid.
114. *SPIS*, no. 7, June 1941, ibid.; it should be noted that the Anṣār had been the original advocates of the boycott which the Khatmiyya had at first opposed.
115. *SPIS*, no. 9, August 1941, FO/371/27382; *SPIS*, no. 21, November 1942, FO/371/35580; Of those involved in the conflict, Yaḥyā al-Fadlī served as Minister for Social Affairs in al-Azharī's government 1953–6; while Ibrāhīm Aḥmad became Minister of Finance under 'Abdallāh Khalīl after independence.
116. *SPIS*, no. 21, Nov. 1942; *SPIS*, no. 22, Dec. 1942, FO/371/35580.
117. Henderson, pp. 540–2, gives all the details as well as the verbatim text of all the communications exchanged between Newbold and Ibrahīm Aḥmad; see also Muddathir 'Abd al-Raḥīm, pp. 127–30.
118. Newbold to all Governors and Heads of Departments, 2 May, 1942, FO/371/31587.
119. 'Note on further association of Sudanese with local and central government in the Sudan', by D. N. Newbold; Huddleston to Lampson, 12 May, 1942, ibid.
120. 'Memorandum on Sudanese nationalism and the Graduates' Congress', enclosure 4 in Lampson to Eden, 22 May, 1942 (secret), ibid.
121. *Istiqlāl*, pp. 42–3.
122. Newbold to Ibrahim Ahmed, 17 July, 1942; Ibrahim Ahmed to Newbold, 23 July, 1942; Newbold to Ibrahim Ahmed, 19 Sept., 1942, FO/371/31587; see also Henderson, pp. 548–50.
123. *SPIS*, no. 22, December 1942, FO/371/35580.
124. Huddleston to Lampson, 18 Nov., 1942, FO/371/31587; see also 'Note on further association of Sudanese with local and central government in the Sudan', signed D. N. Newbold, 10 Sept., 1942, ibid; for details on the Advisory Council see M. 'Abd al-Raḥīm, pp. 135–58.
125. *SPIS*, no. 28, July 1943, FO/371/35580; leading Anṣār tried during that period to discredit the Congress in Egypt and claimed that it did not represent even the educated class. Ibid.
126. *SPIS*, no. 32, November 1943, FO/371/41348; for the attitude of the two Sayyids to the advisory council see below.
127. *SPIS*, no. 33, Dec. 1943, FO/371/41348; according to the report, out of

966 graduates who participated in the elections, only 200–300 were intelligentsia while '... the rest were from the artisan and suk class ...'; *SPIS*, no. 37, April 1944, ibid.

128. 'Extracts from a conversation between Ibrahim Eff. Ahmed, President of Graduates' Congress and Mr. E. S. Atiyah, Public Relations Officer', 7 Jan., 1944, FO/371/41363; Edward Atiyah was Lebanese, educated in Cairo and Oxford, who had served in the Sudan since the early 1920s, first as master in Gordon College and later in the intelligence department and the Civil Secretary's office.
129. The choice of the name Ashiqqā' – brothers on both the paternal and the maternal sides – was politically significant, as it implied the support of the 'Unity of the Nile Valley'.
130. *SPIS*, no. 44, November 1944, FO/371/45972; the number of registered Congress members had risen from 1,300 in 1943 to 9,400, out of whom 4,667 attended the annual meeting. Most of these were defined as '... ignorant Tariqa members ...'. Ibid.
131. *SPIS*, no. 36, March 1944, FO/371/41348; in October 1943, al-Azharī demanded in the committee of sixty that any member of Congress accepting nomination to the advisory council be expelled. He referred specifically to Ibrāhīm Aḥmad and Aḥmad Yūsuf Hāshim, whom he called 'Kalb al-Ḥukūma'; *SPIS*, no. 31, October 1943, FO/371/35580.
132. During the Anṣār annual 'Marriage Festival' in July 1944, a poem was recited, extolling Sayyid 'Abd al-Raḥmān's services to the country and declaring a British intention to reward him with the crown of the Sudan. Despite the Sayyid's charge that this was a Khatmiyya plot to embarrass him, he did not deny his ambitions to become the Sudan's ruler until late in 1945, *SPIS*, no. 40, July 1944, FO/371/41348; see also *Istiqlāl*, pp. 43–4; Killearn to Huddleston, 5 June, 1944, FO/371/41363.
133. Bābikr Badrī, *Ta'rīkh ḥayātī*, Omdurman, 1961, vol. 3, p. 66; *SPIS*, no. 44, Nov. 1944, FO/371/45972.
134. *SPIS*, no. 45, Dec. 1944, FO/371/45972; In April 1945, Sayyid 'Alī was already regretting the close link with the Ashiqqā' and was '... contemplating a withdrawal into the obscurity of his favourite religious background, where he could merely let things slide, leaving himself free to deny complicity or even knowledge if they slid too fast ...' *SPIS*, no. 48, March–April, 1945, ibid.
135. Macintosh to Azharī, 7 February, 1945, FO/371/45984.
136. *SPIS*, no. 48, March–April 1945, FO/371/45972.
137. *SPIS*, no. 51, July 1945, ibid.; al-Azharī justified the government's charges when he promised that the Congress would attempt '... to enforce the educational qualifications at the next elections ...' Ibid.
138. *SPIS*, no. 45, December 1944, FO/371/45972.
139. *SPIS*, no. 48, March–April 1945, ibid.; see also Killearn to F. O., 16 April, 1945, FO/371/45984; apparently al-Azharī had advocated a more moderate resolution by inserting the word 'independent', but was overruled by the more extremist elements.
140. Report of Cairo Police on interview with Azharī, enclosed in Killearn to Eden, 11 July, 1945, FO/371/45984.

141. The six parties represented on the Committee were: Ashiqqā', Umma, Ittiḥādiyyīn, Ittiḥādiyyīn Aḥrār, Ahrār, and Qawmiyyīn. Apart from the Ashiqqā' and Umma, these were in effect factions which had broken away from the two main parties mainly because of the latters' subservience to the two Sayyids; 'The Agreement (Covenant) of the United Parties', (n. d. 25 Aug., 1945?) FO/371/45986; for details on the emergence of the parties see below.
142. Robertson to Haselden, 28 Aug., 1945, ibid.; the word *ḥurr* which was used in the original resolution and translated by the authorities as *free*, might just as well have been employed to denote *independent*.
143. Farquhar (acting British Ambassador in Cairo) to Bevin, 17 Sept., 1945, ibid.; see also *SPIS*, no. 52, Aug. 1945, FO/371/45972.
144. Robertson to al-Azharī, 1 September, 1945, ibid.
145. Azharī to Governor-General, 15 October, 1945, enclosed in Robertson to Mayall, 29 October, 1945, FO/371/45986.
146. Penney to Haselden, 26 November, 1945, ibid.; out of 10,000 Congress members, 5,470 paid their dues for 1945, but only 3,512 actually voted.
147. *SPIS*, no. 30, September 1943, FO/371/35580.
148. *SPIS*, no. 38, May 1944, FO/371/41348; *SPIS*, no. 36, March 1944, ibid.
149. *SPIS*, no. 37, April 1944, ibid.; The riots in Tuti were, according to the government, the result of a misunderstanding of a government development plan. In the clash with the police one of the inhabitants was killed and several were wounded. As the Island's population were Khatmiyya supporters Sayyid 'Alī assumed his favourite role of intermediary with the government.
150. *SPIS*, no. 39, June 1944, ibid.
151. *SPIS*, no. 52, August 1945, FO/371/45972; *SPIS*, no. 53, September 1945, ibid.
152. *SPIS*, no. 38, May 1944, FO/371/41348.
153. The Qawmiyyīn's importance lay in their leader, Aḥmad Yūsuf-Hāshim, who as editor and owner of *al-Sūdān al-Jadīd* was in a position to publicise his party's line; the Aḥrār were a small group, composed mainly of teachers; see 'The Programmes and personalities of the Congress groups contesting this year's elections', Appendix in *SPIS*, no. 43, October 1944, ibid.
154. *SPIS*, no. 41, August 1944, FO/371/41348; *SPIS*, no. 45, December 1944, FO/371/45972; *SPIS*, no. 46, January 1945, ibid.
155. *Istiqlāl*, pp. 46–50; Muḥammad Sulaymān, in his book *al-Yasār al-Sūdanī* claimed that the Umma took its name and its ideology from the Egyptian Umma party which was founded in 1907. Both were supported by the British rulers and advocated cooperation with them. Both were led by members of the local aristocracy and the big landowners but enjoyed too, the support of certain sections of the intelligentsia; Muḥammad Sulaymān, *al-Yasār al-Sūdānī fi 'asharah a'wām* 1954–1963, Wād Madanī 1971, pp. XIX–XX. Four of the founders of the Umma party were among those requesting a full discussion in the advisory council on Sudanese nationality; *SPIS*, no. 43, October 1944, FO/371/41348.
156. 'Constitution of the Nation Party', submitted by 'Abdallāh Khalīl for

approval, 20 Feb., 1945, FO/371/45984; also *SPIS*, no. 47, February 1945, FO/371/45972.

157. Ibid.
158. Ibid.
159. *SPIS*, no. 48, March–April 1945, FO/371/45972; the financial connection between *Dā'irat al-Mahdī* and the Umma was openly admitted by Sayyid 'Abd al-Raḥmān in his memoirs; *Istiqlāl*, pp. 49–50.
160. *SPIS*, no. 50, June 1945 FO/371/45972; see also CMD 7316, *Report of the Governor-General on the Administration, Finance and Conditions of the Sudan in 1945*, Sudan no. 1, 1948.
161. *SPIS*, no. 49, May 1945, FO/371/45972.
162. Robertson to Fouracres, 8 April, 1945, FO/371/45984.
163. Sudan Agent (Cairo) to Civil Secretary (Khartoum), 13 June, 1945 and 9 July, 1945, FO/371/45984; Robertson to Mayall, 25 October, 1945, FO/371/45986.

**Chapter 2** (pp. 67–89)

1. Ismā'īl al-Azharī published his memoirs in the Sudanese daily *al-Ayyām* between 3 June and 6 September, 1957 under the title 'Mudhakarāt al-Ra'īs Ismā'īl al-Azharī'. I am grateful to Prof. Carl Brown of Princeton who put at my disposal his collection of Sudanese dailies dealing with that period, which includes both the al-Azharī memoirs and the articles by *al-Ayyām* editor, Bashīr Muḥammad Sa'īd, on that period (see ref. 37 below).
2. Richard Hill, *A Biographical Dictionary of the Sudan*, Cass, London, 1967, p. 184. Ismā'īl's great-grandfather was killed in the fighting against the Mahdists in Kordofan but his grandfather's uncle, Ismā'īl al-Makki, the head of the Ismā'īliya order at al-Ubayyiḍ, was one of the first supporters of the Mahdi in Kordofan.
3. Among his many friends in Beirut, al-Azharī mentions a Jewish student from Palestine called Neidermann. He also tells of a love-affair he had with an Italian girl but is careful to mention that this was 'before the Italian invasion of Ethiopia'. Mr Zeev Neidermann, a high school teacher (now retired) from Zikhron Ya'acov Israel, confirmed in his talk with me that he had been Ismā'īl al-Azharī's friend during his student days in Beirut. According to Neidermann, al-Azharī refrained from any political activity during his studies. Al-Azharī visited Palestine after WW II and toured Tel-Aviv and Zikhron Ya'acov in the company of Mr. Neidermann.
4. For details see: Henderson (1953), pp. 536–71. See also Enclosed in Huddleston to Killearn, 8 Dec., 1945, FO/371/53249. Azharī to Huddleston, 15 Oct., 1945, Ibid. see also Azharī to Huddleston 7 Apr. 1946, where al-Azharī claims that despite Umma objections, his delegation is qualified to represent the Sudan in the forthcoming negotiations.

5. *Istiqlāl*, pp. 53–57.
6. Ibid., p. 59.
7. Ibid., pp. 61–62.
8. For details see: ʻAbd al-Raḥīm, pp. 159–202.
9. Al-Azharī relates that during the debate about forming the Legislative Assembly, the British Secretary for Home Affairs offered him the post of Minister of Education in the future government. True to his conscience, al-Azharī refused the offer. On the next day, when marching at the head of Sudanese students demonstrating against the assembly he was arrested and sentenced to two months' imprisonment (*Al-Ayyām*, 23 July, 1957).
10. Henderson, (1953) pp. 453–454.
11. *Istiqlāl*, p. 64.
12. The British claim that the assembly was not representative was of course sheer hypocrisy – they were the ones who had lauded the participation of all strata of the Sudanese people in the assembly. See: ʻAbd al-Raḥīm, pp. 186–9.
13. In the first general elections in the Sudan in 1953, the Socialist-Republicans won 3 out of the 97 seats in parliament. According to Sayyid ʻAbd al-Raḥmān the governor-general told him in so many words that the Socialist-Republican party was set up for the express purpose of fighting the Umma (*Istiqlāl*, p. 68).
14. Ibid., pp. 48–9.
15. G. N. Sanderson, pp. 7–8.
16. *Istiqlāl*, pp. 90–2.
17. *The Sudan's Progress towards Self-Government 1951–52*, British Information Services, n.d., pp. 8–9.
18. 'Self-Government Statute', in *Documents on the Sudan*, Egyptian Society of International Law, March 1953, pp. 52–98. This statute, in its modified version, was the basis for Najīb's agreement with the Sudanese parties in January 1953 and for the Anglo-Egyptian agreement signed one month later.
19. For details see: J. S. R. Duncan, *The Sudan's Path to Independence*, Edinburgh & London, 1957, pp. 151–2, see also ʻAbd al-Raḥīm, pp. 200–1.
20. For details of the negotiations see: ʻAbd al-Raḥmān ʻAli Ṭāha, *al-Sūdān l'il Sūdāniyyin*, Omdurman 1955, pp. 91–2. The author was a member of the Umma delegation which took part in the negotiations; see also *Istiqlāl*, pp. 93–5.
21. Ibid., pp. 96–99. When it began to seem that the talks were being bogged down, the Umma spokesmen approached Najīb directly and asked him to intervene (ʻAlī Ṭāha, pp. 101–3).
22. *Al-Ayyām*, 19 July, 1957.
23. *Istiqlāl*, pp. 100–1.
24. ʻAlī Ṭāha, pp. 93–98. See also: J. Marlowe, *Anglo-Egyptian Relations 1800–1956*, Hamden, Conn., 1965, pp. 392–3. Marlowe also cites the mistaken view that Najīb surprised the British by his talks with the Sayyid which resulted in the agreement on the future of the Sudan.

25. *Al-Ayyām*, 30–31 July, 1957.
26. Details in 'Abd al-Raḥīm, pp. 212–27.
27. *Al-Ayyām*, 5 August, 1957.
28. *Al-Ayyām*, 3 August, 1957.
29. Ibid., 7 August, 1957.
30. Ibid., 12 August, 1957.
31. Ibid., 21 August, 1957.
32. Quoted in *Sudan Herald*, 16 August, 1950.
33. Quoted in *Sudan News and Features*, 5 December, 1953.
34. *Al-Ayyām*, 2 September, 1957.
35. *Istiqlāl*, p. 142.
36. Ibid., pp. 143–5. According to al-Azharī, the dismissals were due to personal and not political reasons. (See *al-Ayyām*, 6 September, 1957).
37. The interview was published in full in *al-Ayyām* in December 1954 and again in a series of articles by the journalist Bashīr Muḥammad Sa'īd, published in *al-Ayyām* between 11 and 27 February, 1958.
38. Ibid., 12 February, 1958.
39. 'Alī Ṭāha, p. 120.
40. For the development of the distrust and its political implications see Ch. I; The correspondent of the London *Times* was aware of the importance of this announcement; it was published in *The Times* on 23 August, 1953.
41. *Istiqlāl*, p. 127.
42. 'Alī Ṭāha, pp. 126–127.
43. Ibid., pp. 135–139.
44. Quoted in *al-Ayyām* of 4 September, 1958 in the series of articles by Bashīr Muḥammad Sā'īd.
45. There was strong communist influence in these three organisations and the communists were bitter opponents of the Nasser regime (see *Istiqlāl*, p. 151). For the full text of the Students' Organisation resolution, see 'Alī Ṭāha, p. 144.
46. Ibid., p. 145.
47. *Istiqlāl*, p. 153; *al-Ayyām*, 14 February, 1958.
48. For details see: Bashīr Muḥammad Sa'īd, *The Sudan, Crossroads of Africa*, London, 1956, pp. 75–6.
49. *Al-Jumhūriyya*, 5 August, 1955.
50. Al-Azharī's proposal was published in the *Sudan Weekly News*, 16 August, 1955. See also 'Abd al-Raḥīm, pp. 224–5.
51. The full text of Sayyid 'Alī al-Mīrghanī's statement was published in *al-Ayyām* on 10 February, 1958.
52. *Al-Ayyām*, 15 February, 1958; see also 'Abd al-Raḥīm, p. 225.
53. *Istiqlāl*, pp. 158–9.
54. The only member of the Mīrghanī family who was openly involved in political activity was Sayyid 'Alī's nephew, Muḥammad 'Uthmān al-Mīrghanī, but even he was pressured by his uncle into giving it up after a short time. Thus there was a sort of division of functions between the Mīrghanīs, who were content with religious leadership, and the young generation of educated Khatmiyya followers who were active on the political scene.

55. This view was expounded in Bashīr's article (*al-Ayyām*, 18 February, 1958). Bashīr was then directly involved in the political arena and there is no reason to doubt its truth. It is, however, surprising not to find any reference to it in the Anṣār press and literature of those days.
56. *Al-Ayyām*, 17–20 February, 1958.
57. *Istiqlāl*, pp. 165–6.
58. Ibid., pp. 167–8; *al-Ayyām*, 22 February, 1958.
59. *Al-Ayyām*, 22 February, 1958.

**Chapter 3** (pp. 93–140)

1. J. M. A. Bakheit, Communist Activities in the Middle East Between 1919–1927, with Special Reference to Egypt and the Sudan,' Sudan Research Unit, Univ. of Khartoum, 1968.
2. Ibid.: see also *Secret Intelligence Report* No. 11, February 1927, FO/371/12374; the Soviet agents mentioned in the report were Lumitoff, a Tartar from the Caucasus, and Belkin, a Russian Jew who had previously served in Iraq; It is noteworthy that in 1924 the Comintern established the 'Negro Propaganda Commission' in Geneva, one of whose main tasks was to smuggle leaflets and pamphlets into the African continent.
3. *Secret Intelligence Report* No. 5, June 1926, FO/371/11613; *Secret Intelligence Report* No. 6, August 1926, ibid.; the report signed by Hillelson stated that certain anti-British propaganda sheets in the Sudan had been traced to foreign, probably Greek or Italian, sources.
4. Salah El Din El Zein El Tayeb, *The Student Movement in the Sudan 1940–1970*, Khartoum University Press 1971, pp. 39–41. (Hereafter *Student Movement*).
5. The following, unless otherwise stated, is based on *Lamaḥāt min ta'rīkh al-ḥizb al-Shuyū'ī al-Sūdāni*, Dar al-fikr al-ishtirāki 1960. This brief history of the SCP was written by Maḥjūb in 1959–1960 while he was in prison during the 'Abbūd regime (hereafter *Lamaḥāt*).
6. Saad Ed Din Fawzi, *The Labour Movement in the Sudan 1946–1955* London 1957, pp. 36–37, (hereafter Fawzi).
7. Ibid.; pp. 67–70.
8. *Al-Shafi' Aḥmad al-Shaykh ibn al-ṭabaqa al-'āmila al-Sūdānīyya* ..., Prague 1971. This is a brochure commemorating al-Shafi' which was published by the World Federation of Trade Unions in Prague, shortly after al-Shafi's execution in July 1971 (hereafter al-Shafi').
9. Fawzi, pp. 113–5.
10. Ibid.; see also *Allies for Freedom, Report of the Second Conference of Communist and Workers' Parties within the Sphere of British Imperialism*, Caxton Hall, London, 1954, pp. 107–8.
11. Ibid.
12. Fawzi, p. 116. The Communists ascribed the failure of this strike to the internal strife within the SCP.

13. Ibid., p. 118. The strong influence of the Khatmiyya was probably a
14. Muḥammad Sulaymān, *Al-Yasār al-Sūdānī fī 'asharah a'wām 1954–1963*, Wād Madanī 1971, pp. 11–15 (hereafter Sulaymān); Muḥammad Sulaymān was a member of the SCP; he was founder and first President of the Sudan's Teachers' Union and was elected MP in a graduates' constituency in 1965; under Numeiri, he first served as Sudanese Ambassador to Cairo; during the July 1971 coup he remained passive and now lives in Khartoum as a private citizen; his brother is Aḥmad Sulaymān, one of the leaders of the anti-Maḥjūb faction of the SCP. His book: 'The Sudanese Left during Ten Years 1955–1963', is a compilation of documents, speeches and newspaper articles, presenting communist and leftist views on Sudanese politics.
15. *Al-Ayyām*, 24 January, 1955; quoted in Sulaymān, pp. 85–9.
16. Sulaymān, pp. 104–108.
17. *Al-Ayyām*, 9 September, 1955; quoted in Sulaymān, p. 105.
18. *Al-Mīdān*, 14 November, 1955; in Sulaymān, pp. 152–56; al-Azharī won the vote of confidence by 48 votes while the opposition received 46 votes.
19. For details see below.
20. Sulaymān, pp. 222–24.
21. *Al-Mīdān*, 18 July, 13 October, 1957; in Sulaymān, pp. 278–87.
22. *Al-Mīdān*, 24 February, 1958, Sulaymān, pp. 306–310.
23. *Al-Mīdān*, 24 February, 1958, Sulaymān, p. 312.
24. *Al-Ayyām*, 12 March, 1958, Sulaymān, pp. 315–317; it is interesting to note that the NUP secured the largest support; it received 340,410 votes as against 310,019 votes given to the Umma. The disproportionate representation in Parliament was the result of the new election law. See also *al-Mīdān*, 18 May, 1958, Sulaymān, pp. 319–21.
25. Ibid., p. 317.
26. Ibid., p. 318, quoted from *al-Mīdān*, 13 March, 1958.
27. *Al-Mīdān*, 3 November, 1958, Sulaymān, pp. 349–51.
28. *Al-taḥqīq fī asbāb al-latī adat ilā inqilāb 17 November, 1958* (Wizārat al-'Adl) p. 74, quoted in Sulaymān, pp. 354–56.
29. For details see, R. First, *Power in Africa*, New York 1970, pp. 222–32.
30. *Ṣawt al-Sūdān*, 20 November, 1958, *al-Nīl*, 21 November, 1958; Sulaymān, pp. 357–59.
31. *Al-Ayyām*, 28 November, 4 December, 18 December, 1958, Sulaymān, pp. 360–61; 'Abd al-Khāliq Maḥjūb managed to escape imprisonment until October 1959, when he was finally captured. According to 'Alī 'Abd al-Raḥmān, leader of the PDP, the Umma and the SCP gave their full support to 'Abbūd following his coup. Their attitude changed only after 'Abbūd adopted a more progressive external policy following his visits to the Soviet Union, China, Yugoslavia and the UAR. It was only then that these parties, together with the NUP and the Muslim Brothers, demanded a return to civilian rule; see 'Ali 'Abd al-Raḥmān al-Amīn, *al-Dīmugrāṭiyya wa'l-Ishtirākiyya fī'l Sūdān,* Beirut 1970, p. 92.
32. Sulaymān, pp. 422–8.

33. Sulaymān, pp. 382–4.
34. *Thawrat Sha'ab*, p. 234, quoted in Sulaymān pp. 385–86; on 9 December, 1960, *Ṣawt al-Sūdān* published a declaration, signed by some 35 notables supporting the 'Abbūd regime as the saviour of the Sudan, Sulaymān, pp. 387–90.
35. Sulaymān, pp. 391–4.
36. The SCP, which was fully aware of the leading role played by the leader of the Anṣār in the opposition to 'Abbūd, sent a letter of condolence and appreciation to the Mahdi's family despite its hostility to the Anṣār; *Thawrat Sha'ab*, p. 258; quoted in Sulaymān, p. 395.
37. Sulaymān pp. 396–7; they were arrested in August 1961 and released after six months.
38. *Al-Shafi'* pp. 18–20; see also R. First, *Power in Africa*, New York 1970, p. 247.
39. *Student Movement*, pp. 58–64.
40. K. D. D. Henderson, *Sudan Republic*, London 1965, p. 149; Henderson defines the Jazīra tenants as 'a highly privileged section of the Community, gentlemen-farmers dependent more and more on hired labour'. The Jazīra project had been financed by the Sudanese tax-payer and therefore the government had a good case in trying to retain a substantial share of its profits.
41. Muṣṭafā A., 'al-Ḥizb al-Shūyū'ī al-Sūdānī yunāḍil fī sabil istiqlāl wadīmuqratiyyat bilādihī', *al-Waqt*, August 1962, pp. 36–43.
42. Henderson, (1965), pp. 146–9.
43. Declaration of the SCP, 1 August, 1961; in *Thawrat Sha'ab*, p. 380, quoted in Sulaymān pp. 410–12.
44. *Thawrat Sha'ab*, pp. 381–87; declaration of the SCP, 12 December, 1961; in Sulaymān, pp. 413–21.
45. The Political Bureau of the SCP, 9 March, 1963, in Sulaymān, pp. 422–28.
46. *Thawrat Sha'ab*, p. 258, in Sulaymān, pp. 407–9.
47. The following account is based mainly on Yusuf Fadl Hasan, 'The Sudanese Revolution of October 1964', *The Journal of Modern African Studies*, Vol. 5 (1967) pp. 505–9.
48. Yusuf Faḍl Hasan, p. 507; see also al-Bustānī M., 'Ba'd al-iṭāḥa bi'l-diktātūriyya al- 'askariyya fī'l-Sūdān,' *al-Waqt*, December 1964.
49. The three were: Aḥmad Sulaymān, al-Shafi' Aḥmad al-Shaykh and al-Amīn Muḥammad al-Amīn. The reason why 'Abd al-Khāliq Maḥjūb did not join the Cabinet was, according to the Lebanese journalist Fu'ād Maṭar, that the party realised that the post-revolutionary honeymoon would not last and hence regarded it as unwise to 'burn' the SCP's secretary general, see Fu'ad Maṭar, *al-Ḥizb al-Shuyū'ī al-Sūdānī naḥarūhu amm intaḥara*, Beirut 1971, pp. 21–2 (hereafter Maṭar).
50. S. R. Smirnov, 'The Sudan', in S. R. Smirnov, (ed.) *A History of Africa 1918–1967*, (Moscow, 1968) pp. 174–75. Smirnov claims that the communist-attempted general strike was blocked by the police and the army. According to Henderson, (1965) p. 216, the strike failed as it was denounced by the railway and motor transport unions for political reasons

while the Jazīra cotton growers refused to be involved. The negative attitude of the Khatmiyya leaders to communist tactics may also explain their failure, especially amongst the railway workers.

51. The 'Graduates' constituencies' were first established in the 1953 elections in order to provide for greater representation of the intelligentsia.
52. Henderson, (1965) p. 225.
53. Hassan 'Abdallāh, 'Ma'rakat al-dīmuqrāṭiyya la tazāl mustamirra', *Al-Waqt*, 2 (1966). The accurate number of SCP members is not known. According to *The World Today*, London, January 1965, there were 10,000 party members at that time.
54. *Al-Anwār*, 4 December, 1964. According to the PDP leader, 'Alī 'Abd al-Raḥmān al-Amīn, (pp. 125–26) the SCP knew only too well that the sole reason for its success in the 1965 elections was that the graduates had only two alternatives: either to vote for the communists or to abstain. This was due to the fact that the NUP was at the time co-operating with the Umma in the government, while the PDP decided to boycott the elections. The results of the 1968 elections tend to prove this claim, as the SCP lost all but three of the graduates' constituencies, mainly to former PDP candidates (the PDP had united with the NUP in December 1967 to form the Democratic Unionist Party).
55. *Al-Anwār*, 15 May, 1965; *al-Nahār*, 6 May, 1965.
56. *Al-Nahār*, 12 May, 1965; see also below.
57. *Al-Ḥayāt*, 13 November, 1965.
58. R. Omdurman, 14 November, 1965 – BBC, 16 November, 1965.
59. *Al-Jumhūriyya*, 14 November, 1965.
60. *Al-Ahrām*, 16 November, 1965.
61. R. Omdurman, 21 November, 1965 – BBC, 23 November, 1965.
62. R. Omdurman, 22 November, 1965 – BBC, 24 November, 1965.
63. R. Omdurman, 8 December, 1965 – BBC, 11 December, 1965.
64. *Al-Akhbār*, 13 December, 1965; *al-Ḥayāt*, 15 December, 1965.
65. R. Omdurman, 17 December, 1965 – BBC, 20 December, 1965.
66. The case was first brought to court on 23 December (*al-Thawra*, 24 December, 1965). On 29 December, the hearing was postponed to 5 January, 1966 (*al-Ahrām*, 30 December, 1966); the government, however, refused to give in despite a warning by the Supreme Court that the judges would resign (*al-Akhbār*, 3 January, 1967).
67. *Al-Anwār*, 19 January, 1966; *al-Akhbār*, 1 June, 1966; 6 June, 1966.
68. *Falasṭīn*, 12 December, 1966.
69. *Le Monde*, 4 October, 1966.
70. *The Morning News*, 1 January, 1967; *Le Monde*, 30 December, 1966.
71. *Al-Akhbār*, 10 March, 1967; for details regarding the founding of the Socialist Party, see below.
72. *Al-Dustūr*, 7 April, 1967.
73. *Al-Ahrām*, 21 April, 1967.
74. One of the best articles describing the situation is that by Aḥmad Ḥamrush in *Rūz al-Yūsuf*, 1 May, 1967; See also *al-Ahrām*, 19 May, 1967.
75. *Al-Ḥayāt*, 4 October, 1967.

76. *Rūz al-Yūsuf*, 4 December, 1967.
77. *Rūz al-Yūsuf*, 15 January, 1968.
78. *Al-Akhbār*, 1 January, 1967. According to *Rūz al-Yūsuf*, 2 February, 1967, the communists refused to join the new party. It seems, therefore, that only one faction of the communists joined the new party. See *al-Muṣawwar*, 10 March, 1967; and also Abdel A. El-Ghannam, 'Die Kommunistische Partei im Sudan', *Afrika Heute*, 15 June, 1967.
79. *Rūz al-Yūsuf*, 8 January, 1968.
80. *Al-Ḥayāt*, 8 May, 1968; *Le Monde*, 8 May, 1968.
81. *Al-Ṣafā'*, 5 December, 1968; *al-Ḥayāt*, 26 November, 1968. 'Abd al-Khāliq Mahjūb, who had just been married, was at the time touring Eastern Europe, *al-Ḥayāt*, 11 October, 1968.
82. R. Omdurman, 25 May, 1969 – D. R., 26 May, 1969; for details see P. K. Bechtold, 'Renewed Intervention by the Military in Sudanese Politics', paper presented to the annual meeting of MESA, Toronto, November 1969.
83. Ḥusayn 'Abd al-Rāziq, *Haqā'iq al-Ṣidām ma' al-ḥizb al-Shuyū'ī al-Sūdānī*, Beirut 1972; pp. 23–5 (hereafter Rāziq).
84. For details see below.
85. Maṭar, pp. 27–8.
86. Maṭar, pp. 23–4.
87. *Africa Confidential*, 20 June, 1969.
88. Rāziq, pp. 23–5; see also Maṭar, p. 48, who claims that due to their position, the pro-communist members of the RCC managed to infiltrate SCP members into the Military Academy and the Secret Services.
89. Maṭar, pp. 25–6; Rāziq, pp. 27–9.
90. *Al-Ḥayāt*, 13 October, 1969; *New York Times*, 29 October, 1969.
91. MENA, 11 October, 1969 – I.M.B., 11 October, 1969; *al-Ahrām*, 12 October, 1969; *al-Ḥayāt*, 18 October, 1969.
92. *Al-Ḥayāt*, 7 July, 1969; *Niḍā al-Waṭan*, 10 July, 1969. At the University of Khartoum, Maḥjūb reacted strongly against those who attacked the communists. See MENA, 11 October, 1969 – D.R. 13 October, 1969; *al-Ahrām*, 14 October, 1969; *al-Jadīd*, 24 October, 1969.
93. MENA, 28, 29, and 30 October 1969 – I.M.B. 29, 30 and 31 October 1969.
94. J. Shaw, 'Crisis in the Sudan', *Marxism Today*, April 1971.
95. For details on the internal strife within the SCP regarding these problems, see below.
96. This does not agree with the view expressed in *al-Ṭalī'a*, 5 May, 1970, pp. 141–147, which claims that the SCP and the trade unions supported the use of arms against the Anṣār most enthusiastically.
97. Rāziq, pp. 30–2; Maḥjūb was allowed to return to the Sudan in July 1970, following pressure from Nasser, but was immediately put under house arrest, as were several other leaders of his faction.
98. *International Affairs Bulletin*, Vol. 5, No. 1 (March 1971) pp. 25–26 (this Bulletin is a bi-monthly publication of the International Department of the Communist Party of Gt. Britain). Following the conference mentioned

above, the anti-Maḥjūb faction left the SCP and set up its own communist party. For details see below.

99. MENA, 16 November, 1970 – I.M.B., 17 November, 1970.
100. *Al-Akhbār*, 13 April, 1971.
101. 'To the masses of the Sudanese People from the Central Committee of the Sudanese Communist Party, on the Events of 16th November'. Khartoum, 16 November, 1970 (official translation). See below, ch. 5, C.
102. In the 'Report of the Central Committee of the Communist Party of Sudan' September–November 1971 session, Egypt was accused of actually initiating the events of 16 November in order to impose the Tripartite Federation on the Sudan.
103. 'Ḥiwār bayn al-Ra'īs Numayrī wal-Ṭalī'a', *al-Ṭalī'a*, 12 December, 1970, pp. 11–25; see also *al-Ṭalī'a*, 7 July, 1970, pp. 138–142.
104. The Five-Year plan had been drafted by Soviet experts. It envisaged an increase in the Gross National Product from £S564 m. in 1969/1970 to £S833 m. in 1974/1975 (an average annual rise of 8.1 per cent as compared to an annual rise of 4.7 per cent in the previous five years). The plan called for the investment of £S95 m. by the Soviet bloc and some £S25 m. by West-European countries; see also *al-Kātib*, July 1970, pp. 80–98.
105. Although Numeiri did not mention the SCP, its opposition to the socialism as proposed by him was well known.
106. R. Omdurman, February 12, 1971 – D.R. 12 February, 1971. It should be noted that the motif of Islam – later on elaborated upon by Numeiri – was not mentioned at this stage.
107. 'Statement by the Communist Party of Sudan', 12 February, 1971 (official translation). Full text printed below, Ch. 5, D.
108. Communist opposition to a number of reforms introduced at Khartoum University at that time is a good illustration. These included the introduction of Arabic as a medium of tuition instead of English; and a reform enabling more students from lower brackets of income to be accepted by the University. The communist-dominated Students' Union declared a students strike against these measures; see Rāziq, p. 41.
109. *Daily Report*, 27 April, 1971.
110. R. Omdurman, 26 May, 1971; for details see Rāziq, pp. 43–45.
111. Document reprinted in Rāziq, pp. 86–91.
112. Maṭar, pp. 45–6; according to rumours, Maḥjūb was in fact hiding in the palace under Numeiri's own roof, while the police were searching for him all over the country; Rāziq, pp. 44–45.
113. Another version, explaining why the coup was executed so suddenly, is that al-'Aṭā' feared that the SCP's central committee, which was scheduled to meet on that day, would decide against a coup and thus Maḥjūb who supported it would find himself in a minority; *Africa Confidential*, 2 June, 1972.
114. R. Omdurman, 19 July, 1971 – BBC 21 July, 1971.
115. Two leading communists, 'Azz-al-Dīn 'Alī 'Āmir and Muḥammad Maḥjūb (the secretary-general's brother) who were travelling to the Sudan

on the same plane, were probably not noticed by the Libyans and thus were saved; see Rāziq, p. 10.

116. Maṭar, pp. 59–65; the two Egyptian delegates were Aḥmad Ḥamrūsh, then editor of *Rūz al-Yūsuf*, and Aḥmad Fu'ād, director of Bank Miṣr, both known for their leftist views.
117. Rāziq, p. 53.
118. Rāziq, p. 60.
119. Rāziq, pp. 56–7; see also El Mahdawi, 'Dark Days in The Sudan', *The African Communist*, 47 (1971) pp. 62–7.
120. 'In Memory of our Independence Anniversary'; Central Committee Sudanese Communist Party, December 1971 (official translation).
121. According to one report, 624 persons were killed in the few days following Numeiri's counter-coup, among whom 156 were communists; see A. Sylvester, 'As the dust settles in Sudan, President Numeiri must face realities', *New Middle East*, 37, October 1971, p. 12.
122. R. Omdurman, 3 August, 1971 – BBC 5 August, 1971.
123. Maṭar, pp. 39–41.
124. *Information Bulletin*, 16, 1971.
125. *Le Monde*, 12 February, 1972. It is noteworthy that the Chinese refrained from any protest against the execution of Maḥjūb and his colleagues, yet greeted Numeiri for his success, *Hsinhua*, 26 Julyand 13 October, 1971.
126. *Al-Niḍā'*, 8 August, 1971; see also *World Strength of the Communist Party Organisations*, 24th Annual Report, Bureau of Intelligence and Research, (Washington 1972), p. 128; according to this report, the number of active members of the SCP was 5000–10,000. However, this is only an estimate as the same number was given in all previous reports.
127. 'Report of the Central Committee of the Communist Party of Sudan'; Sept.–Nov., 1971. Session. See below, ch. 5, E.
128. Ibid.
129. Ibid.
130. Ibid.
131. 'In Memory of our Independence Anniversary'; Central Committee, Sudanese Communist Party, December 1971 (official translation).
132. The Funj Sultanate ruled over parts of the Northern Sudan between the 16th and 19th centuries. It was conquered by Egypt in 1820–21. The Mahdist movement ousted the Turco-Egyptians from the Sudan in 1881–85 and was in turn overthrown by the Anglo-Egyptians in 1896–98.
133. *The African Communist*, 51 (1972) p. 71. See also *WMR* vol. 14 No. 9 (Sept. 1971), p. 51, where under the heading 'The Terror in the Sudan' the writer denounces the execution of Maḥjūb and his colleagues and the 'manhunt for Communists and other patriots'.
134. Ibid; see also *Africa Confidential*, June 2, 1972.
135. Ibid.
136. Klime Čorbe; 'Sudan at the Crossroads', *Review of International Affairs*, Belgrade, March 5–20, 1972.
137. For details, see Christopher Gandy, 'Sudan 1972: Pragmatism Replaces Ideology', *New Middle East*, 42–3, March–April 1972, pp. 14–16.

138. According to a report in *Africa Confidential*, 28 July 1972, the pan-Arabists have been trying to sabotage the solution in the South in order to enhance their own policies.
139. Sylvester, op. cit., p. 13; see also Maṭar, p. 39–41, who states that Numeiri's Minister of the Treasury, Muḥammad 'Abd al-Ḥalīm, had accused the Soviets of charging higher prices for their exports to the Sudan, as early as 1970.
140. *Africa Confidential*, October 6, 1972.

**Chapter 4** (pp. 141–168)

1. *Lamaḥāt*, pp. 10–13; 49–54.
2. Ibid, pp. 16–17.
3. *Al-Mīdān*, 22 July, 30 July, 1956; in Sulaymān pp. 232–3.
4. Ibid. pp. 242–56; quoting from *al-Mīdān*, 22 October, 1956; *al-Ra'y al-'Ām*, 17 November, 1950; Matar, (p. 19) claims that the friendship between Nasser and Maḥjūb was forged during the trying period of October–November 1956.
5. See for instance: Memorandum to Ismā'īl al-Azharī, signed by the AIF, 4 April 1955; quoted in Sulaymān, pp. 121–30.
6. *Al-Mīdān*, 19 December, 1957; 23 December, 1957; in Sulaymān pp. 289–97.
7. *Al-Mīdān*, 24 February, 1958; in Sulaymān, p. 312.
8. The anti-Maḥjūb faction later claimed that this decision was part of Maḥjūb's plan to dissolve the SCP and to found instead a broad National Democratic Front together with al-Ṣadiq al-Mahdī; see *al-Nahār*, 29 March, 1971.
9. Rāziq, pp. 37–8.
10. Maṭar, pp. 94–5, quoting Maḥjūb's statement on Arab Unity in February 1970; see also Dr. Amer Izzedine, 'Popular Resistance is Being Organized', *Africasia*, 16 August, 1971.
11. 'Abd al-Khālig Maḥjūb, 'Ra'y al-Shuyū'īyīn al-Sūdānīyīn fī'l Waḥda al-'Arabiyya', *al-Ṭarīq*, 8 (1971) pp. 9–16; see also Rāziq, pp. 36–37.
12. Maṭar, p. 88.
13. Declarations of the Political Bureau of the SCP on 'The Current Situation of the Arabs', 18 August, 1970; quoted in Maṭar, pp. 186–90. Full text printed below; ch 5, A.
14. Maṭar, p. 186.
15. Ibid. p. 188; it is noteworthy that neither Numeiri's regime nor Qādhāfī's are defined as revolutionary or progressive.
16. The term 'educated' refers to all those who had received high school or college education and who were included in the definition of 'graduates'.
17. Fawzi, p. 5; the author states that in 1952 there were 205,986 employees in the Jazīra scheme.
18. *Student Movement*, p. XII; quoted from the introduction of Ja'far M. A. Bakheit, who was at the time Professor of Politics at the University of Khartoum.

19. This may be clearly seen in the election results of the students' union ever since its foundation. In the 1969–70 elections, the Muslim Brothers gained 32,920 votes and the SCP 22,295, while all the other groups together received only about 16,000; ibid, pp. 17–18.
20. *Al-Ayyām*, 5 October, 1954, in Sulaymān, pp. 63–8.
21. Maṭar, pp. 18–19.
22. *Istiqlāl*, p. 141.
23. *Al-Mīdān*, 14 October, 1954, in Sulaymān pp. 63–4, (fn. 1).
24. Quoted from a speech in the Sudanese House of Representatives by the communist leader Zarūq on 16 August, 1955; Sulaymān, p. 139.
25. Ibid. pp. 147–50, quoted from *al-Mīdān*, 13 October, 1955.
26. *Al-Ṣarāḥa*, 15 June, 1956, in Sulaymān pp. 217–221; see also interview of 'Abd al-Khāliq Maḥjūb with Fu'ād Maṭar in April 1965; Maṭar, pp. 84–7.
27 Ibid, pp. 17–20; according to Maṭar, these so-called 'illiterate Marxists' constituted the majority of the SCP.
28. *Lamaḥāt*, pp. 35–6.
29. Ibid, pp. 37–8.
30. For details see *al-Ra'y al-'Ām*, 23 March, 1955; *al-Mīdān*, 23 Feb., 1956; *al-Ṣarāḥa*, 13 March, 1956, in Sulaymān, pp. 114–17, 205–12.
31. *Information Bulletin*, 25 March, 1965, pp. 42–50.
32. 'Alī 'Abd al-Raḥmān al-Amīn, 123–5.
33. For details, see M. O. Beshir, *The Southern Sudan Background to Conflict*, London 1968.
34. Quoted in Sulaymān, pp. 60–62.
35. Ibid. pp. 7–10.
36. Ibid. pp. 24–26; most of the teachers at that time were English.
37. Ibid. pp. 142–146.
38. *Information Bulletin*, 4, 1965.
39. *Round-Table Conference on the Southern Sudan*, Khartoum 16–25 March, 1965, 'Sudan Informazioni' News Agency Documents, pp. 172–180.
40. Ibid. p. 177.
41. Ibid. pp. 203–206; See also *Humanité*, 15 May, 1965, which published a lengthy interview with Maḥjūb dealing among other subjects with the South.
42. According to Garrang, Numeiri adopted 'the entire programme of the Sudanese Communist party on the question of the Southern provinces', see J. U. Garrang, 'Imperialist Conspiracies Against Sudan' *New Perspectives*, August 1971, p. 56.
43. A Revolution in Action, No. 2 'Regional Autonomy for the South', speeches by Joseph U. Garrang, published by the Ministry for Southern Affairs (Khartoum, n.d.).
44. *Nile Mirror*, 24 September, 1970.
45. Ibid, see also J. U. Garrang, 'Imperialist Conspiracies Against Sudan'. *New Perspectives*, (August 1971). Garrang maintained that there was a well devised imperialist conspiracy to encourage the Southern separatists.
46. J. U. Garrang, 'The Southern Sudan Problem', *Comment*, 10 October, 1970, p. 653.
47. See for instance 'An Open Letter to Comrade Alexei N. Kosygin and

Comrade Leonid Brezhnev,' signed: Colonel Joseph Lagu, on behalf of the *Anya-Nya* AEGIS Committee, (n.d.); also 'Southern Sudan Lives, Arab-Soviet Genocide must fail!' published by the Union of Black Sudanese Students in America, (26–29 December, 1970).

48. Report of the Central Committee Meeting and its decisions, 8 October, 1970, reprinted in Maṭar, pp. 169–175. (Full text translated below, ch. 5, B.).
49. Ibid. p. 171.
50. *Al-Ḥawādith*, 14 January, 1972.
51. The following is a summary of 'Abdel Khalek Mahjoub's Report on the Political Situation, in the Country, the Changes that have taken place since the Previous Meetings and the Tasks of the Party and the Revolutionary Movement in Defending and Promoting the Revolution', *Information Bulletin*, 35, (March 1965) pp. 42–50.
52. 'Full text of the Statement, issued by the Central Committee of the Communist Party of the Sudan on Elections, May 13, 1965', *Information Bulletin*, 57, (October 1965), pp. 36–44.
53. *Al-Nahār*, 26 March, 1971; this is the first of a series of articles on the SCP written by Fu'ād Maṭar between 26 March and 3 April, 1971.
54. *Rude Pravo*, 2 February, 1965, quoted in *Information Bulletin*, 35, (March 1965).
55. *La Voix du Peuple*, 16 January, 1968 (weekly organ of the Belgian CP); according to the statement, the 'Revolutionary Trend' within the SCP was founded in January 1967.
56. *Al-Nahār*, 29 March, 1971.
57. *Al-Nahār*, 1 April, 1971. See below, ch. 5, C.
58. See for instance Hasan al-Ṭāhir Zarūq, 'Adawā' 'alā al-waḍ' al-siyāsī fī'l Sūdān,' *al-Ṭalī'a*, September 1966; also 'Declaration of the Central Committee', 12 November, 1965, in *al-Waqt*, No. 3 (1966) pp. 24–6.
59. *Al-Nahār*, 26 March and 1 April, 1971.
60. 'Rede des Genossen Abdel Khaleg Mahgoub', in *Internationale Beratung der Kommunistischen und Arbeiterparteien, Moskau 1969*, Prag 1969, pp. 552–61.
61. Rāziq, pp. 18–23 and 79–85.
62. 'Abd al-Khāliq Maḥjūb's Report to the Conference of Communist Cadres, February 1970, *Information Bulletin*, 16 (1971), translated from *al-Ḥuriyya* 26 July, 1970; see also Maṭar, pp. 99–147.
63. Deliberations of the central committee of the SCP, 8 October, 1970, in Maṭar, pp. 163–8.
64. Maṭar, pp. 176–8.

# List of Works Cited

(does not include British parliamentary papers, archival sources and newspaper articles)

(does not include British parliamentary papers, archival sources and newspaper articles)

'Abd al-Nūr 'Ubayd, *al-Thā'ir al-awwal*, Khartoum n.d.

'Abd al-Rahīm, Muddathir, *Imperialism and Nationalism in the Sudan*, London 1969

'Abd al-Rāziq Ḥusayn, *Ḥaqā'iq al-ṣidām ma' al-ḥizb al-shuyū'ī al-Sūdanī*, Beirut 1972

*Allies for Freedom*, Report of the Second Conference of Communist and Workers' Parties within the Sphere of British Imperialism, Caxton Hall, London 1954

al-Amīn, 'Ali 'Abd al-Raḥmān, *al-dīmuqrāṭiyya wa'l-ishtirākiyya fi'l-Sūdān* Beirut 1970

Asad, Talal, *The Kababish Arabs*, London 1970

Badrī, Bābikr, *Ta'rīkh ḥayāti*, vols 1–3 Omdurman 1960/61

Bakheit, Jaafar Muhammad Ali, 'Communist activities in the Middle East 1919–1927, with special reference to Egypt and the Sudan', University of Khartoum 1968

Barclay, H. B., 'A Sudanese Religious Brotherhood al-Ṭarīqa al-Hindīya' *MW*, vol. 53, 1963

Beshir, M. O., *Educational development in the Sudan, 1898–1956*, London 1969

Currie, James, 'The educational experiment in the Anglo-Egyptian Sudan', *Journal of the African Society*, vols 33–34 (1934/35).

Duncan, J. S. R., *The Sudan's Path to Independence*, Edinburgh 1957

Fawzi, Saad Ed Din, *The Labour Movement in the Sudan 1946–1955*, London 1957

Hasan, Yusuf Fadl, 'The Sudanese Revolution of October 1964', *The Journal of Modern African Studies*, vol. 5 1967

Hasan, Yusuf Fadl, (ed.), *Sudan in Africa*, Khartoum 1971

Henderson, K. D. D., *The Making of the Modern Sudan*, London 1953
——, *Sudan Republic*, London 1965
Hill, Richard, *A Biographical Dictionary of the Sudan*, Cass, London 1967
Hill, Richard, *Egypt in the Sudan 1820–1881*, London 1959
Holt, P. M., *Holy Families and Islam in the Sudan*, Princeton Near East Papers, No. 4, Princeton 1967
Holt, P. M., 'The Sons of Jābir and their Kin: A Clan of Sudanese Religious Notables', *B.S.O.A.S.* vol. 30 (1967)
—— *A Modern History of the Sudan*, London 1961
—— *The Mahdist State in the Sudan 1881–1898*, London 1970
—— *Studies in the History of the Near East*, Cass, London 1973
Ibrāhīm 'Abdallāh 'Alī, *al-Ṣirā' bayn al-Mahdī wa'l-'Ulamā'*, Khartoum 1968
Kedourie, Elie, *The Chatham House Version and other Middle-Eastern Studies*, Cass, London 1970
MacMichael, H. A., *A History of the Arabs in the Sudan*, 2nd impression, Cass, London 1967
—— *The Anglo-Egyptian Sudan*, London 1934
al-Mahdī, al-Ṣādiq (ed.), *Jihād fī Sabīl al-Istiqlāl*, Khartoum n.d.
Mahgoub, Mohamed Salih, 'The Sudanese Press', *S.N.R.* vol. 46 (1965)
*Manshurat al-Imām al-Mahdī*, vol. 2 Khartoum, 1964
Maṭar, Fu'ād, *al-Ḥizb al-Shuyū'ī al-Sūdani naḥarūhu amm intaḥara*, Beirut 1971
Nur, S. M., *A Critical Edition of the Memoirs of Yusuf Mikha'il*, unpublished Ph.D. thesis, London 1963
Said, M. Beshir, *The Sudan Crossroads of Africa*, London 1965
Sanderson, G. N., 'Sudanese nationalism and the independence of the Sudan', Symposium on Islamic North Africa, London 1971
Shuqayr, Na'ūm, *Ta'rīkh al-Sūdān al-qadīm wa'l Ḥadīth wajughrafiyatuhu*, Cairo n.d. [1903]
Slatin, R. C., *Fire and Sword in the Sudan*, London 1896
Smirnov, S. R. (ed.), *A History of Africa 1918–1967*, Moscow 1968
Sulaymān, Muḥammad, *al-Yasār al-Sūdānī fī 'asharah a'wām 1954–1963*, Wād Madanī 1971
Ṭaha, 'Abd al-Raḥmān 'Alī, *al-Sūdān li'l Sūdāniyyin*, Omdurman 1955
Voll, John O., *A History of the Khatmiyya Tariqah in the Sudan*, unpublished Ph.D. thesis, Harvard University 1969
Warburg, Gabriel, *The Sudan under Wingate*, Cass, London 1971

# Index

Arabic names, with few exceptions, are listed according to alphabetical order of first names.